CHESNEY
THE MIDDLE CLASS MURDERER

JONATHAN OATES

First Edition published 2016 (Hardcover)
This Edition 2019 (Softcover)

Copyright © Jonathan Oates, 2016, 2019

The right of Jonathan Oates to be identified as the author of this work has been asserted in accordance with the Copyright, Designs & Patents Act 1988.

All rights reserved. No part of this book may be reprinted or reproduced or utilised in any form or by any electronic, mechanical or other means, now known or hereafter invented, including photocopying and recording, or in any information storage or retrieval system, without the prior permission in writing of the publishers.

Unless otherwise stated, images are from the author's collection. Whilst every effort has been made to credit all images to the appropriate source/copyright holder, the author apologises for any oversight, which we would be happy to correct in future editions.

ISBN: 978-1-911273-09-7 (hardcover)
ISBN: 978-1-911273-09-7 (softcover)
ISBN: 978-1-911273-09-7 (ebook)

Published by Mango Books

www.mangobooks.co.uk
18 Soho Square
London W1D 3QL

CHESNEY
THE MIDDLE CLASS MURDERER

Contents

Acknowledgements 1
Introduction 3
1 Dreadful Discovery in Ealing, 1954 5
2 A Young Man, 1908-1926 17
3 A Death in the Family, 1926 35
4 Investigations, 1926-1927 60
5 The Trial of John Donald Merrett, 1927:
    Case for the Prosecution 73
6 The Trial of John Donald Merrett, 1927:
    Case for the Defence and Verdict 91
7 Peace and War, 1928-1945 109
8 Post War Years, 1945-1951 138
9 Countdown to Tragedy, 1951-1954 171
10 Denouement, 1954-1955 193
Conclusion 219
Bibliography 221
Index 227

Acknowledgements

I would like to thank all those who have assisted in the production of this book. The staffs at the National Archives, the National Maritime Museum at Greenwich, the Guildhall Library, the British Library, the London Metropolitan Archives, the National Records of Scotland, the Edinburgh City Library, Edinburgh University Library and Edinburgh City Archives for the production of the documents, newspapers and books without which this book could not have been written. Staff at other institutions, such as Hastings Cemetery Office, Waitaki School, Malvern College, Edinburgh Cemeteries and elsewhere have also generously helped with their time. Elspeth Willis read part of the script and made comments. Paul Lang also helped with the research and provision of pictures. David Leslie has also been helpful. Mike Quincey's sailing knowledge was useful for chapter 7. Paul Fitzmaurice's and Lesley Smithson's legal knowledge was put to use over William Henry Milner's will. John Gauss pointed out my many grammatical and other English errors. Robert Clack allowed the author use of relevant newspaper articles about Gerda Schaller. Finally, Lindsay Siviter, a walking Newgate Calendar, assisted with lending useful material.

This book is dedicated to Angela.

About the Author

Jonathan Oates obtained a PhD from Reading University in History in 2001. Apart from being Ealing's Borough Archivist since 1999, he has had 26 books and over 30 articles published on a wide variety of historical subjects; criminal, military, local and genealogical. He has a particular interest in 1940s and 1950s crime. This book is his third biography of a major post war British murderer.

Introduction

Unlike most killers who surface in the press as headline news once they have committed their murders, Chesney attracted the headlines twice; in 1926/1927 and in 1954. In both instances the crime was one of murder. For the reader of the national press, Chesney was the man who had got away with one murder whilst a young man, but nearly three decades later killed again, but ended his own life rather than risk the hangman performing that same office.

There is a sense that his life and crimes were almost in the realm of fiction. Agatha Christie's best selling books of mysterious murders dealt with the middle and upper middle classes. Characters were professional people, monied men and women who employed servants and were from privileged backgrounds. Murderers who had obvious motives had established alibis which the detective had to break. The motive was very often monetary. Real life crime is usually much different, with killers and victims usually from working class backgrounds and whose motivation often included lust and sadism. Certainly known murderers in the 1940s and 1950s such as John Christie or Gordon Cummins, 'the Blackout Ripper' would never have featured in an Agatha Christie novel. Nor would killers who killed on the spur of the moment or/and confessed immediately.

Yet Ronald John Chesney, who hit the headlines in February and March 1954, does fit the bill. He was from a wealthy family, attended public school and university and served as a Royal Navy officer in an active role in the Second World War. He was a gambler and a womaniser. Yet he also acquired a sizeable criminal record from his teens until middle age. He is also credited with three murders; for one he tried to establish an elaborate alibi.

Chesney was the subject of two books which were published shortly after his final crimes, both by journalists, which is not uncommon, as well as one part study in a wider survey of post war multiple murderers.[1] He has been cast as a larger than life figure who bestrode the criminal underworld of Europe in the 1930s to 1950s, as well as committing three murders, the first whilst he was but in his teens. However, much of these books are unsourced and so reliant on sources whose provenance is unprovable; chiefly people who knew Chesney in his later life. Where they can be checked, parts of these accounts resemble fiction.

This account relies on proven sources compiled at the time of events or shortly afterwards, and uses the police and judicial files unusable by previous authors as they were only released for public inspection in recent years. Chesney's war records shed another light on his character, as do archives held in Scotland about his earlier criminal career. There is a revealing magazine article by his wife about his sailing exploits. Nor have other sources, known to the genealogist, been hitherto used to reconstruct both his life and that of those around him. Newspapers are another source which help fill in details of his non-lethal crimes. This book spends far more time dealing with his early life and first crimes; previous books have only spent a little time on this in order to focus on his later activities.

This new study aims to recreate the life and times of one of Britain's most notorious criminals who was motivated by the lack of money, caused by his own capacity to lose it and his inability to work in a lawful profession. It begins with the shocking discovery of his final crimes, then steps back into his past before working forward and concluding with the denouement and fall out caused by his death.

---

1 McLeave, Chesney: *The Fabulous Murderer* (1954); Tullett, *Portrait of a Bad Man* (1956); Phillips, *Murderer's Moon* (1956).

1
Dreadful Discovery in Ealing, 1954

Residential northern Ealing was a very quiet place in the daytime and after dark. There is no reason for anyone but residents to visit there; no shops, no pubs nor any places of entertainment. It is not a thoroughfare to another location. Non-residents would only go there to meet someone else who lived there.

The evening of Wednesday, 10 February 1954 was different, despite a temperature that night close to freezing. There was a man who was on the prowl there. Perhaps the first to detect his presence was housewife Betty Cooper of 6 Helena Road. To the right of her house was a public footpath which ran along the backs of the houses in Montpelier Road. Whilst she was listening to her favourite radio play, The Unguarded Hour, at a quarter to nine, she heard 'the sound of slow, heavy footsteps passing through the lane'. At a quarter past ten she heard them again. On neither occasion did she see whoever made them.[1]

Others who were abroad that night did so, however, with the benefit of a half moon as well as the street lights. One was an eighteen-year-old trainee secretary called Patricia March. Resident at flat 16 of The Orchards on Montpelier Road which backed on to Helena Road, she was taking her dog for a walk at half past ten. She later recalled:

> I saw a man, aged about 49, height six feet one inch, heavy build, dark hair, clean shaven, wearing a dark overcoat and a black

---

1   TNA, MEPO 2/9542.

> *trilby hat walking along outside the Orchard towards me. He had a very pronounced limp and I think his left leg was shorter than his right. I noticed him because at first I thought he was drunk and it frightened me. He came up suddenly out of the dark.*

She quickly walked off in order to avoid meeting him and so did not see where he went.[2]

There was another witness. This was Peter Henderson, a middle aged store manager who lived at flat 2 of Cecil Close, which adjoined Helena Road. As with Miss March, he was another nocturnal dog walker. He saw the man at the corner of Mount Avenue and Helena Road. He recalled, 'He appeared to be looking around and up and down the road, and his attitude made me suspicious of him'. The man saw Henderson and walked quickly up Helena Road, away from him. He seemed to have a limp. Henderson crossed the road and saw the man looking back at him several times to see if he was being followed. Henderson briefly saw the man's face in the light of a street lamp.[3]

That night at number 22 Montpelier Road, a home for elderly people, the proprietor, the 71-year-old Mrs Mary Ann Menzies was making her final rounds of the night. Elizabeth Whitmore, aged 80 and a resident, was brought in her milk and medicine in bed, as it always was. Mrs Menzies left the drink and quietly shut the door. The elderly lady drank it and fell asleep. Mrs Menzies also looked into another room, this one shared by two elderly men; George Cummings and John Clark, to see that all was well. Cummings went to the toilet in the can under the bed a few minutes later. Another elderly resident, Miss Edith Jell, met her as she was going to bed and said goodnight.[4]

But everything was not quite as peaceful as it appeared. Mrs Clara Eccles could not sleep well, heard noises in the night and wondered if it was Mrs Menzies' daughter, Mrs Isobel Veronica Chesney, 42-years-old, coming home late (this was not the case; she had already returned home by 9.30). Clark later said to his room mate, 'Do you hear the water?' Cummings said no. Yet he heard a thud and the shout 'Oh' downstairs. He thought that someone might have fallen over. Clark thought that the sound of running water at midnight meant that there had been a burst pipe somewhere, but he had not heard the thud or shout. They went to sleep. Elsewhere, Margaret Rawle of no. 21

---

2 TNA, MEPO 2/9542.
3 Ibid.
4 TNA, MEPO 2/9542; *Illustrated* [rest of title unknown], 24 April 1954.

Montpelier Road, heard her landlady's dogs barking at both 12 and 2am. This was not usual.[5]

Meanwhile, in the street, Fred Daye had been visiting a friend at 24 Montpelier Road and left late; at about 1.20 am. He saw a car at the junction of Hillcrest Road (which is a continuation of Montpelier Road eastwards) and Hanger Lane. It stopped to offer a man a lift. The man, however, hurried on. Daye commented:

> He obviously did not wish to be given a lift, neither did he wish to be recognised, as after the first stalled turn towards him, he turned back and continued walking on swiftly as before, keeping his head turned away from me.

The man carried a brown Gladstone bag.[6]

Thursday, 11 February 1954 was a day unlike any other in the young life of eighteen-year-old Eileen Georgina Thorpe of Hanwell. She had only been working as housemaid at Sunset Home, the old people's home at 22 Montpelier Road, for a few weeks. Normally she was awoken by Mrs Menzies at 6.30, but today she was not. At a quarter to eight that morning she rose from bed, put on a coat and went to the bedroom on the first floor of the three-storey detached house to find one of her employers, Mrs Chesney.

She later recalled:

> She was not in her room but the couch appeared to have been slept on, as the bedclothes had been disturbed. I noticed that the electric fire in the room was alight. I took it for granted that Lady [Mrs] Menzies was attending to one of the old people upstairs, so I went into the kitchen and started getting the breakfast ready.
>
> At about 8.15 am I took some tea up to Mrs Chesney's room but she was not in the room. Her bed appeared to have been slept in as the bedclothes were disturbed. I became very worried when I could not find either Lady Menzies [who slept on the settee in a ground floor front room] or Mrs Chesney.

She then found that the front door was locked and bolted from the inside. Clearly no one had left by that way (it was usual for the door to be locked at night time). She began to ask some of the house's residents whether they had seen either of her employers recently.

5 Ibid.
6 TNA, MEPO 2/9542.

Mrs Whitmore told her that Mrs Menzies had been to see her in her room on the previous night. Cummings, one of the few male residents, told her that she had called into his room at one in the morning.[7]

There seemed little else to do at the moment because the residents' breakfasts needed preparing and serving. This is what Eileen proceeded to accomplish. Some time between nine and ten, Eileen had the time to investigate. She found that the back door – which led to the garden and the outside toilet – was open. It was usually locked at night. She returned to her other duties and began washing up the breakfast crockery.[8]

Clark later recalled, 'I guessed something was wrong next morning when no tea came at the usual time. I dressed and went to ask Eileen, the maid, what was wrong. "They must be out" she said, "All their doors are locked".'[9]

It was then that she was interrupted by Mrs Alice Lindus, who told her, 'There is an ambulance at the door'. Eileen unlocked and unbolted the front door and saw two ambulance drivers with an elderly patient. These men were Peter James Heaslewood and Frank Harley. They had just been to Greenfields Nursing Home at 1 Courtfields Gardens, West Ealing, in order to collect one Mrs Dane, leaving at about 9.40 and arriving at 22 Montpelier Road just before ten.[10]

Eileen said, 'I can't understand it, but Mrs Chesney and Lady Menzies seemed to have disappeared in the night', though Heaslewood thought she said, 'I am in a state, with a new patient arriving and Mrs Chesney and Lady Menzies missing'. Harley thought her words were, 'I don't know, she went out during the night'. The men queried this, 'are you sure?' and she replied, 'Yes, come and have a look yourselves'. Once Mrs Dane had been made comfortable in the house, the two men had a brief look around part of the premises. They looked in Mrs Menzies' room and in the garden (possibly no more than a glance through the French windows) and the garage, which contained a Ford 10hp. Nothing untoward was found.[11]

Heaslewood was content to leave, but Harley was more anxious. He told Eileen they would contact the police, but she was reluctant for

7   TNA, MEPO 2/9542.
8   Ibid.
9   *Illustrated* [rest of title unknown], 24 April 1954.
10 TNA, MEPO 2/9542.
11 Ibid.

them to take this step because she had only been recently employed and did not want to cause problems for her employers who might in turn dismiss her because of it. In any case they left at about 10.20 and informed the police at Ealing Police Station, about one mile south on the High Street.[12]

The police were prompt to act. At 11.15 two plain clothed men from CID visited the house. Eileen told them what happened, and they left soon afterwards, presumably taking brief details to be filed as a missing persons' report, for there were no obvious signs of foul play. At about 12.25, Miss Phyllis McNeish (1917-1998), of 40 Mount Park Road, Ealing called at the house, but could not find her aunt or cousin. She assumed they must have gone out. She then called at John Nixon-Pearson's house on 21 Gordon Road, but neither he nor his wife could help (he was an adopted son of Mrs Chesney). She then contacted Mrs Chesney's adopted daughter, Elizabeth Ann Trull (1933-) of 16b Sutherland Road, to ask after them. Faced with more negative news, they decided to go to 22 Montpelier Road. Mrs Trull took a taxi and arrived first, at about ten past one, Frederick Robert Trull (1924-1998), her husband, joining her fifteen minutes later, cycling over. He found her in the lounge with Miss McNeish. Nothing seemed out of the ordinary whatsoever and Eileen had told them, 'everything is under control'.[13]

Trull explained what happened next:

> We then went to the room next to the lounge, and I noticed an envelope on an armchair just inside the room, which had two large spots of blood on it. There was a dark blue frock of Granny's [Mary Menzies] near the window on the floor, with a lot of blood stains round the collar. I felt the collar but it was dry. Similar bloodstains were on the wall and floor.
>
> I thought this was rather strange and my wife and I and Auntie Phyllis who also noticed it, said "It's probably blood from one of the old people who died in the house last week". This was a reference to Mrs Emily Ellis, a resident who died a day or two previously and who had been administered to by Mary Menzies. Aunt Phyllis noticed Granny's dentures were on the mantelpiece also one of her slippers was on the armchair and she said, "I am beginning to think

12 Ibid.
13 Ibid.

something is really wrong".[14]

They then looked for any message for them, but instead saw a key on the kitchen table which was then ignored. They looked at Mrs Chesney's room. They saw that all her coats and shoes were there, as was her handbag. A single slipper lay by the bed. The only item of clothing that was missing was her dressing gown. The curtains had not been drawn and the clock had stopped at 1.10. Miss McNeish said, 'I am really worried now'. After all, she would hardly have left the house without any of these outdoor clothes. She must still be on the premises, therefore.[15]

They had a cursory look at the lounge on the ground floor. Miss McNeish recalled:

> We did look into the ground floor front lounge on the right hand side of the hall at the rear. In this room I examined, but did not touch, a chest of drawers...The room was being used as a junk or store room. I did see what I thought was just bundles and curtains.[16]

Meanwhile, Trull found that the bathroom was locked. His wife informed him that this was probably because one of the old people was using it. Trull remembered the key they had seen downstairs, but did nothing about it and instead inspected the cupboards where he found nothing untoward. Miss McNeish looked in the garden and the sheds there. Eileen told him, 'I have just remembered the back door was open this morning'. A search of the cellar and pantry was made, and the garage was examined again. In the garden they found the imprint of muddy boots. Mrs Trull knew that her mother slept on a settee on the ground floor, but though made up for a sleeper, it had not been used.[17]

The Trulls needed to return home now. It was two o'clock and their eleven month old son Christopher needed to be collected. Fifteen minutes later, Miss McNeish rang the police and explained her concerns to DS Munsie. Munsie and his superior, Detective Superintendent Edmund Walter Daws (1903-1961), newly appointed head (4 January 1954) of CID for T Division (which covered much of outer west London), agreed to pay a visit. Daws had been born in

---

14 TNA, MEPO 2/9542.
15 Ibid.
16 Ibid.
17 Ibid.

Battersea and his parents ran a furniture business; his two siblings died in infancy. Initially employed as a maintenance engineer, he joined the police in 1927, rising to sergeant in 1936, inspector in 1944, chief inspector in 1949. In 1946-1947 he was in Australia to investigate a fraud case involving a London suspect, Claude Albo de Bernale. He also worked in the Flying Squad, known as Flaps Daws and dealt with race course crooks and pickpockets, often called in by county forces to deal with such gangs. He had many commendations for his work, chiefly concerning the apprehension of thieves. He had a tall, angular, stooping body. In 1950-1951 he worked with the Post Office investigative department in breaking up a gang of safe thieves. A colleague wrote of him, 'Daws had acquired a formidable reputation in the criminal world for the care and persistence with which he carried out his inquiries'. Daws was often chosen for delicate assignments, including the investigation of misdeeds among the Metropolitan Police. In 1950 he married Gladys Amelia Williams and they still resided in Battersea. The police arrived at 22 Montpelier Road and began by searching the grounds behind the house.[18]

Eileen remembered the key in the kitchen and thought it was that to the bathroom. She said, 'Let's see if this key fits the bathroom door'. Mrs Trull, who had returned, replied, 'Come on. You come with me'. They went upstairs, Eileen holding the key. According to her:

> *I went to the bathroom, which is on the same floor as Mrs Chesney's room, opened the door with the key and on looking inside saw a woman in the bath. I thought it was Mrs Chesney. Her feet were at the tap end of the bath, she was partly clothed, her legs were bare and her face was a mauve colour. I ran to the landing and saw Mrs Trull on the stairs, I shouted to her "There's a body in the bath, at least I'm not sure".*[19]

She began screaming and so Daws rushed to the bathroom to see what was the matter. It is uncertain what the time was now; Daws claimed it was 2.20, Eileen and Miss McNeish stated it as being 2.45. He described the scene in his report, 'Mrs Chesney was lying in the bath on her right side with her head towards the door; the lower part of her clothing was damp and her hair was wet and soapy'. There

---

18   TNA, MEPO 2/9542; Hatherill, *A Detective's Story* (1971), p.157; Thomas, *Villains' Paradise* (2005), pp.163, 240; Webb, *Deadline for Crime* (1955), p.52; *The Times*, 10 January 1947; information from Scotland Yard.
19   TNA, MEPO 2/9542.

was some bedding at the side of the bath, which was empty of water. There was a box of soap flakes in the room but no towel. There was nothing that he could do immediately, so he locked the door and went downstairs again. He went to the lounge on the ground floor which had been dismissed as a junk room by the others earlier on and made another shocking discovery, for hidden under the cushions piled there he saw that:

> *Mary Menzies was lying on her face with her arm extended down her side, palm uppermost, whilst her left arm was bent double and tucked under her body. On her right leg was a stocking and on her right foot a slipper. The left leg and foot were bare. Closer examination revealed that her head was covered with a tartan headscarf and she had a stocking (which apparently was the stocking from the left leg) tied tightly round her neck with a granny knot at the back. A blue belt was also tied round her neck. The body itself was covered the head being covered with a loose chair cover.*[20]

Blood had soaked through the scarf and onto the carpet. There were several smears of blood on the wall near to where Mrs Menzies' corpse had been found. These may have been caused by the body being dropped nearby and rubbing against the wall or from a blow to the head. There was also evidence in the adjacent ground floor front room. Smears of blood were on the door and blood spots were on the armchairs. On the top of the bookcase in the front room was a small metal coffee pot (now at the Crime Museum) with its lid missing. Ominously there were bloodstains on the pot and a dent in its side. There were also bloodstains near to the bookcase. Daws concluded, 'A thorough examination of the room clearly indicated that a terrific struggle had taken place and that afterwards, the room had been cleverly tidied up so that, at a casual glance, no one would appreciate that anything had happened there'.[21]

Mrs Chesney's death yielded fewer clues. However, in her room were found a number of bottles of brandy, gin, port, whisky, sherry and stout. Bloodstains were found on her bedclothes, which had been tidied up, probably by someone with blood on their hands. Downstairs, Daws learnt that the French windows on the ground floor were defective and that they could be held in position by a heavy

---

20 TNA, MEPO 2/9542.
21 Ibid.

stone on the outside and a wood screw was found on the floor, and thus opened there quietly. Daws found it was possible to enter the house via the back of the house, which had a broken fence, and the French windows without the police officers in the house being aware of the fact. Other discoveries included a quantity of ammunition for an automatic pistol; 20 of which were loose in a coal scuttle.[22]

Dr Allan Massey of 47 Uxbridge Road, Hanwell, arrived at 5.15 and pronounced both women were dead (curiously enough the local police surgeon was not contacted; when the *Daily Mirror* rang him for his comments he was able to profess ignorance). Police officers took statements from the nineteen elderly residents, as well as Miss Thorpe, the Trulls and Miss McNeish. A large white tarpaulin was spread over the carriageway, covering an area eight by ten yards, in order to preserve any footsteps that might be there in the soft, damp gravel soil. With the aid of torches, officers examined the steps leading to the front door for the sign of any footsteps, as night closed in on them. The ground on the side of the house and the gravel drive at the front were also examined.[23]

At about 5pm Dr Robert Donald Teare (1911-1979) of 90a Harley Street, arrived at the house, following a call from the county coroner, Dr Harold Broadbridge. Teare was employed by the Home Office and was one of the three major postwar pathologists who handled the bulk of such work in and around London (just over four years ago he had carried out post mortems on the bodies of Beryl and Geraldine Evans, murdered at 10 Rillington Place, in what was to be, in retrospect, his most controversial work). A colleague referred to him thus, 'a solid, likeable man with a good sense of humour, competent both in the field and the witness box'. He carried out post mortems on the two corpses. An hour later, Detective Chief Superintendent Thomas Barratt (who had also been involved in the Evans murder enquiry) arrived. Fingerprint men from Scotland Yard came and began dusting throughout a number of rooms. Photographs were taken in the dining room and of various artefacts, such as a lampshade. The residents, three of whom were bedridden, were conveyed elsewhere in county council ambulances; one destination being Percy House in Isleworth, after having been told that there had been a burglary.[24]

22 Ibid.
23 *Middlesex County Times*, 13 February 1954.
24 *Middlesex County Times*, 13 February 1954.; Simpson, *Forty Years of Murder* (1978), p.233; *Illustrated* [rest of title unknown], 24 April 1954.

Teare found that there was a small abrasion on Mrs Chesney's left cheek and small bruises on her elbows, but that otherwise her body was unmarked. She had been wearing a cardigan and a nightdress. There was also a considerable amount of alcohol in her blood; 0.186%. She would therefore have been drunk at time of death, which had been caused by drowning. She had been wearing a wrist watch which had stopped at 2.30. Mrs Menzies had sustained five wounds on her scalp; above her left ear and on her temple - caused by the coffee pot - and there were pressure marks on her neck. The back of her right hand and her knuckles were bruised where she had tried to defend herself. She had probably been struck whilst in a kneeling position.[25] He took samples of the hair and blood of both victims, and clippings from their fingernails; these were placed in separate envelopes for further examination.[26]

It was reported in the press that a large cache of letters addressed to Mrs Chesney and stretching back to the 1930s, was found in her bedroom, in a trunk, totalling about 3,000 in all. It was alleged that many were from her various lovers, some of whom were married and of these, several were of high social standing. None of these letters are known to have survived (certainly the family deny that they have them and the police files do not include them), though a few from her husband were reproduced in books about the case written in the 1950s, so these allegations cannot be verified. One newspaper stated, they 'revealed that she could command the deep affection of her acquaintances – an affection which she seldom reciprocated'. Motive for murder seemed obscure, however. According to Duncan Webb (1917-1958), a crime journalist, Daws stated, 'This beats the flipping band. It might be robbery, it might be revenge. The old lady might have disturbed a burglar. If she did she could not have cried out very loud, since the dogs were not disturbed'.[27]

Conrad Phillips, writer and journalist, approached the scene in the early evening and described it thus:

> *I was late arriving in Montpelier Road. Night was climbing up the sky. A line of cars and vans queued up outside moved slowly. As soon as one was loaded with old people another would drive through the*

---

25 TNA, MEPO 2/9542.
26 LMA, COR/MW/1954/184/162-3.
27 Webb, *Deadline for Crime* (1955), pp.53-4; *Sunday Despatch*, 14 February 1954.

front gateway.

A crowd of newspapermen near the gate, guarded by two policemen, were struggling to get intros. to their stories. This murder bristled with angles. It was the sort of story Shakespeare could have gone to town on.

Members of the Murder Squad, including Dr Lewis Nicholls, head of the Yard's forensic laboratory, Chief Detective Superintendent Tom Barratt, Superintendent Daws and Superintendent Livings, kept entering and leaving the house.

Somebody had planned the perfect murder, but it had "come unstuck" they said... [later] I left Montpelier Road and had a drink with some of the Murder Squad boys. There was no doubt that Chesney killed his wife and mother-in-law.[28]

Later that evening the corpses were taken to Acton Mortuary, just south of the Town Hall on Acton High Street and Miss McNeish officially identified the bodies on the following day.[29] In the next few days, police made door to door enquiries and checked on all those who arrived and left the country by aircraft to northern European destinations. One odd fact that did emerge was that in the previous summer a young man had often come to the house. He had pounded on the door late one night and the police had had to be called. Aged between 25 and 30, the police wished to question him, though he was never apparently identified.[30]

On Saturday, 13 February, Daws put the following insertion into the confidential police newspaper, *The Police Gazette*:

MURDER

At 2.30 p.m. 11th inst, the bodies of Isobel Veronica Chesney, aged 42 years, and her mother, aged 68, were found in a nursing home which they conducted.

It is desired to trace John Donald Merrett, alias Ronald John Chesney and John Donald Milner, 46, 6ft., heavy build, fresh complexion, brown hair, small pencil moustache, grey eyes, ears pierced, usually wears ear-ring in left, scar bridge of nose, right wrist and first right finger, wearing blue grey mixture two-piece suit, knitted waistcoat, light blue shirt with dark stripe, bow tie, light grey leather shoes

---

28 Phillips, *Murderer's Moon*, pp.177-8.
29 *Middlesex County Times*, 13 February 1954; TNA, MEPO 2/9542.
30 *Aberdeen Evening Express*, 12 February 1954.

> with crepe soles and brown gloves. Speaks fluent German and French and has good knowledge of Arabic, Spanish and Egyptian. Embarked at Harwich on 4th inst. for Hook of Holland but is believed to have returned to this country.[31]

The public were merely told that the police were seeking to interview a middle-aged man, bearded and possibly sporting a gold ear ring, to assist them in their enquiries.[32] Rumours abounded that a hired killer was responsible and had been seen driving a car along the road on previous days, stopping outside number 22.[33] Another theory was that a man who had had an affair with Mrs Chesney had killed her due to jealousy. The police made enquiries in Tangier, Holland and elsewhere.[34]

This was shocking news for the inhabitants of this part of Ealing where violent crime was rare. It had been 18 years since north Ealing had seen a murder committed. This had taken place in a house not too far away from Montpelier Road, at 16 Winscombe Crescent in the nearby Brentham Garden Suburb. Arthur Wheeler, an insurance clerk, and his wife had become friendly with Linford Derrick, a tennis coach. One night, after an evening that the two men had spent together, Derrick returned to his friend's house and killed him. Derrick confessed, but alleged he struck the deadly blows in self defence because Wheeler accused him of adultery with his wife. Derrick was found guilty of manslaughter and was given a custodial sentence; he was lucky to escape with his life.[35]

The question was who was Merrett/Chesney/Milner and we shall begin to address this in the next chapter.

---

31 Tullett, *Portrait of a Bad Man* (1956), p.183.
32 *Middlesex County Times*, 13 February 1954.
33 *Daily Mail*, 13 February 1954.
34 *Empire News*, 14 February 1954.
35 Oates, *Foul Deeds and Suspicious Deaths in Ealing* (2006).

2

A Young Man, 1908-1926

John Donald Merrett had been born in Levin, a small town in the Manawatu-Wanganui district, of the North Island, New Zealand, on 17 August 1908, the son of Bertha and John Alfred Merrett. Very little is known about his early life because he never left any written record and there was no one alive after his death in 1954 who was able or willing to comment on those formative years. Nor did he often talk about his youth and upbringing to anyone in later years. So we shall begin a summary of his family's background and his role within it.

Bertha had been born in Chorlton, Lancashire, on 19 December 1869 and was baptised in the parish church of St. Clement's on 30 January 1870. Her father was William Henry Milner (1834-1899), an auctioneer's son and her mother was Elizabeth Anne Cordingley (1840-1905), daughter of a gentleman. The family was then living at Brookfields, a house in Edge Lane, Chorlton, four miles to the south of Manchester and continued to do so until at least 1881. Bertha had an elder brother, James (1861-1930), and two elder sisters, Mary Louisa (1864-1935) and Annie Eliza (1865-1940), all of whom had been born in Chorlton, where the family had lived at Parker Street from at least 1861-1868. Their parents had married in Cheetham Hill on 5 September 1860. The Halifax born Milner was a wine and spirit merchant. He had been partner to one Robert Whittaker, who had been a witness at his marriage, but the partnership was dissolved in 1864. He was certainly affluent; the family had three domestic servants in 1871 and could afford to send their children away to be educated privately; Bertha and Annie went to a boarding school on North Park Road, Knaresborough, by 1881. By 1884 he owned the Granby Hotel in Harrogate. He was also active in the community and was chairman of the Chorlton Rate Payers' Association by 1881.[1]

Little is known of the family's life. They were certainly well to do, with none of the three daughters having to earn their own livings. In 1881 James was articled to an architect. Mary was married in Altrincham in 1891 to the Rev. William Chadwick (1862-1934), Vicar of St. Paul's church, Sale. They had no children. Possibly Bertha was travelling abroad in 1891 as she is not noted as living in England at that time. However, all was not well. By 1901 at least, James was incarcerated in a private asylum in Church Stretton, Shropshire, where he died on 16 July 1930. Given that the asylum records no longer survive, we cannot know of what ailment he was suffering from and later it was thought that this might be of significance if it ran in the family. However, Annie stressed that his illness had been brought on by himself.[2]

Milner died on 23 May 1899 at The Gables, Birkdale, Southport and left his family well provided for; his will left £78,184 17s 9d, with a net value of £56, 198 17s 5d, a handsome sum indeed. His widow received £1,000 per annum, his son was given an annuity of £600 per annum, whilst the daughters equally received half that amount. After various legacies to friends and employees, the residue was left in trust for the three daughters and their children on reaching the age of 21, and this was to become of the utmost importance in later decades in ways unforeseen in 1899. His three daughters clearly held their father in high esteem for they had a stained glass window at St. Paul's church in Sale as a memorial to him, a window in the east side of the church representing St. Luke and St. Timothy and costing £80.[3]

His widow and Bertha lived in a more modest dwelling in 1901, at 9 Westfield Road in Birkdale, with two servants. Mrs Milner died four years later and left £9,354 5s 4d in her will. Some of this went to various local charities, but the residue was left to her daughters. After her death on 20 March 1905, major changes took place in her

---

1   *York Herald*, 29 March 1884; *Blackburn Standard*, 1 June 1864; *Manchester Guardian*, 17 March 1882; census returns, 1861-1881.
2   Census, 1891-1901, marriage and death certificates; Roughead, *Trial of John Donald Merrett* (1929), p.140.
3   *Morning Post*, 1 July 1899; *Cheshire Observer*, 30 September 1899; Milner's will.

youngest daughters' lives. Annie married Walter Edward Penn (1882-1959), an artist, and they settled in Bosham, Sussex. Bertha married John Alfred Merrett in New Zealand in 1905, allegedly having met on a voyage with Annie to Egypt. She certainly arrived at Auckland on the Rimutaka on 23 November 1905, at which time she was unwed.[4]

Again, little is known of the marriage and thus Merrett's early years. Little has been written about Merrett's father, described as an electrical engineer, who managed a dry milk factory in 1908. He had been born in London on 25 July 1879, the first child of John Henry Merrett, an accountant's clerk, and Ellen Rose, his wife. They lived in 11 Malvern Road, Hornsey, north London, from at least 1881-1891. The family were certainly doing well for in 1891 Merrett senior was now an accountant, there were two more children and a domestic servant. His eldest son attended private schools from 1883-1891 and then the Mercers' Company School until 1898. He was then a student at Finsbury Technical College from 1898-1900, where he studied engineering and mathematics (being in the highest class), passing the College Certificate and winning the Mitchell scholarship. At the college he had cleaned and overhauled boilers.[5]

Merrett's first job was as an apprentice at the Telegraph Construction and Maintenance Company, from August 1900 – September 1901, whilst living as a boarder in 59 Pelton Street, Greenwich, described as a cable machine fitter. He also took evening classes at Finsbury Technical College at this time. In September 1901 he began working for the Escher Wyas and Company, based in Greenwich. By the end of 1902 he worked at Gebruder Hemmer Neidsenfels. He quickly moved to another post as chief engineer for Messrs Hames R. Hatmaker at 28 Boulevard, Malesherbes, Paris, working there from March 1903 to December 1903.[6]

He then took an even bigger step and took a job in January 1904 as chief engineer to Messrs James Nathan and Co, in Wellington, New Zealand. He was also employed as a manager of a dried milk factory (where milk is evaporated for increased shelf life and reduced transport costs). In 1905 he resided at Bunnythorpe near Palmerston, in Manawatu-Wanganui, New Zealand, and was listed as an engineer. From 1906-1908 he was the consulting engineer at Levin. Since 1905

---

4   *Lancashire Evening Post*, 1 May 1905; Roughead, *Trial*, p.3; census returns, 1881-1891.
5   ancestry.com.
6   Ibid.

he had been an associate member of the Institute of Mechanical Engineers.[7]

Following the marriage with Bertha and the birth of his son, the family moved to St. Petersburg. They seem to have sailed from Wellington on the Athenic to London on 5 November 1908. Merrett senior was manager in Russia for the Anglo-Russian Dust Destructor Company from 1908-1909. From then on he was a consulting engineer, a consultant for spinning mills and factories in that city, Riga and Moscow. The work included advising on planning extensions to factories, designing power plants, contracts for installing power plants and electrifying mills and designing lighting installations. The annual value of his work was £0.25m. Finally he acted as an agent for firms in Manchester. In 1914 he was resident at 65 Nevsky Prospect and became a full member of the Institute of Mechanical Engineers.[8]

Although his career was doing exceptionally well, not so his marriage. Merrett's parents split up at some time in the 1910s but it is unknown why and when. Certainly in 1911, Merrett senior was residing with his widowed mother in her house in 137 Palmerston Road, in Southgate, north London, whereas his wife and son were not then resident in England. The son later told a girlfriend they split in 1914 but Annie Penn claimed it was 'a long time before the war'. She said, 'He practically deserted her'. The reason for this is unknown. They were certainly not divorced; to do so at this time was possible as desertion was grounds for such, but it was very unusual, garnered much publicity and was expensive. Nothing is known about what Merrett senior did during the First World War, and he certainly does not appear to have served in the armed forces. He briefly went to the USA in 1919, then returned to England in the same year. He went to Algiers in 1924 and later resided in India, where he may have been employed on the huge system of railways there. On 21 July 1927, in Bombay and now a widower, he re-married. He returned to England in 1929 and may have retired by November 1935 as his name no longer appears in the Mechanical Engineers listings.[9]

Mrs Merrett and her son were in Vevey in Switzerland, where she tended British officers in hospital during the First World War. It was here that she met William Jenks of Calverley Road, Catford, London, in

7 ancestry.com.
8 Ibid.
9 Roughead, *Trial*, p.131; FindMyPast, ancestry.com

early 1915 and he became her financial adviser. He persuaded her to invest £1,014 in war bonds by 1924. She also met, in 1916, one Major Thomas Blackburn (1882-1972), OBE, of the 7th battalion of the King's Own Scottish Borderers. Blackburn had been in the battle of Loos in September 1915 and suffering serious leg wounds, had been captured. He then had had his leg amputated and endured nearly a year in a POW camp at Mainz. In May 1916 he was repatriated to the Chateau d'Oex in Switzerland where he remained until September 1917. He described her as being a 'very upright and charming' woman. Mrs Merrett also took out a patent on a fireless cooker on 18 June 1917; an oven with heat retaining chambers. So perhaps when she returned to England shortly afterwards, it was not surprising that she was employed by the Ministry of Food.[10]

On 18 March 1918 she took ship from Plymouth to Auckland. By 1919 mother and son lived at Hillsbrook, Havelock North, a suburb of Hastings near Hawke's Bay and on the east coast of the North Island, New Zealand, though they may not have stayed there for long. She became friends with Mrs Bertha Hill of Oamaru, South Island. Merrett finally had some stability at the highly rated Waitaki Boys' High School, Waitaki Avenue in North Otago, on South Island. He began as a boarder in the third term of 1919, but had become a day pupil in 1921. The school had been founded in 1883 and was a boys' public school for both boarders and day pupils, based on the English Public School model, described in 1928 as 'one of the best known in New Zealand'. Its motto was *Quanti est sapere* (how valuable is knowledge) and in the 1920s the headmaster was Frank Milner (1875-1944). Donald Saxton, a master there, later claimed Merrett 'bore an odd resentment towards his mother'.[11]

However, Merrett's time at the school was not without distinction. In 1922 he won the class prize for French; in the following year he won that for German. One of his assets throughout his life was his skill with languages; indeed it provided a later 'career opportunity' for him (his mother thought that he would thrive in the Diplomatic Service). Yet there was another side to his character which was also noticeable from an early age apart for linguistic ability; controlled violence. In 1923 he won the school's junior level boxing championship. And, in

---

10 Ibid, pp.3, 131; National Records of Scotland, AD15/27/18; TNA, WO339/10556; information from David Leslie.
11 McLeave, *Chesney: The Fabulous Murderer* (1954), p.12; information from Waitaki School.

the same year he won a senior national scholarship. From about 1920 he was a member of the school's Officer Training Corps, which would have given him the rudiments of military skills.[12]

Merrett's younger years were very peripatetic indeed. Nowhere did he put down roots and nowhere did he make lasting friendships. His only constant was his mother, who clearly wanted to do the best for him that she could. He was an only child. Many boys at this time had lost their fathers during the Great War, so Merrett's being without his father would not have been so very unusual. It is not certain, what, if any relationship Merrett had with his father. He never referred to him in later life and never saw him again as an adult. He may well have believed that his father died in Russia in 1917 as his mother presumably told him and never cared to investigate the claim. It is possible he resented his mother for his father's absence. She is not known to have had any other male companion in these years after she parted from her husband.

Merrett left Waitaki School in the first term of 1924 and he and his mother returned to England, travelling first class on the Port Caroline from Wellington to London. They docked on 20 July 1924. Mrs Merrett, who rented Whitehorn Cottage at Mortimer, near Reading, made her last will and codicil that year at Reading, directing that her entire estate be made over to her son on reaching the age of 25; hitherto, it should be administered by the Public Trustee and Jenks, to provide funds for his education. These executors would also act as his guardians, but Jenks renounced this responsibility.[13]

Merrett attended Malvern College in Worcestershire from the autumn term of 1924 to the summer term of 1925. Again, he was probably a boarder. This was a prestigious boys' public school, founded in 1862 and which opened its doors to boys three years later. The first headmaster was Rev. Arthur Faber. At this time there were several hundred pupils, divided into houses. One famous pupil was C.S. Lewis, the Christian writer. In 1924 the headmaster was Frank Sansome Preston, MA of Pembroke College, Cambridge and the President was the Bishop of Worcester. He had 44 assistant masters under him, some of whom were clergymen and the others former army officers, and nine specialist staff, including some female teachers. The three sided quadrangle building, designed by Mr C.F. Hansom, was dominated by

---

12 Information from Waitaki School; Edinburgh University Archives, IN1/ADS/STA8.
13 Roughhead, *Trial*, p.17.

a bronze statue of St. George, the war memorial for the 457 Old Boys killed in the First World War. The school was made up of ten houses and the School House (Merrett was in the latter; Mr F.U. Mugliston was the housemaster). There were 575 boys at the school. School facilities included a chapel, library, gymnasium, workshops, racket courts, covered fives courts, cricket pitches, a swimming pool, a rifle range, a sitting room and a schools mechanical engineering centre. It was divided into Lower, Middle and Upper. English, French, Latin and Maths were taught in the Lower School, with Science in the Middle and Classics, History, Science, Maths and Modern Languages in the Upper.[14]

Apparently, academically, he did well, especially in Modern Languages (no surprise here, given his record at his previous school) though it is unknown whether he passed his School Certificate. A letter from his mother claimed, 'I have heard from Malvern the other day he had taken Honours in Higher Mathematics, the last examination he took before he left there; but it is satisfactory, as he left a good record as regards school work while he has been at college'. His career there was not unchequered. On one occasion, he told his mother that a friend had invited him to spend some days with his family at their house. His mother happily acceded to the request, but must have been shocked to hear, a few days later, that her son had not turned up. He was later found at a seaside resort on the south coast, 'having a good time'.[15] At this time, Mrs Merrett maintained her friendship with Mrs Hill who had also returned to England.[16]

Schooling at an end, the next question was how to deal with his future. Mrs Merrett turned to Major Blackburn, now secretary to the Agricultural College in Edinburgh, married and resident at 13 George Street, Edinburgh. Merrett had a desire to join the Royal Navy, but his mother thought this was impracticable. Instead she thought he should study for the Diplomatic service and utilise his undoubted flair for languages. Blackburn was not without influence at Edinburgh University, so it was decided she and her son should live in Edinburgh, where he could attend the university there, but they stayed for a fortnight in Bosham to be with Annie Penn. Edinburgh University, founded in 1583, was the sixth oldest in the English speaking world

14 *Kelly's Worcestershire Directory*, 1924, p.190.
15 Roughead, *Trial*, p.195; NRS, AD15/27/1.
16 Ibid, p.125.

and an extremely prestigious one, with many famous alumni including Robert Louis Stevenson and Arthur Conan Doyle, and being known for Medicine and Law.[17]

Merrett was interviewed by the University Faculty of Arts Adviser and was assigned to Mr William King Gillies (1875-1952), a noted classical scholar and Rector of the Royal High School, Edinburgh, as his tutee. Although term began on 1 October, entry during the academic year was not uncommon (Evelyn Waugh entered Hertford College, Oxford, in January 1922). Merrett matriculated at Edinburgh University on 12 January 1926, the first day of term, student number 3,708 for the academic year, 1925-1926. Apparently he had matriculated at London University in the previous month. At Edinburgh he was registered on the Master of Arts degree course. This was a three year course, made up of five subjects, leading to exams. The Faculty of Arts was one of six faculties at the University and was located at the Old College on South Bridge, on the site of the murder of Darnley in the sixteenth century.[18] Virtually nothing is known about Merrett's university career. Less than one in twenty then attended university and for many the work there was far from onerous.

We need to examine Mrs Merrett's financial position. In 1925 she opened an account with the branch of Midland Bank at Boscombe.[19] Her income was £700 per annum, about the same as that of a doctor and so firmly middle class. £100 of this came from her own estate, the remainder being from the interest in her parents' estates. On her decease, the interest from the former would go to her son and that from the latter would do so, but to a smaller degree.[20] Annie Penn described her sister as 'an extremely careful person about money matters, and an excellent business woman. I know that she kept accounts; I have seen her account book'.[21] Bertha Hill agreed with this, stating that her friend was 'Very clever in everything' and 'She discussed planning her money and making things pan out, like one might, but she never expressed any feeling of difficulty whatever'. She was also a devout Christian; a prayer book being found in her room.[22]

---

17 Roughead, *Trial*, p.131; NRS, AD15/27/1.
18 NRS, AD15/27/1; EUA, IN1/ADS/STA8; Edinburgh University Calendar, 1925-1926, p.50.
19 Roughead, *Trial*, p.195.
20 Ibid, p.197.
21 Ibid, p.131.
22 Ibid, pp.127, 22.

After a brief stay at Waverley Hydropathic, a hotel in Melrose, on the Scottish borders, mother and son began to live at 7 Mayfield Road, Edinburgh, the house of Elizabeth Hardie, on 4 January 1926. Occasionally a tutor would visit in the evenings to coach Merrett for his studies. He once took his mother to a students' union dance and to the Fountainbridge Palais. They eventually left because they were unable to entertain friends at the house. The Merretts then lived in Mrs Joan Sharp's boarding house at 33-35 Palmerston Place from 25 January to 10 March. Merrett was not popular with the others there and was referred to as being 'not a talking boy' or what later would be called being a sulky teenager. Callers sometimes came to visit Merrett and he was meant to study in his room in the evening but often left surreptitiously and stayed out late. Mrs Sharp recalled, 'he was not truthful. I think sometimes he told his mother he had been or not been to places which tales were not true'. Blackburn recalled, 'The boy's inclinations ran in the direction of gaiety and dancing'.[23]

Mrs Merrett arranged with Robert Anderson, a house agent, at 7 Drumsheugh Place, Edinburgh, to rent rooms in Buckingham Terrace (a few minutes walk from Palmerston Place), to commence from 10 March until the end of June. The rent would be for £50, payable in two halves, with the first instalment paid on 2 March and Anderson duly received a cheque for £25 on that date and another £25 ten days later. One reason for this new accommodation was that Blackburn suggested that a self contained flat would be more suitable than a boarding house for the boy's studies; clearly his mother was concerned about her son and had confided in the major.[24]

The Merretts moved house to 31 Buckingham Terrace, just off Queensferry Road, one of the major thoroughfares into the city centre from the west, and took the rooms on the first floor. These houses have three floors, cellars and attics. The street consists of 40 houses, divided into one block of 34 (numbers 1-34) and then one of six (35-40) is sheltered from the main road by a strip of tree lined land which in 1927 was railed around. This was part of the Learmouth development as an extension west of the New Town, after Dean Bridge opened. It was one of the streets designed in the 1860s by John Chesser (1820-1893), who did much to shape the new Edinburgh of the Victorian

---

23 Ibid, pp.207, 197; NRS, AD15/27/1.
24 Ibid, p.196.

age. It was the first street in Edinburgh to offer bay windows and has been deemed the first and best of Chesser's terraces. These were of sympathetically paired houses, with well considered architectural details, balconies above the front doors and sloping gardens at their rear, aimed at being for the middle classes. There were no shops and no street life. And it 'breathes an atmosphere of gentility'. Certainly in 1926, there was a nursing home, a private hotel, two majors, a solicitor, a Lady and an OBE holder among its residents. Nearby are two churches and Stewart Melville's College, a well established private school.[25]

However, by the 1920s, as with many houses, number 31 was subdivided as flats in response to changing socio-economic demands. Their flat consisted of a front bedroom and an adjacent sitting room. At the back of the flat was the kitchen, the bathroom and another bedroom. They needed someone to do the cleaning and one Mrs Henrietta Sutherland, a 27-year-old separated from her husband, Hugh, because of his excessive drinking, heard of their need. She began her employment there on Wednesday, 10 March, working there from nine until twelve that morning. She was employed elsewhere on the next day, but performed her housekeeping duties at no. 31 for each of the subsequent mornings.[26]

Edinburgh, historically Scotland's capital, was the seat of government, Church and judiciary and was the second largest city of Scotland, with a population in 1921 of 420,281. It had a significant middle class, with above average ownership of cars and consumer goods. Its population had a high degree of retired people, of single women and professionals, many who had lived and worked abroad. There was only a limited industrial base; publishing, printing, brewing and the North British Rubber Factory, so the impact of the post 1918 economic downturn was limited. It was exactly the type of place and society that Mrs Merrett would appreciate.[27]

On Sunday the 14th, Mrs Sutherland overheard a conversation between the Merretts. She asked her son to write a letter about a missing cheque book. Mrs Merrett said little that was memorable to her servant, but on Monday the 15th told her that she had had a hard

---

25 Pevsner, *The Buildings of Scotland: Edinburgh* (1984), pp.397-8; *Kelly's Edinburgh Directory*, 1927.
26 Roughead, *Trial*, plan and p.61.
27 Information from Elspeth Wills.

life, though did not seem dispirited. She mentioned that her husband had died in the Russian Revolution, a story that she had also told her son. It is not certain why she said this because it was untrue; possibly it saved her the embarrassment of not having to explain that she and her husband were living apart; possibly she believed it to be true. However, although Mrs Sutherland did not see much of the Merretts together, she thought that they were on excellent terms.[28]

Various accounts are given about the state of Mrs Merrett's temperament at this time. Mrs Agnes Mary Anderson, an old friend, who visited her in early March thought she was in good spirits. Mrs Sharp, the boarding house keeper whom the Merretts had stayed with, stated, 'Mrs Merrett was very cheerful and bright, and was a person of very methodical habits'. She did not think she was 'excitable'.[29] Nor did Elizabeth Hardie, saying she was nether excitable nor nervous, but she noted, 'She did things on the spur of the moment as far as he [Merrett] was concerned.'[30] She also claimed that she spoke in a silly way to her Pekinese dog and to herself, but did not think she was in poor mental health.[31] Bertha Hill said she was 'Highly strung, emotional, [had] a keen grip on life and everything it concerned'. She recalled the two of them seeing a tramp which unnerved Mrs Merrett, but discounted this as an instance of character. Little things might affect her, before she could think through them and that she became a little more upset than most people.[32]

Relations between mother and son were thought to be good, at least on the surface. Mrs Merrett told her bank manager in Boscombe on 4 March, 'Donald has done well at the University, and has quite settled down to the life here'.[33] Elizabeth Hardie saw a great deal of the two in early January, and recalled that they got on well together, that they were on affectionate terms and that there were no disagreements. She thought that Merrett was attached to his mother and behaved 'Quite as a son ought to behave towards his mother'. Apparently he even took her to dances once or twice. As to Mrs Merrett, 'She struck me as a very loving mother...She was devoted to the boy in every way. That

---

28 Roughead, *Trial*, pp.65-6.
29 Ibid, pp.196-7.
30 Ibid, p.208.
31 NRS, AD15/27/1.
32 Roughead, *Trial*, p.127.
33 Ibid, p.196.

was what struck me'.[34] Mrs Anderson, said that Mrs Merrett was 'very proud of her son, being an only child, and was looking forward to his having a successful career at the university'. The two planned to visit France at Easter in order that the lad might increase his proficiency in French by practical experience.[35]

Yet he was, in fact, living a less than exemplary life. Edwin Muir, writing in the 1920s, gave his view of vice in the city:

> Nowhere that I have been is one so bathed and steeped and rolled about in floating sexual desire as in certain streets of Edinburgh. This desire fills the main thoroughfares and overflows into all the adjacent pockets and backwaters: the tea rooms, restaurants and cinema lounges.[36]

It cannot be known whether Merrett indulged in such vices, but he was certainly not averse to female company. This may well have been reciprocated as Agnes Anderson remarked of him, 'He was a handsome boy and looked much older than he was'.[37]

He was spending a lot of his time and money at the Dunedin Palais de Danse, (also known as the Assembly Rooms), self proclaimed 'Greatest of all Dance Halls', there being several then in the city, on 10 Picardy Place, which had opened in 1922, and was located just to the east of the city centre. It opened in the afternoon; entry price one shilling, and in the evenings for two shillings and six pence. In March 1926, the Romany Revellers' Band, who had also performed on the BBC, were one of the bands employed; another was Bert Ralton and his Havana Band. On Friday evenings there were special dances, such as a Theatrical Carnival Ball on 5 March; on the 16th was a Grand Cinema Ball. There were also charity balls for good causes such as the Edinburgh Boys' Brigade. This was not a seedy den of vice, but a fairly respectable establishment where popular ballroom dancing took place, and where tea and sherry were commonplace beverages. George Armstrong Scott, a clerk and dance instructor employed there, claimed Merrett went there two or three times a week from January 1926. He added, 'Merrett I think was an enthusiastic dancer but I could not call him a very good dancer'.[38]

34 Ibid, pp.207-8.
35 NRS, AD15/27/1.
36 Fry, *Edinburgh: A History of the City* (2009), p.378.
37 NRS, AD15/27/1.
38 Roughead, *Trial*, p.198; *Edinburgh Evening News*, 16 March 1926; NRS, AD15/27/1.

Elizabeth Helen Christie, a dance instructress, known as Betty, who had been employed there since August 1925, thought Merrett was a frequent visitor; three or four nights a week and sometimes once or twice per week on afternoons, too. The Palais employed eleven dance teachers to teach the Charleston, the waltz, the foxtrot, tango and blues for five shillings a lesson (no booking needed). Individual dances cost sixpence each. Merrett danced with other girls, but he paid her a great deal of attention. He bought her two rings, one worth £2 5s and the other £2. He also paid to spend time with her outside the dance hall, a recognised practice at the time. This cost 15s per afternoon, £1 for an early night and 30s for a late night. She said, 'we became what one might call "good pals". He sometimes booked me out for the afternoon. I was once down at Queensferry [known as Edinburgh by sea and site of a huge funfair] for tea with him, and I have also been down to the Marine Gardens with him'. Apparently Merrett 'never seemed to be in want of it [money]'. She also remarked, 'He was inclined to dance a little too vigorously, at times such as a young romping boy might do. He behaved like a kid sometimes'. Yet she thought he was well behaved, 'Donnie always behaved very decently to me'. Girls such as Betty were not necessarily tarts, but were probably not the type of young woman that middle class parents would like to see their sons with. He also allegedly began gambling at this time and his losses added up.[39]

It is often stated that Merrett's mother was wholly unaware of her son's extra-curricular activities, but this was not the case. Joan Sharp recalled that she had been told that Merrett had been 'naughty' once or twice and should study more steadily. Mrs Merrett told Donald Saxton, master at the Waitaki School, 'Donald is wayward and appears to have no respect for me'. Major Blackburn recalled his friend telling him that she knew her son spent more money than he possessed and that he sometimes went out to the Dunedin Palais de Danse. She had taken him to task over it. He said, 'Donald's conduct was causing his mother some uneasiness and grief'. Mrs Penn recalled that 'I gathered that Donald had been giving her some uneasiness. He had got into an escapade associating with persons his mother did not approve of, but I understood that this matter was satisfactorily arranged'. Yet he did deceive her over the scale of his night life. Matters were worse than

---

39 Ibid, pp.149-150; *Edinburgh Evening News*, 17 March 1926; NRS, AD15/27/1; *Woman's Sunday Mirror*, 6 October 1957.

she knew, for the boarding house keeper was aware that Merrett was given a latch key and sometimes went out in the evenings without his mother's knowledge. At 31 Buckingham Terrace he often kept his bedroom door locked as he slept in the day time, and may have had a rope in his room, nailed to the bottom half of the window allegedly in case he fell out of the window whilst walking in his sleep. In reality this was Merrett's discreet way of leaving the flat and re-entering it later on.[40]

A rather odd incident occurred on the morning of Sunday, 14 March, when Mrs Merrett rang PC William Oliver. Apparently Merrett was locked in his bedroom without his key and so could not leave. The officer arrived half an hour later. One suggestion was that Merrett could get out of the window and inch himself over to the balcony in front of the living room, perhaps using a rope. No such athletics were needed. Mrs Sutherland found the missing key outside the front door and it was used to unlock the door. Merrett could not explain why he had lost his key.[41]

Merrett was also spending money in another way. In very early February he went to Messrs Hardy Brothers, 101 Princes Street, Edinburgh's major shopping street, overlooked by the castle, a gunsmiths, and inquired of Charles Nichol Stott, an assistant there, for a pistol. Doubtless well aware of the 1920 Firearms Act, Stott told him that registered dealers could only sell guns to those possessing a firearms certificate and that he would have to apply to the police to obtain one. Obtaining a licence was easy; the supplicant needed to be fourteen or more, to be sane and sober, to be trustworthy and to have a need for a gun. On 12 February he went to the West End Police Station and met PC William Davidson. He gave him an application form for a firearms licence. Merrett explained that his father was dead, told him about his educational history and current status, that he needed a gun because he intended to go to France during the Easter holidays with university friends, and that he would use the pistol to shoot small game, birds and trees in the woods there. The policeman forwarded the application and a report of his interview to the Central Police Station.[42]

The application was processed promptly. PC Murdo McLean of

---

40 NRS, AD15/27/1; McLeave, *Chesney: The Fabulous Murderer* (1954), p.14.
41 NRS, AD15/27/1.
42 Roughead, *Trial*, pp.151, 198.

the firearms department dealt with it and later commented, 'there seemed to be no objection to the certificate being granted'. On the following day Merrett returned to the shop with his certificate and bought a .25 calibre automatic pistol, costing £1 17s 6d, and 50 rounds of ammunition for a further 7s 6d, paying in cash. Merrett told Stott that he needed the gun because he proposed going abroad. Merrett's friend, George Scott, was aware that he had a gun, as was Miss Christie.[43]

The little gun was a cheap make and was made in Spain. It had an effective safety catch. A fair amount of force was required to squeeze the trigger. It could hardly be discharged by accident. The gun's magazine held six cartridges and after each discharge, another cartridge would come into the chamber and so be ready to fire again. The cartridge, when fired, was automatically ejected from the pistol, usually to the right of the firer. It would also discharge a small amount of smoke.[44]

Guns are often carried by people who do not know how to use them. They carry them in order to feel powerful; inadequates attempting to satisfy their own ego. This makes them all the more dangerous, both to themselves and others. He later told a girlfriend that a gun was necessary, alleging, 'Mixing with the kind of people I did, I decided to be armed'.[45]

There will be some question as to whether Mrs Merrett knew about her son's gun. The answer is probably not. Blackburn was convinced that she knew nothing of it. This was because he believed he knew her so well that if she had known of it she would have mentioned it to him, as she did her other concern about her son. They had known each other for 10 years, after all. Mrs Penn also believed that her sister knew nothing about the gun, and she did write to her, confiding in her concerns about her son.[46] On the other hand, it is possible that she did not tell all about her son, especially if it was something that was embarrassing. Merrett later claimed that his mother had found the weapon and had confiscated it.

---

43 Ibid, pp.151, 198; NRS, AD15/27/1.
44 Ibid, pp. 151-3.
45 Hastings, *The Other Mr Churchill* (1963), pp.60-61; *Woman's Sunday Mirror*, 6 October 1957.
46 NRS, AD15/27/1.

Then there was another significant purchase. In early March, he went into a motor cycle shop on Greenside Place. He told James Cairns, the joint manager there, that he wanted a second hand cycle. At that time, Cairns had a customer who wanted to sell an AJS motorcycle and so he arranged a sale between the two parties. It was about £28. Merrett could not buy immediately, but left a cheque as a deposit and returned two days later with the cash and so became the proud owner. On 16 March he and Scott went on 'a run' with their motor cycles. Merrett had an accident and sustained some cuts which required dressing.[47] All this cost money and was beyond Merrett's weekly allowance of ten shillings (his mother also bought him clothes on top of this). We shall soon see how he financed these purchases.

To the outside world, Mrs Merrett maintained the pretence that all was well, writing on 26 February, 'Donald has taken to life at the Varsity'. She had regular dealings with her banks. On 4 March she wrote to the Boscombe bank and asking for her pass book to be made up so she could see how she stood financially. She was then living at Palmerston Place, and so the bank sent the book there by post and it noted that the balance then stood at £286 2s 4d. Eight days later, her cheque book having been lost, she requested that another be sent; later she believed it to have been destroyed, yet as we shall later see, this was not the case.[48]

His mother first had a better intimation of how exactly the land lay when she received the following letter:

The Clydesdale Bank Ltd.
George Street
Edinburgh, 13 March 1926
Mrs Bertha Merrett,
31 Buckingham Terrace.

Dear Madam,

We beg to advise you that we have to-day paid a cheque on your account which makes the balance £22. Might we suggest the advisability of drawing on your Boscombe account a sum sufficient to put your account here in order.

Yours faithfully,

---

47 Roughead, *Trial*, pp.199, 198.
48 Ibid, pp.195-6.

> R.J.L. Hendry,
> Manager[49]

It is not certain when Mrs Merrett read the letter. Another letter was sent shortly afterwards:

> The Clydesdale Bank Ltd.
> George Street
> Edinburgh, 16 March 1926
> Mrs Bertha Merrett,
> 31 Buckingham Terrace.
>
> Dear Madam,
>
> We think it well to advise that cheques have been paid by us on your account which make it overdrawn to the extent of £6 11s 3d.
>
> Yours faithfully,
>
> R.J.L. Hendry,
> Manager[50]

The letter was undoubtedly received on the morning of the 17th.

This state of affairs had come about because a number of cheques had been made on Mrs Merrett's accounts from 2 February onwards, of which she was wholly unaware of. She took care of her money and kept a separate account book to record her expenditure and needless to say, none of these payments were known to her until she was notified of the effect they were having on her bank account. Between 2 February and 11 March there had been eleven cheques withdrawing cash from the Clydesdale Bank account, totalling £79 17s 6d. From the Boscombe account from 8 February to 16 March, eleven cheques for rather larger amounts, the total value of £194 19s 5d, had been used to remove money from her account. In total, £274 16s 11d had gone; a sum equating to nearly half her annual income had been taken in six weeks. In all cases, the payee was her own son. He had simply presented cheques bearing his mother's signature to the bank branch, and the cashiers had duly cashed them. He was known to the staff for he and his mother had visited there and there was no obvious reason why this should have caused suspicion.[51]

---

49 Ibid, p.23.
50 Ibid, p.24.
51 Ibid, pp.193-5, 322.

However, once the second letter arrived, as it did on 17 March, Mrs Merrett learnt that her finances were in the gravest condition. A crisis was close at hand.

3

A Death in the Family, 1926

Wednesday, 17 March was to be a critical day in the life of John Merrett and his mother. There are various accounts of what happened on that morning on the first floor of 31 Buckingham Terrace and these will be revealed as we proceed in a chronological order; they conflict with one another and so it is up to the reader to decide for themselves which is the most likely of scenarios.

Mrs Sutherland made various statements as to what she did or not witness on that morning. I will present what seems to be the most likely account, which was her final version and was corroborated by Merrett. According to her:

> On the morning of the 17th of March I got to the flat at just about nine. I did not have a key of my own, so I had to ring. I was let in by Mrs Merrett. When I got in I went right to the kitchen to take my hat and coat off. Having taken them off, I went into the dining-room. Mr Merrett [this was unusual; he had usually left by nine and rarely said anything to her] and Mrs Merrett were both in the room when I first went in. Mrs Merrett was putting some of the things off the table into the drawers of the bureau – the salt cellar, sugar bowl, and such things.[1]

Nothing could have been more ordinary or commonplace. Mrs Sutherland continued her narrative:

---

1 Roughead, *Trial*, p.61.

> *When I went in the first time, some of the breakfast things were still on the table. I started to clear them away. I took them to the kitchen. When I left the room, Mrs Merrett was at the bureau, getting out what I thought was writing material. I cannot remember where... [Merrett]... was at that time. Mrs Merrett did her writing on the big table on which the breakfast things were. When I left the room on the first occasion, Mrs Merrett was still collecting the things. I washed up the dishes in the kitchen. Having finished with the dishes, I went into the sitting room again to do the fire-place. There was no fire on at that time. When I went in to do the fire-place Mrs Merrett was sitting writing at the big table, and ...[Merrett]... was sitting reading behind the big chair in the recess. As I went in at the door and saw Mrs Merrett sitting writing, her left side was a little towards me. Her back would be towards the bureau, but not straight on. I did not do the fire at that time, as I saw they were both engaged in the room, so I just came out.*[2]

Again, this could have been just like any one of the previous days when Mrs Sutherland had been employed at the flat. The next moments were anything but.

> *After leaving the sitting room I made to go to the kitchen, and on my way I opened the coal-cellar door and took out a pailful of coal that I had ready to take into the kitchen along with the ash-bucket. I then went to do the kitchen fire-side. I had just got started on the kitchen grate when I heard the shot.*[3]

At this point - the time was about 9.40 am - she was just making to bend down but she suddenly got up. As well as the shot she heard Mrs Merrett scream once and once only, immediately after the explosion. Mrs Sutherland stood stock still with shock, later claiming 'I did not know what to do'. She then heard a thud as if someone was falling and then heard some books fall to the ground in the hallway. A few seconds later:

> *[Merrett] came out into the kitchen and said his mother had shot herself, and he seemed very much upset. He made to put his hand on my shoulder. I thought he was going to cry.*

Instead he said, 'Rita, my mother shot herself'.

---

2 Roughead, *Trial*, pp.61-2.
3 Ibid, p.62.

Mrs Sutherland told him that she thought that his mother had seemed perfectly fine when she had admitted her to the flat, and he replied that he had been wasting her money, and that he thought his mother had been worried because of that. They were now walking out of the kitchen into the hallway. According to Mrs Sutherland, 'We both went into the sitting room together. When I went into the sitting room I saw Mrs Merrett lying on the floor with her head towards the door'.[4]

She described the scene:

> *The chair was at the other side where her feet were like at the other side of her body…I did not go up to Mrs Merrett when I saw she was bleeding so much. She never moved while I saw her. [Merrett] was besides me at the time…I went right to the telephone.*[5]

The telephone was on a small table in the hallway. She picked up the handset and asked to be put through to the police (rather than to fetch medical assistance), for she did not know the number. Merrett stood by her side whilst she telephoned, and Merrett completed the call as she was uncertain how to spell his surname. Then, in her words:

> *I remained beside him whilst he was telephoning. After he had finished telephoning we both went back to the sitting-room. Mrs Merrett was still lying there. She had not moved. She was still bleeding. [Merrett] asked me to help him with his mother on to the settee. The settee was to the right hand side of the fireplace between the door and the window. I said "Oh, I think we had best leave her"…We both stood in the room, and then when I said we had best leave her Donald made to take my hand and said, "Let us go out: I cannot stand to look at it any longer". We both walked out of the room, and I opened the outside door and made to go down the stair, in order to meet the police.*[6]

Merrett did nothing to make his mother more comfortable or assist her in any way. The first policemen on the scene were constables Thomas Gray Middlemiss and David Izatt, both aged 28. Middlemiss had just come on duty and was in Queensferry Street, when a police ambulance came along. Driver Edgar told him there had been a shooting accident at 31 Buckingham Terrace. According to Middlemiss:

---

4   Ibid, pp.62-3.
5   Ibid, p.63.
6   Ibid.

> *I went with the ambulance. At the foot of the stair I met [Merrett]... and the tablemaid or housemaid Mrs Henrietta Sutherland...I asked what was wrong and...[Merrett] said that his mother had shot herself. I went up the first floor stair and into the sitting room, and found Mrs Merrett lying on the floor. She was lying in front of a kind of writing desk or something. There was a good deal of blood about, and she was still bleeding. She was unconscious.*[7]

Izatt recalled his colleague asking Merrett whether the reason behind the shooting was financial and the latter replied, 'No, I think my mother is well off'. Middlemiss could see that Mrs Merrett was moving and trying to breathe, choking with blood in her throat. Once they were both upstairs, the constables put Mrs Merrett's still living body on a stretcher to be taken by ambulance to the city's Royal Infirmary on Lauriston Gardens. Built in 1872-1879 by the Bryces it replaced an earlier foundation of 1738. At the scene of the shooting there were two contentious points. These were the location of the weapon and the letter which Mrs Merrett had commenced writing before the shot was fired.[8]

Mrs Sutherland recalled seeing the pistol, which was the one that Merrett had bought in the previous month, on the top of the bureau. It was bloodstained. Izatt thought the gun was lying by the body, on the right hand side. However, PC Middlemiss, who had picked it up, after being told where it was, was not sure whether he took the bloodstained gun from the floor or from the bureau. He rolled it up into a paper and put it in his pocket. No one ever troubled to dust it for fingerprints; a crucial omission, for they could have revealed who had fired the fatal shot.[9]

Apparently Mrs Sutherland said to them, 'would he please take it away as I did not like it lying there'. The gun was later examined and was found to have five cartridges loaded, one in the breach ready to fire and four in the magazine, as one would expect after one bullet had been fired from a fully-loaded six shot gun.[10]

Izatt recalled in a newspaper interview nearly three decades later:

---

7   Roughead, *Trial*, p.77.
8   Ibid, pp.78, 83.
9   Ibid, pp.64, 78.
10 NRS, AD15/27/1; Ibid, p.79.

> *He [Merrett] was absolutely cool, calm and collected...he made no move to assist her. She was in agony on the floor, while he just waited for us to arrive...I shall never forget it – the sight of young Merrett standing so coolly near his mother.*[11]

Mrs Sutherland saw a letter lying under an envelope on the writing bureau, but she could not see its contents. Nearby was a letter addressed by Mrs Merrett. It was never taken by the police and subsequently disappeared.[12]

Middlemiss and Izatt then went with Merrett in the ambulance to the surgical out-patients' department. In the corridor, Middlemiss spoke with Merrett. The police officer said,

> *'I wonder what went wrong with your mother? How has she come to do this?'*
>
> *'Money matters.'*

This was in direct contradiction to what he had just told Izatt.

> *'What do you mean by "money matters" – too much or too little?'*
>
> *'No, just money matters.'*

Nothing more was said until the two left the hospital and returned to 31 Buckingham Terrace in a taxi. Needing to know more in order to write his report, Middlemiss asked again about the reason for the shooting, which was assumed to be a case of attempted suicide. Merrett told him the same, but added that his mother was writing a letter at the bureau whilst he was sitting at the other side of the room when he heard the shot. He told how he then went to his mother and then left the room to see Mrs Sutherland in the kitchen and then they rang the police. Middlemiss asked who owned the pistol and Merrett said he did. He was then asked about having a firearms certificate but he could not produce it immediately. Merrett told him he had it so he could go shooting in France whilst on holiday. He later said that Merrett did not 'give it [the information] freely or willingly' as 'he is a fellow that I could not really tell you what he is'. Merrett told him that his father had died in the Russian Revolution. On returning to the flat he spoke to Mrs Sutherland, who said she had been in the kitchen when the shot was fired and then Merrett entered to tell her

11 *Daily Mail*, 17 February 1954.
12 Roughead, *Trial*, p.64.

that his mother had shot herself. She was clearly distraught, for on their return, she was in the upstairs flat talking to the maid there as she was too frightened to remain alone downstairs. Middlemiss later made a report of the interviews to the desk sergeant at West End Police Station at Torphichen Street. At the time he believed he was reporting an attempted suicide.[13]

Shortly after all this, at 10 am Detective Inspector David Fleming of the City Police arrived on the scene with Sergeant William Henderson and they questioned Mrs Sutherland. Fleming was the senior officer in charge of the investigation. Born at St. Andrew's Fife on 10 August 1876, he had been a clerk before being appointed as a policeman on 16 June 1896. He was five feet eight and a half inches in height, had brown hair, blue eyes and a fresh complexion. Although he had had two injuries to his foot in 1908 and 1912, generally his health was very good and he had only had occasional days off for minor ailments. The only stain on his record was in February 1906 when he had had his monthly leave suspended for dubious conduct concerning a pawnbroker transaction. By 1907 he was a detective constable and he became a 1st class detective inspector on 16 July 1922, with an annual salary of £360. He was thus an experienced officer of almost 30 years standing.[14]

They had already been informed that this was a case of suicide. Mrs Sutherland was feeling confused about what had just happened, as she later explained:

> Well, I spoke to them, but I do not know what I said to them, because I was mixed up at that time. I had been upset by the whole incident, because I had only been there a few days, and I did not know what had happened when I heard the shot.[15]

According to Fleming, Mrs Sutherland gave a rather different statement to the one given earlier in this chapter. He stated:

> I asked Mrs Sutherland what had happened. And she told me that she had been in the kitchen about half past nine and heard a shot, and on going into the lobby saw Mrs Merrett fall off the chair and onto the floor **and a revolver falling out of her hand**. [author's emboldening]

13 Roughead, *Trial*, pp.78-81; NRS, AD15/27/1.
14 Edinburgh City Archives, ED6/13.
15 Roughead, *Trial*, pp.64-5.

Henderson agreed, later stating, '[she] saw Mrs Merrett falling from her chair to the floor, and a revolver falling from her hand'. He added that the witness 'stated that Mrs Merrett was sitting at the table writing letters, or a letter, and...Donald, as she termed him, was sitting beside the fireplace in a chair, reading a book'. Although she was 'a little bit' agitated, there seemed no reason to doubt her accuracy.[16]

Fleming and Henderson went into the sitting room. Fleming saw Mrs Merrett's letter on the table. It had not been finished. It was to a friend in Stirling, mentioning the fact that she had got a flat at last, and that there had been trouble finding a maid, but that had been resolved. Fleming noted 'There was nothing about money troubles in it'. He said that the last word was not smudged or blurred and that there was no evidence that the writer had suddenly been stopped in her writing of the letter. He left the letter on the table and forgot all about it. It was never seen again. He also noted the two letters from the bank about her financial situation. He concluded that this was a case of suicide and returned to the police station to give the necessary instructions as to a charge being considered, that of attempted suicide. Until 1961 suicide was a criminal offence in the United Kingdom and anyone attempting it would be brought to trial with the possibility of facing a custodial sentence.[17]

The police investigation and the officers responsible for it have been much criticised. One contemporary writer noted, 'Two intelligent schoolboys, visiting the locus that morning, could better have observed and reported what they saw and did than the officers responsible for that duty'. A later writer likened them to the incompetent fictional American policemen, the 'Keystone Kops'.[18] There was no attempt to collect the evidence at the scene nor to dust for fingerprints (and testing the automatic could well have been decisive one way or another) or take photographs of the scene of the shooting nor of the victim, for example. The letter that Mrs Merrett was writing at the time was not preserved, nor was there any search for the discharged cartridge case. It was certainly not a case that was treated with an open mind. Because they believed that this was an attempted suicide, little effort was taken to rigorously investigate it.

However, it is not uncommon for the busy – or the lazy – to look

16 Ibid, pp.87-8, 206-7.
17 Ibid, pp.87-8, 93.
18 Ibid, p.28.

no further if a conceivable solution is ready at hand. Unlike the case in detective fiction, police officers have to deal with numerous cases at the same time. It is also possible that they chose to believe the apparently respectable youth whereas had the shooting taken place in a less affluent district they may well not have done so. More pertinently, nor was there then any obvious motive why he should have shot his mother. It should also be noted that suicides were far more common than murder and that matricide was extremely rare; from 1911-1925 there were two trials in Edinburgh for matricide and in only one of these the accused was found guilty. The police erred; but their mistake was not unnatural.

The six officers who had a part in the investigation were a diverse group. As said, Fleming had nearly 30 years of experience. Henderson had 25 years, and nearly 13 in the detective force (he was to end his police career in 1936 as a 3rd class Detective Lieutenant). His police record noted his 'smart arrest' of shop breakers and 'exceptional tact and energy' in enforcing the gaming laws. PC Victor Gibson had joined the Force in 1914 and retired as a 1st class Sergeant in 1948. He had been highly commended in 1920 for bravery in arresting an armed robber and was later highly commended for 'special zeal and efficiency'. PC William Watt had nearly a dozen years experience in the police by 1926 (less four years in the army in wartime). Middlemiss had five years experience as a constable and Izatt six; in 1923 the latter was commended for 'tact and efficiency' in arresting would be burglars. None of these men were inexperienced novices, therefore.[19]

At the Infirmary, Dr Richard Bell was a surgeon in the out-patients' department. He was the first to examine the injured woman. He had to cut some of her hair away to better see the wound:

> *She was suffering from a wound in the head. I examined the wound to see whether there was any blackening or tattooing around the wound, but I could not find any. The hair round the wound did not smell of any explosive. I examined it specially to see if it did. I cleared away some of the hair so as to get better observation. The patient's clothing was spoiled both by blood and vomiting.*

He did not remove the blood. He also spoke to Merrett, asking how the shooting occurred, and he told him that he was in the room, heard an explosion and saw that his mother was wounded. Bell then sent

19 ECA, ED6/13.

her to the surgical theatre in ward 16 and from there she was taken to ward 3, which is where the hospital put attempted suicides. It had barred windows and locked doors, so was in effect a detention ward. Although Bell had qualified as a doctor only two years previously, it is worth noting that he had seen military service as an army officer in the First World War and in doing so had earned the Military Cross. Therefore, it can be assumed that he had experience of gunshot wounds.[20]

At half past twelve, Dr Roy Stanley Holcombe examined her, having been informed she had tried to commit suicide. He noted that she had a wound through her right ear, which had entered the skull. The entry wound was small, about the size of a pencil, 'very, very small, but well defined'. There was no sign of blackening or tattooing by gunpowder particles in the region of the wound, but there was a slight reddish discolouration around it. Bell wiped the blood away from and inside the ear with a swab after he had examined the wound. By now she was conscious. Dr Holcombe was relatively inexperienced, having only qualified as a doctor in the previous year.[21]

Elizabeth Fraser Grant was one of the nurses attached to ward three. She saw Merrett and later recalled:

> He asked me if his mother was still alive, and I said, "Yes, and she has spoken to us". He asked me, if his mother got better, not to tell her what happened, as he did not wish her to know anything about it…I proceeded to ask him what happened, and he said he found his mother in the drawing room about 9.45 with a bullet wound – or "shot in the face" were the words exactly. I said "Has she been worried about anything?" He said, "Yes, she has been worried about money matters". Before he left I asked if his mother was in a normal state that morning and the night before and he said, "Yes, and she has been quite normal that morning and the night before."[22]

That day Mrs Merrett complained of the pain she was in and wanted to know its cause. Holcombe recalled, 'I just said "Oh, you have had a little accident, Mrs Merrett" and that was all. I did not force the matter at all. I did not tell her straight out that I thought it was a case of suicide'. She was perfectly rational and coherent at this point.

---

20 Roughead, *Trial*, pp.101-102; *Medical Directory*, 1927; NRS, AD15/27/1.
21 Ibid, p.103.
22 Ibid, p.113.

However, he thought at once that she might not survive the wound.[23]

Fleming made out a charge sheet at West End Police Station to the affect that Mrs Merrett had attempted suicide. Colonel George David St. Clair Thom (1870-1935), was superintendent of the Royal Infirmary and later that day he received a letter from the police, which clearly stated their view as to what had happened:

> Police Station
> West End
> Edinburgh
> 17 March 1926
>
> *I have the honour to inform you that Bertha Milner or Merrett, now detained in No.3 Ward, Royal Infirmary, is a prisoner charged with attempted suicide, and I am directed by the Chief Constable to ask you to be good enough to inform the lieutenant on duty at the High Street, Edinburgh, the date and hour on which it is proposed to discharge the accused, in order that arrangement may be made for taking her into custody.*
> *Your obedient servant,*
> *Hugh Ross, Sergeant.*[24]

At about 2pm Merrett met Miss Christie outside her place of employment. He did not initially mention what had happened to his mother, but as he had done on previous occasions, booked her out for the afternoon. However Miss Christie noticed he was white faced 'and very upset', so asked him what was wrong. He replied that his mother had had an operation and that he was unsure whether she had shot herself or had had an accident with his gun. He explained that he had been in the sitting room, reading and that the maid was in the kitchen when the shooting occurred. Thinking that having tea at Queensferry might take his mind off his troubles, she suggested they go there. They travelled on his motorcycle. They may have patronised the Marine Gardens Ballroom there, 'Scotland's most popular ballroom', where teas could be obtained from 2.50-5 and from 7.30-10 for as little as a shilling each. Furthermore, at this time, Jefferies and his 'world famous' Rialto Orchestra were playing. Yet all this was not an effective remedy. 'He was greatly upset at tea time and I do not think he ate anything' she recalled. Then they went to the flat

---

23 Roughead, *Trial*, pp.104, 107.
24 Ibid, pp.95, 203-4.

at Buckingham Terrace, where they were met by George Scott, who was told a similar version of the morning's incident as that relayed to Miss Christie. They then went to the hospital where Merrett saw his mother. Miss Christie gave the staff there the telephone number of the Palais, with Scott as Merrett's reference there. However, Nurse Grant thought this conversation occurred in the evening at her initiative and she verified the number.[25]

Nurse Grant met Merrett again. She was busy so had little time to converse with him. However, she asked him if he had any relatives and he replied in the negative. She persisted, 'You have no brothers or sisters?' He again replied with a no. She also asked him 'Haven't you a soul in the world now but yourself?' A final no was given.[26]

They then returned to the Palais, perhaps at four o'clock. Merrett booked Betty off for the evening. He collected a suitcase to take to the Country Hotel in Lothian Road, where Scott had already booked a room for him. They had another visit to the hospital, where he saw his mother. Merrett also sent a telegram to Bertha Hill, which read, 'Mother ill, please come at once, asking for you. Donald'. She replied 'Very grieved, how is mother, just leaving to stay Hampstead but will postpone and come immediately if you shall need me. Awaiting reply'. He did not do so immediately, and in need of relaxation, they went to the Caley Picture House, on Lothian Road. The film they watched was *The Teaser*, a romantic comedy, starring Laura La Plante (then Universal Studio's leading actress) and Pat O'Malley. According to the advert in *The Edinburgh Evening News* the film was:

> *The chronicles of a naughty eyed bedimpled young lady who decided that if she couldn't have the man she wanted, she would make it interesting for her more fortunate sisters. The solution of this tangle of love and laughter comes in an hilarious and astounding denouement.*

Apart from the main feature there was an Andy Gump comedy and picture of 'topical interest' (presumably a newsreel). The day's performances concluded at 10.30. Afterwards the couple went back to the Palais. According to Scott, Merrett did not venture inside as usual.[27]

---

25 Ibid, pp.149-51, 114; *Edinburgh Evening News*, 12 March 1926.
26 Ibid, pp.113-14.
27 Ibid, pp.150, 198, 114, 125; *Edinburgh Evening News*, 17 March 1926; NRS, AD15/27/1.

That evening, Mrs Sutherland felt unwell. Being a panel patient of Dr Rosa, she called on him and was seen by his son, Dr Lewis George Rosa at 28 Pitt Street. He made up a prescription for her and they talked. The conversation turned to the shooting earlier that day. Dr Rosa later thought that she had told him, 'whilst she was in the [sitting] room she observed her mistress remove her false teeth, and that struck her as a strange thing. Later she proceeded to leave the room and turned her back on her mistress, and as she was leaving the room her mistress shot herself'. Dr Rosa took this to mean that Mrs Sutherland had seen Mrs Merrett fall from her chair. He thought that Mrs Sutherland looked tired and was worried by the shooting, but that she was otherwise composed. She also told the doctor that she felt very sorry for Merrett because he was very young.[28]

Also that evening, at another house in Buckingham Terrace, William Roughead (1870-1952), an amateur criminologist who attended every major murder trial in Edinburgh from 1889-1949, was having dinner with friends. His hostess, knowing his interest in crime, told him that a murder had taken place in that very street. An errand boy had passed on this piece of information. Roughead was shocked and intrigued, 'Such an incident occurring in so respectable a residential quarter was appetizing indeed.'[29]

On Thursday, 18 March Merrett passed the afternoon and evening with Miss Christie, booking her out as usual. Scott also saw him on this day. He visited the hospital that day, having that morning sent another telegram to Bertha Hill, reading, 'Nervous breakdown, bad, wants you, enquire RI, my address. D'. She replied, 'Leaving King's Cross tonight' and took a train from that north London station, and made the journey northwards to Edinburgh, letting the hospital staff there know of her intended arrival. Merrett was also told that she was coming. He cashed another of his mother's cheques for £30 in his name.[30]

Later that day, Mrs Merrett spoke to Nurse Grant about what had happened on the Wednesday morning. The latter recalled:

> *Nurse Innes and I were attending Mrs Merrett, making her bed and changing her, and she said, "What has happened? It is so*

---

28 Roughead, *Trial*, pp.204-5, 71.
29 Roughead, *Classic Crimes* (1951), p.413.
30 Roughead, *Trial*, pp.198, 150, 125, 322, 11.

> *extraordinary." She could not understand it – or words to that effect. I said I did not know what had happened, could not she tell me, and she said she was sitting writing at the time when suddenly a bang went off in her head like a pistol. I said, "Was there not a pistol there?" and she said "No, was there?" in great surprise. I think it was here when she asked me if the X-ray had not shown anything. I said I could not tell her that. So I continued then to ask her if she was quite sure she was writing at the time of the accident, and she said, "Yes, quite sure. Donald can tell you; he was standing beside me, waiting to post the letter."*

Grant thought that Mrs Merrett was mentally alert. She reported the conversation to Dr Holcombe.[31]

Nurse Jean Innes was also present and she overheard the conversation. She verified what Mrs Merrett had said, 'she said "Donald was standing beside me waiting to take them [the letters] to the post, and suddenly something burst in my head, just like a pistol shot"'. Dr Holcombe then talked to Mrs Merrett. He was unable to tell her outright that she was suspected of having attempted suicide by shooting. Mrs Merrett said much of what she had already recounted, but added that when her son was standing next to her, she told him, '"Go away Donald, and don't annoy me" and the next I heard was an explosion and I do not remember any more'. He then asked her to whom she was writing the letter to, but she said 'Oh, I do not know'. She was in great physical pain throughout these days.[32]

Meanwhile, Charles MacPherson, the Public Prosecutor for the City, was told about the shooting incident. He received a charge sheet which he passed as a matter of routine, without much consideration, to the city police surgeon, Professor Harvey Littlejohn of Edinburgh University (and of he, more anon). Proceedings, however, would wait until Mrs Merrett was recovered enough to face the charge.[33]

On the morning of Friday, 19 March (the last day of the second term at Edinburgh University), Mrs Hill arrived in Edinburgh. It was six in the morning and she went straight away to the Royal Infirmary. She found her friend, but she was asleep. Not wanting to disturb her, she asked for Merrett's current address and was told he was staying at the Country Hotel. Having located him there, she told him of having

---

31 Ibid, pp.112-3.
32 Ibid, pp.104-5, 122-24.
33 Ibid, p.203.

discovered that Mrs Merrett had been shot, but asked him how it happened and whether someone could have entered the room to do the deed. His reply was 'No, because I was there.' He told her that he was standing near her but his mother said, 'Go further back, I cannot write, you overlean my shoulder', so he did so, then heard the shot and saw his mother's fall. They discussed the revolver; he said he needed it for a trip to France. 'Fancy having it loaded,' she said. Mrs Hill was still uncertain and uncomprehending, 'But if she did it, what would be her reason for doing such a thing?', to which Merrett told her about money worries being on her mind.[34]

She later related, 'he did not want to discuss the matter with me or to volunteer information and what he did say was only in reply to questions'. He was certainly evasive, 'he seemed to avoid speaking about his mother and rather spoke to me about the sights of Edinburgh'.[35]

The two had breakfast and then went together to the Infirmary. Mrs Hill went to see her friend, who was now conscious and seemed pleased to see her. They later had a conversation about what had happened. Mrs Merrett said:

'Why am I here? What has happened to me?'

Mrs Hill had been told by the nurses she must not tell what the real reason was.

'You have had a fall.'
'But my left side is injured.'
'You have had a fall on this side and it has injured your leg.'
'No, I have not had a fall. I was writing a letter.'
'To whom?'
'Mrs Anderson, and a pistol went off under my ear.'
'How could it? Did you see the pistol?'
'No.'
'Did you handle one?'
'No.'
'Was there one there?'
'No.'

34 Roughead, *Trial*, pp.125-6; NRS AD15/27/1.
35 NRS, AD15/27/1.

Not wanting to excite her friend anymore – though she had been clear throughout the conversation - she gave her a drink and left. She later related that she 'seemed to be in full possession of her faculties' and 'never insinuated to me that her son or anybody shot her'.[36]

Mrs Merrett had also asked her friend to write to her sisters, Mrs Chadwick and Mrs Penn. This she did; Mrs Penn being then on holiday on the Riviera with her husband (they later met in London to discuss matters further). She also gave Mrs Hill some money (12s 6d) to pay Mrs Sutherland. Mrs Hill saw Merrett again that day, but returned to London that night after having being lent £2 for the return fare from him. Merrett seemed in a hurry and had not spent much time at the hospital. However, he did go back in the evening when the doctor was making his rounds of the patients.[37]

It was then that he met Dr Holcombe. This was the first day that the doctor saw him there. He asked him how the shooting happened. Apparently:

> *He said his mother was sitting down writing letters, and she said to him "Go away, Donald, and don't annoy me", and he went over to the corner of the room, and the next he heard was a shot, and he looked round and saw his mother falling to the ground with a revolver falling from her hand.*

The doctor also discussed Mrs Merrett's condition with her son, telling him that it was very serious, but she had a chance. Merrett then said,

> 'So, it is still on the cards that she will recover?'
>
> 'Yes. Where there's life there's hope.'

Merrett wondered whether his mother's sisters should be informed of what happened and the doctor agreed. The youth said that the sisters were not on the best of terms but that he would contact them to give them the opportunity to visit.[38]

On the 19th, PC Watt received a telephone call from the hospital to call there, at ward 16. He went along and Dr Holcombe told him of Mrs Merrett's statement. Once he had heard it he telephoned the details to the CID. He asked whether he should take a statement, but was told

---

36 Ibid.
37 Roughead, *Trial*, pp.126-7.
38 Ibid, pp. 105-6.

that a detective officer would be despatched to take a statement from her instead. Watt felt that he had discharged his responsibilities in this aspect of the case, assuming another would take the statement from her.[39]

Fleming was the detective who went. He arrived at the Infirmary to see Dr Holcombe, but could not find him. He returned on the next day when he met the doctor. Holcombe repeated the remarks that Mrs Merrett had made to him two days previously and said that her death might be imminent. It is not clear why Fleming did not take a statement from her; clearly he did not want his first impressions of the case to be disturbed. However, he thought that some further action was needed. That afternoon, at the Gorgie Police Office, Fleming asked PCs Watt and Gibson if they had seen either Merrett or Mrs Sutherland. On their remarking in the negative, he told them to interview both of them (they claimed that they were instructed thus on the following day). Fleming clearly did not see the matter as a high priority as he felt no need for him to personally interview the witnesses, but felt he could delegate it to junior colleagues.[40]

No urgency was thought to be required. The constables saw Mrs Sutherland on Sunday, 21 February. Their purpose, in the light of contradictory statements, was to ascertain whether what she had told their colleagues on the Wednesday morning was correct. Watt took the following statement from Mrs Sutherland:

> *I was employed as a maid for a few hours daily at 31 Buckingham Terrace, and about 9.40 am on Wednesday, 17 March 1926, I had occasion to go into the dining-room where I saw Mrs Merrett, who was sitting writing, and her son, Donald, was sitting in a corner, reading. I then went to the kitchen, returned to the coal-cellar, and saw Mrs Merrett, still writing, and returned to the kitchen again. When working at the grate there I heard a shot, and a sound as if someone had fallen. Then the boy came to the kitchen door and informed me that his mother had shot herself, and requested me to 'phone the police. I then entered the dining-room and saw Mrs Merrett lying on her back with her head towards the door, and the revolver lying on the drawers near the writing table. I never at any time heard her threaten to commit suicide.*[41]

39 Roughead, *Trial*, p.85.
40 Ibid, pp.88-9.
41 Ibid, p.83.

Watt asked her whether she had seen Mrs Merrett fall off her chair as she had informed his colleagues a few days ago. She said she may have said that but that she was so excited at the time that she could not remember having done so. However she did not explicitly deny that she had said that. Watt took her new statement as being truthful.[42]

Constables Gibson and Watt saw Merrett at the Country Hotel on the same day, to ask him for additional information about the shooting. He told them that he heard a shot, saw his mother fall from the chair. He said that his mother was worried about money but never talked about suicide. According to the officers, 'Merrett gave us the story quite voluntarily and without any hesitation'.[43]

Merrett, still cashing cheques from his mother's cheque book, found another purchase he wished to make. He called on the Rossleigh Motor Company, Shandwick Place, on Monday, 22 March. There he saw James Donald Paton, a salesman employed there. He made an order for a HRD motorcycle and sidecar, explaining he could make a part payment with his AJS motorcycle. The item he desired cost £133 8s; with accessories, £139. He would receive £30 for his current machine. Merrett said he needed a new motorcycle for general use and occasional racing. Over the next few days he paid cash; on 23 March, £20, 24 March, £15, 26 March, £20 and 27 March £15, a total of £70. He eventually acquired it in the following month.[44]

On Tuesday the 23rd March, at the hospital, Nurse Grant received a telegram from Mrs Penn, asking how her sister was. She checked with Dr Holcombe how she should deal with the enquiry. Then she sent a telegram back, stating that Mrs Merrett was very ill and recommended that she come straight away. Her other sister could not come due to her ill health and her clerical husband could not be spared from his Easter duties. That evening, when Merrett visited the hospital, the nurse told him what she had done. Nurse Elizabeth Wilson recalled, 'He was generally in a hurry and had little time to wait'. She also remembered that his mother said to her, 'Where is that bad boy?' on several occasions; further proof that she had not been wholly hoodwinked by her son.[45]

---

42 Ibid.
43 NRS, AD15/27/1.
44 Roughead, *Trial*, p.197.
45 Roughead, *Trial*, pp.116, 140; NRS, AD15/27/1.

The 23rd was the last night that Merrett stayed at the Country Hotel, where he had occupied room 17. Isabella Grant, the hotelier, said that he only mentioned her mother's condition to her once. He only stayed in the hotel to eat breakfast and to sleep, though he did little of the latter. This was because he was always late returning to his room and on one occasion stayed out all night. He requested that he might have a latch key so he could let himself in at any hour, but was told this was unnecessary because there was a night porter. He never left his contact details, but he behaved perfectly well and promptly paid the bill.[46]

Mr and Mrs Penn travelled up from London at night, arriving in Edinburgh between six and seven on the morning of the 24th, but found Mrs Merrett was asleep when they first came to the hospital, so returned later that day. Merrett arrived at the ward with them, at about 10 a.m. Hitherto Mrs Penn had believed her sister was suffering from pneumonia.[47] Mrs Merrett was now awake and was very happy to see her. She was perfectly sound mentally (Dr Holcombe concurred on this point). Mrs Penn later recalled what her sister told her:

> *She first of all asked me if I would look after Sister Grant; would I find her a present &c., that she had been so good to her. She asked if we would at once go to the flat and look after Donald. She was perfectly clear, and asked us if we would go to a certain church to hear certain music. She spoke of the kindness she had received. She asked me if I would get an ear specialist for her. She said that they had said that she had had a fall... She said she was in doubt about that fall. She said she was sitting at the table writing when a sudden explosion as if Donald had shot me went off in her head. She asked me particularly if I would look after Donald for her, mentioning that Edinburgh was a particularly wicked city, &c.*[48]

Mrs Merrett also asked her sister to go to the flat and to take her fur coat. Walter Penn was not present during this conversation. He did speak to his sister-in-law later and she told him, '"Walter, you have been awfully good, and I have been most unkind at times. You will forgive me, won't you?"'. She did not speak to him of what had happened on the past Wednesday. However, he recalled that they did talk about health matters:

46 NRS, AD15/27/1.
47 Roughead, *Trial*, pp.116, 144.
48 Ibid, p.132.

> *She seemed to be very much upset at not knowing what had happened to herself. She seemed at a very great loss, because she said she had very great pain in her ear, and knowing that I had suffered all sorts of things with my own ears, I suppose she was hoping I could give her some explanation about it, and she mentioned the noises she experienced in her ear. I said, trying to soothe her, "That is nothing; I have very great noises in my own ears sometimes". Then she said on another occasion that she could not move her arm.*[49]

Mrs Penn recalled asking her sister about her son owning a gun, and Mrs Merrett replied, 'Oh Donald has lots of things that I don't know of'.[50]

On this occasion or, more likely, on the following day, the Penns heard a less than encouraging prognosis of Mrs Merrett's condition. They had been hoping for the best, but a doctor, probably Dr Holcombe, told Mrs Penn 'that he was very much afraid there was no hope whatever'. This naturally upset Mrs Penn greatly. Her husband took her to a nurse's room nearby where they could have some privacy. There was then a potentially significant exchange between the two and Merrett:

> *When she was sitting down she looked across at Donald, who was on one of the settees, and she said "Donald, didn't you do it?" and Donald said, "No auntie, I did not do it, but if you like I will confess". I said to him at once "What a ridiculous thing, boy! You cannot do a thing like that".*[51]

Penn telegrammed Jenks to come up to Edinburgh and he arrived on Friday, 26 March. He and the Penns went to the hospital. There is some doubt over which day the three of them had a meeting with Merrett in a room in the hospital; Mrs Penn inferring it was on the 24th and her husband on the 26th, but both are clear that the three of them and Merrett were all present, so the latter date seems more likely. There, Mrs Penn asked her nephew what had occurred on the crucial morning. He said he had not seen what happened. He could not suggest who shot her or that it was suicide. They all discussed the matter and concluded that the shooting was accidental, but it was unclear who made the suggestion.[52]

49 Ibid, pp.142-3.
50 NRS, AD15/27/1.
51 Roughead, *Trial*, p.143.
52 Ibid, pp.133, 144.

All four went back to the flat. They continued their discussion. They concluded that the pistol was in the secretaire drawer and that it might have been taken out with papers that were stored there and that it might have gone off accidentally. Merrett then suggested suicide, but his aunt was emphatic that it could not have been so. She said, 'I knew my sister intimately, and, of course, I could not think of such a thing'. At one point (no later than 30 March) Merrett also explained why the pistol came to be in the secretaire and his uncle recalled:

> he said that on the Saturday previous he was going out with it, and, as soon as his mother saw his pistol, she said "Donald you shall not go out with that. You will give me that pistol" and according to his statement, she took it from him and put it into the second lower drawer on the left hand side of the secretaire, and there the pistol was.[53]

The Penns tried to work out exactly what had happened. Penn had three or four hypotheses. One was that she might have leaned round in her chair and taken something out of the drawer and caught hold of the gun, not realising what it was and that her thumb had got into the guard, lifted it out and it had gone off. He also conducted a search of the room, which the police had not undertaken, and found the cartridge case which had been ejected from the magazine when the gun had been fired. He took it to the West End Police Station on the day that he had found it, pondering the question of whether it was not the duty of the police to undertake such searches. This may have taken place on 27 or 28 March.[54]

However, it was only on 30 March that Fleming was informed both of Penn's finding and of the statement Mrs Merrett had made to her sister on 24 March. He and PC William Johnston then went to 31 Buckingham Terrace, where the Penns were staying, together with Merrett after his brief sojourn at the hotel. Penn pointed out to the police officers where he had found the cartridge. Fleming then took a statement from Merrett himself. It read as follows:

> I am the only son of Bertha Milner or Merrett, about fifty-six years. We arrived in Edinburgh on 4th January, 1926, from Waverley Hydropathic, Melrose. We resided at 7 Mayfield Road, c/o Hardie,

---

53 Roughead, *Trial*, pp.133, 145.
54 Ibid, p.145.

and remained there about a fortnight or three weeks, when we removed to 35 Palmerston Place, a boarding house, and remained until we took a flat at 31 Buckingham Terrace, c/o Crooke, on 10th March, 1926. The reason for coming to Edinburgh was to attend classes at the University. In February, 1926, I applied for a certificate for an automatic pistol, as we thought of going abroad to Bailleau, near Paris, at the Easter holidays. She allowed me 10s a week, sometimes extra for outside meals. I also purchased a motor cycle three weeks ago, £27. After coming to the flat at 31 Buckingham Terrace everything was in good spirits and getting on all right. When in Palmerston Place she got on me for going out too much and neglecting my lessons. This was when we came to Edinburgh first. On 16th March, 1926, we had a Miss Macglashan 7 Ann Street, visiting us, there just being the three of us. Mother went to bed, I having retired before her. About 8.30 am on the 17th March I got up and dressed and had breakfast. Some letters arrived in the morning, and one was an intimation from the Clydesdale Bank in George Street to the effect that she had overdrawn her account. After breakfast I went into my room, which adjoins the dining-room, and mother got the dishes removed. When I returned to the dining room, mother was sitting at the table writing, when I saw an envelope my mother had addressed to Mrs Anderson, 64 Murray Place, Edinburgh [actually Stirling], I pointed out the mistake and she said, "Go away, you worry me." I went to the other side of the room to get my books, when I heard a report and saw my mother in the act of falling to the floor. I rushed over to my mother and saw the maid in the hall, where I said, "Mother has hurt herself". She fell on the left side, and the revolver was lying beside her right hand. I telephoned for the police, and they removed the body to the Royal Infirmary, where she was detained... In the dining room there is a writing bureau with three drawers. About noon on Saturday, 13th March, I had the pistol and loaded it with six cartridges, one being in the breach, and the safety catch on. I was going to the Braids [an open space just to the south west of Edinburgh] to shoot rabbits. I wanted to take it on the Sunday morning, but she took it from me and put it into the small drawer in the writing bureau. I think I told my mother to be careful, that it was loaded. I never again saw the pistol.[55]

Merrett added, as a result of further questioning, that on the morning of the shooting he lifted the gun and placed it on the corner of the

---

55 Roughead, *Trial*, pp.89-90.

bureau. He said he tried to lift his mother, but despite his strength, failed (there were no witnesses to this). All this was before he left to see Mrs Sutherland. The statement confirms the final one of Mrs Sutherland and does away with the one made to Dr Rosa about seeing the gun fall from Mrs Merrett's hand – as she was in the kitchen it would have been impossible for her to have done so.[56]

The two police officers also spoke to Mrs Sutherland on the same day. Fleming had read the report made by PC Watt, which contradicted her statement made to him on the day of the shooting. She made no excuse for changing her story and claimed not to remember what she had said to him on the 17th. He also asked Merrett where the missing cheques and counterfoils were and he professed not to know. So the police searched the rooms. They were found in Merrett's room. They also found an envelope addressed to his mother at their former address and a letter from the bank. His mother's account book was also there. He also asked about the letter that Mrs Merrett had been writing on the 17th, but Merrett told him that he had destroyed it. The two letters from the bank were still in existence and Fleming removed these. Merrett added, incorrectly, that he had paid £5 for the gun and said his mother knew nothing of it, contradicting earlier statements that he had made, and that his mother had bought the motor cycle for him. Fleming also found 38 loose bullets in a drawer in Merrett's room, suggesting that he had discharged six prior to the day of the shooting; perhaps he had been indulging in target practice or showing off to friends.[57]

Over the next few days, Mrs Merrett's health began to decline. On Thursday the 24th her sister said that she had developed delirium; Dr Holcombe stating that this occurred in the evening and that this was the first sign of an inflammation of the brain coming on. Two days later she fell unconscious after being incoherent on the preceding day. She died early on Thursday, 1 April; fifteen days after she had been shot. Dr Holcombe completed the death certificate and cause of death was recorded as 'Basal Meningitis, following a bullet wound in cranium'.[58]

Merrett's lack of concern for his mother had struck the nurses.

---

56 Roughead, *Trial*, pp.90-3, 100.
57 Ibid.
58 Ibid, pp.133, 103-4, 108, 12.

Elizabeth Grant told him off for not meeting Mrs Hill at the railway station; he excused this by saying he had to cancel all his mother's fifteen appointments. Nurse Grant said, 'I was struck by the callousness of Donald's behaviour in view of his mother's serious condition'. She never let mother and son be alone, 'Somehow I did not feel sure of him'. Mrs Elizabeth Wilson remarked, 'He was generally in a hurry and had little time to wait'. On one day he did not visit, claiming he had a football match instead. However, he was present at time of death, albeit asleep in the side room when his mother died. Mrs Wilson, nurse in charge, awoke him and told him of the news. That day he telegraphed Mrs Hill to let her know that his mother had died.[59]

Harvey Littlejohn (1862-1927), Professor of Forensic Medicine of the University of Edinburgh since 1906 and author of *Forensic Medicine Illustrated by Photographs and Descriptive Cases*, was called upon to undertake the post mortem, which he conducted on the day of her death. He extracted the bullet from her skull and passed it over to Fleming. His report was made four days later:

> *I certify upon soul and conscience that by instructions of the Procurator Fiscal of the county of Midlothian, on Thursday, 1st April, in the mortuary of the Royal Infirmary, I examined the body of Bertha Milner or Merrett.*
>
> *The deceased was a well-nourished and apparently healthy woman of about fifty years of age.*
>
> *There was a perforating wound of the antihelix of the right ear, less than a quarter of an inch in diameter, and behind this was a larger wound which passed into the skull immediately posterior to the meatus or external entrance of the ear. These wounds were healthy in appearance.*
>
> *With these exceptions, there were no recent marks of external violence.*
>
> *On removing the skull cap, the brain membranes were found to be inflamed and infiltrated with purulent matter. The brain was uninjured, but embedded in the bone of the base of the skull, close to the sella turcica, there was a nickel plated bullet of small calibre. The direction of the wound, judging by the external wounds and the position of the bullet where found, was horizontal and slightly*

---

59   NRS, AD15/27/1.

> *from behind forwards, the bullet lying about an inch anterior to the external wound.*
>
> 'The various organs of the chest and abdominal cavities were normal and healthy. Both ovaries and the appendix had been removed by operation at some previous time.
>
> *I am of opinion that death was due to meningitis, the result of a bullet wound.*
>
> 'There was nothing to indicate the distance at which the discharge of the weapon took place, whether from a few inches or a greater distance. So far as the position of the wound is concerned, the case is consistent with suicide. There is some difficulty in attributing it to accident, although such a view cannot be wholly excluded.[60]

This being Scotland there was no inquest; unusual deaths being reported to the Procurator Fiscal for him to take the necessary steps to order an investigation if he deemed it necessary. He saw no reason at this time to do so.

None of this was made public until after the death of Mrs Merrett; her initial shooting had gone unreported. This initial anonymity may have been in recognition of her respectability. A Scottish newspaper, *The Sunday Post*, reported Mrs Merrett's death, quoting from both Merrett and Mrs Sutherland. It referred to her death as being 'a pathetic accident', though also noted, 'What actually happened is not perfectly clear'.[61] *The Scotsman* on 2 April 1926 also noted her death and referred to it as being an accident, too.[62] The *Edinburgh Evening News* on 2 April had a small column headed 'Edinburgh Shooting Tragedy...West End Sensation'. It stated that 'The circumstances attending the tragedy are somewhat obscure, but from information gathered it appears to have been the result of an accident'. It stated that Mrs Merrett had taken the gun bought for use in France on holiday from the drawer of the writing bureau and had contrived to accidentally shoot herself.[63]

So that was, apparently, that. Mrs Merrett was dead and buried in Section E, Lair No. 244 in Piershill Cemetery, off the Portobello Road, to the east of the city centre, on Saturday, 3 April. The headstone's

---

60 Roughead, *Trial*, pp.154, 313.
61 *Sunday Post*, 4 April 1926.
62 Roughead, *Classic Crimes*, p.413.
63 *Edinburgh Evening News*, 2 April 1926.

message read as follows:

> *BERTHA MERRETT*
> *AGED 56 YEARS*
> *YOUNGEST DAUGHTER*
> *OF THE LATE W.H. MILNER*
> *ESQ. OF MANCHESTER*
> *PASSED OVER*
> *TO THE FULLER*
> *LIFE OF CHRIST JESUS*
> *APRIL 1ST 1926.*

Possibly she was buried as a suicide, in which case the church service would have been altered accordingly.[64]

Yet her death was not the last word.

---

64 Gravestone of Bertha Merrett; Roughead, *Trial*, p.12.

4

Investigations, 1926-1927

Not everyone was certain that Mrs Merrett had died by her own hand or by accident. PC Middlemiss was one, claiming that 'after I reported the matter I was beginning to think different things, just the same as the public'.[1] Nurse Grant recalled 'I remember myself reading in the newspaper that it was an accident'. She had a conversation with Mrs Penn, with the latter being against the idea that her sister died by her own hand and was pleased that the shooting was deemed an accident.[2]

Slowly but surely those in authority began to have suspicions about the death. The Procurator Fiscal's Office was puzzled about the affair from 17 June onwards. This was partly because of the matter of Merrett's trip to London (described hereafter) and his disreputable lifestyle. Yet, as the Procurator Fiscal's deputy noted, a month later, there was 'no provable motive for his murdering his mother' apart from the fact that he was her heir (but would not inherit until he was 25, seven years later). It was known that he had forged cheques to gain her money when she was ill, however, presumably because the bank had alerted them of their suspicions. The Rt. Hon. Patrick Balfour, 2nd Baron Kinross (1870-1939), a KC and Advocate of the Scottish Bar, had been Advocate Depute from 1922 to 1925. He voiced his concerns to the Solicitor General in July, wanting the case to be

1 Roughead, *Trial*, p.81.
2 Ibid, p.120.

reinvestigated and noting both the inadequate police work hitherto and the general concern among some in the city about the case. A meeting with the Chief Constable took place in September. Forgery, not murder, was their immediate concern and evidence for the latter seemed scanty despite the suspicious circumstances, though suicide was now deemed an impossibility. Yet they believed that the charge should be made, 'it does place the accused under a suspicion so heavy as to justify his trial by jury'. It was in this month that the police took statements from all those concerned, most of whom later appeared at the trial.[3]

Despite having initially concluded that Mrs Merrett died by her own hand, Littlejohn was now having doubts, as well, and Sir Sydney Smith (1883-1969), a fellow pathologist (and like Merrett, had been born in New Zealand and attended Edinburgh University), recounted their meeting in his memoirs:

> *I was in Edinburgh on vacation that summer, and Littlejohn consulted me about the case. He told me that he was worried about it, and by then, no doubt, the police were too... "What do you think?" Littlejohn asked me when I had gone through all the evidence. "It looks to me like murder," I said. I hesitated to advise my old teacher but it seemed to me that there was one obvious course to be taken. "Why don't you make some experiments with the weapon that killed her?" I suggested. "Find out if a discharge close to the skin would cause powder-marks."*[4]

It was in August that Littlejohn made the necessary experiments. He received the pistol used in the shooting from the Procurator Fiscal and had similar cartridges to the ones used from Mr Hardy's shop, Eley's smokeless cartridges .25. He then experimented by shooting from various distances in order to see the amount of blackening and tattooing caused. It will be recalled that Dr Holcombe stated that there were none around the entry wound on Mrs Merrett.[5]

The results were as follows. At half an inch there was intense blackening around the bullet hole with over an inch diameter, and a further two inches of darkening by smoke and particles of powder. At an inch there was blackening for a three quarters of an inch in

---

3 NRS, AD15/27/1.
4 Smith, *Mostly Murder* (1959), pp.142-3.
5 Roughead, *Trial*, p.314.

diameter. However at six inches there were only a few particles of ingrained powder. At nine and twelve inches there was no blackening around the bullet hole. At three inches range there was no blackening but numerous particles of ingrained powder over an area of one and a half inches in diameter. At three inches there was also a ring of blackening for two thirds of an inch and tattooing three quarters of an inch. At two inches distance was blackening for three inches diameter and tattooing for three quarters of an inch.[6]

Littlejohn concluded:

> From the foregoing experiments it is evident that, if the discharge took place with the muzzle at a distance of 3 inches or less from the skin, there would have been definite evidence of such a near discharge which Dr Holcombe would have recognised if present. This evidence would not have been removed by the blood or by the washing of the wound, but would have remained for many days.[7]

This led the professor to make the following deductions about the cause of death which contradicted his findings of earlier that year:

> In considering the question of a possible accidental discharge of the pistol by the deceased, I am of opinion that this is not easily conceivable when one considers (1) the position in which the pistol must have been held, viz., behind the ear and not less than 4 inches from it; (2) the angle at which it must have been held, with the muzzle pointing forwards; and (3) the considerable force required to discharge it.
>
> Intentional self-infliction is in my opinion equally inconceivable.
>
> The suicide, as a rule, leaves nothing to chance. He holds the weapon close to his head in a natural position and fires at the temple or side of the head in front of the ear. The wound always shows the character of a "near" discharge.
>
> In the present case the discharge was not a near one. The wound was in a very unusual position, while the direction, considered along with the distance of the discharge, indicates that the hand and arm must have been in a strained position – a most unlikely circumstance in a would be suicide. With the weapon held in such a position, the person could have had very little knowledge of what part of the head he would hit, also a very strong point against self-

---

6   Roughead, *Trial*, p.314.
7   Ibid.

infliction.

From these considerations I am of opinion that suicide was in the highest degree improbable.

The direction of the bullet wound, the position of the wound, the distance at which the discharge took place, all point to the weapon having been fired by another party.[8]

On 30 November, Littlejohn wrote to John Glaister (1856-1932), Professor of Forensic Medicine from 1898 at Glasgow University and the City's police surgeon. He had suggested to the Crown that Glaister's opinion be obtained, and that the Procurator Fiscal had already written to him. Littlejohn, having access to the gun used, offered to help Glaister all he could.[9]

Glaister clearly agreed, so on 8 December, he made similar experiments and two days later Littlejohn wrote up the results. These experiments were made on cardboard and human skin. Glaister also made a report in order to try and answer the question as to how Mrs Merrett had met her death. He put to himself four questions; what was the appearance of the wound when admitted to hospital, the direction of the wound, leading to ascertaining the distance from gun to head and the mode of causation.[10]

Using the reports of Dr Holcombe and Littlejohn, and the results of the experiments, he noted that blackening was only visible from a bullet fired at three inches or less distance, but no blackening had been found on the body. The entry of the bullet was horizontal and slightly upward, and slightly from behind. This, in his opinion, cast doubt on this being a suicide. His experience of suicides was that they tended to adopt the easiest and most certain position in order to kill themselves; usually into the mouth, to the temple or forehead. However, in this case, the head, right arm and hand would have to be in a very constrained position, straining the hand further back from the shoulder and pulling the shoulder very much backwards. He thought the bullet was fired from at least four and probably over six inches away.[11]

---

8   Ibid, p.315.
9   Glasgow University Archives, FM/2B/20/3.
10 Roughead, *Trial*, p.316.
11 Ibid, p.318.

His conclusion was similar to that of Littlejohn, but was a little equivocal:

> *Taking all the facts of the wounding in this case, while I am unable to exclude absolutely the possibility of the production of such a wound as in this case by self-infliction, the improbabilities so outweigh in my mind the possibilities that I have come to the conclusion that the head injury which caused the death of Mrs Merrett was not self-inflicted.*[12]

The Crown also proceeded to investigate whether Mrs Merrett's cheques had been forged. Gerald Francis Gurrin, a handwriting specialist of London and a Fellow of the Royal Microscopical Society of England, with 22 years' experience of disputed and forged documents, was called in to make examinations. On 4 November he made his report. He had divided his material into three groupings; documents bearing Mrs Merrett's signature which were disputed (56 cheques), documents which bore the undoubted signatures of the deceased and finally examples of the handwriting of her son. He had to ascertain which, if any, of the signatures in the first group were forged and if so, was there anything to connect them to those in the third class. In other words, could he prove whether Merrett had forged his mother's signatures on her cheques?[13]

He began by familiarising himself with the characteristics of Mrs Merrett's handwriting. He thought they had been executed with speed and precision. He then looked at those signatures in group one and found that they were very heavy and unnatural and that they were suspiciously alike one another. He thought that 29 of them were created by two signatures existing, one being created by use of a carbon copy.[14]

Although the signatures in the first group were forged, he could not detect any of the peculiarities of the writer's own style. He concluded, 'there is nothing to enable me to form an opinion as to whether the 29 signatures, which I do not believe to have been written by Mrs Merrett, were written by J.D. Merrett'.[15]

Other experiments were made. These were by the expert witnesses called on Merrett's behalf and were conducted by Robert Churchill

12 Roughead, *Trial*, p.319.
13 Ibid, p.182.
14 Ibid, pp.183-4.
15 Ibid, pp.185-6.

(1885-1958), a gunsmith of Leicester Square, London, who had been often used as an expert witness in shooting cases since 1910, and the even better known Sir Bernard Spilsbury (1877-1947), Home Office pathologist. Sydney Smith noted in his memoirs:

> To counter Littlejohn's expert evidence they [the defence] put up Sir Bernard Spilsbury, the Home Office pathologist, who was very brilliant and very famous, but fallible like the rest of us – and very, very obstinate. In England, where he has always appeared for the Crown, many murderers were justly convicted on his evidence. Now he was making one of his rare appearances for the defence. With him was Robert Churchill, often described as the expert on ballistics. Robert Churchill was famous, too, and I am sure he was an excellent gunsmith. He was also stubborn and dogmatic. He and Spilsbury often appeared together in shooting cases, and they were indeed a formidable team.[16]

Sir Bernard was a very well-known and highly esteemed pathologist, popular with both public and the press. He had presented scientific evidence in numerous high profile cases, such as that of infamous wife murderer Dr Crippen in 1910 and that of serial killer George Joseph Smith of Brides in the Bath fame, in 1915, as well as a host of others. Dr Cedric Keith Simpson (1907-1985) wrote 'he was undoubtedly the authority on his subject and an unchallenged expert of the greatest integrity, pretty well unchallengeable...a lucid but firm witness using as few words as were necessary, he had for twenty years been head and shoulders above anyone in the country in this branch of pathology'. Yet others were less certain about his talents. John Cassells, KC, noted, 'It will be a sorry day for the administration of criminal justice in this land if we are to be thrust into such a position that, because Sir Bernard Spilsbury expressed an opinion, it is of such weight that it is impossible to question it'.[17]

Opinion is still divided about Sir Bernard. A biography produced shortly after his death was very praiseworthy of his talents. But a more recent study has been extremely critical and has accused him of being party to miscarriages of justice. The veracity of his conclusions on the Crippen case and that of Smith have also been queried. Yet other authors applaud him as 'the Father of CSI'. Bob Odell's study of

---

16 Smith, *Mostly Murder*, p.144.
17 Simpson, *Forty Years of Murder* (1978), pp.29-30.

famous twentieth-century pathologists gives a more balanced verdict – a great man, but as Sydney Smith observed, fallible at times. Just before this case he gave controversial conclusions in the Norman Thorne murder case, arguing that Thorne had killed his girlfriend and not, as other doctors contended, that she had committed suicide by hanging. Laymen, such as Sir Arthur Conan Doyle, thought Spilsbury was in the wrong, too, in this instance.[18]

Spilsbury and Churchill also decided to make tests regarding the effects of blackening caused by shooting. Churchill argued that shooting at inanimate targets would prove nothing, so Spilsbury contacted London hospitals to let them know that he wanted some human flesh for such experiments. They were provided with an amputated leg of an elderly woman. Wrapping it up in brown paper they travelled down to Churchill's shooting grounds in Kent by train. They had not got the gun used to shoot Mrs Merrett, but used a similar one (a .25 calibre pistol). This therefore devalued the worth of the experiments. They did, however, use ammunition from Hardy's shop.[19]

When the pistol was fired at a portion of the skin at the range of one inch, there was some blackening on the right side of the wound and rather less on the left hand side. They also fired at white cardboard, too. At one inch, a shot caused an inch worth of blackening around the hole, but at two inches there was only slight blackening. At six inches there was no blackening. Blackening was less distinct on the skin than the cardboard, according to Spilsbury. Dampening the cardboard with water resulted in a wider deposit of powder on the surface.[20]

Churchill was not happy with the value of these experiments. He later explained to his biographer that this was the case because the reaction of dead flesh is different to that of living flesh. The evidence was therefore insignificant. But at the time he kept his doubts to himself.[21]

The Crown took other steps in their furtherance of the case. On 9 November, James Robertson, an Edinburgh surveyor, went to the flat, accompanied by PC Izatt and Mrs Sutherland. They showed him the sitting room and pointed out to him the location of the furniture at the

---

18 Rose, *Lethal Witness* (2007); Evans, *The Father of Forensics* (2007).
19 Hastings, *The Other Mr Churchill* (1963), pp.117-18.
20 Roughead, *Trial*, pp.221, 229-31.
21 Hastings, *The Other Mr Churchill*, p.118.

time of the shooting. With this knowledge and the evidence of his own eyes, he drew a plan of the room.[22]

The Penns had remained at 31 Buckingham Terrace until the end of the lease, in June 1926, retaining Mrs Sutherland as their servant. They occasionally talked about the case, but Mrs Penn did not show any great hostility towards Merrett. They looked after him as best they could because the Public Trustee (responsible for the trust fund set up by the later William Milner for the use of his heirs) would not initially settle the bills that needed paying, so the Penns paid from their own resources. After all, Mrs Penn had promised her sister that she would do so.[23]

The young man continued his carefree existence. On the day of his mother's death he went to the Palais between 12 and 1. Two days later, on the day of his mother's funeral, he had tea with Miss Christie, but he did not dance on that occasion. As ever, he never seemed to be in want of money. At some stage at this time, Blackburn had a few words with him, 'I was disappointed that he had let me down [he had been the lad's sponsor at university]. I spoke to him severely about his having neglected his studies and even having neglected attendances at the classes. He had nothing to say'. Merrett also became acquainted with George Scott's brother at this time. This was James Aitchison Scott, then a 24-year-old taxi driver. This was because Merrett often employed him as a taxi driver in the days following his mother's death. He ran up an £11 bill with trips to the countryside and to dance halls. Scott thought that Merrett looked older than he was, perhaps 21/22-years-old, and that he was 'quite smart and quite able to look after himself'. Yet he did not think he was callous, 'So far as I could make out I think Merrett was greatly attached to his mother and that her death was a great blow to him'.[24]

Merrett continued to frequent the Dunedin Palais, dancing with other girls, some he brought with him and others whom he found there. He seemed no longer to want to dance with Betty. However, she noticed his habits were different, 'It was quite apparent to me that he was not spending so much after his mother's death as he was doing before'. Not surprisingly; his previous source of money had run out.[25]

22 Roughead, *Trial*, pp.76-7.
23 Ibid, pp.72, 141.
24 Ibid, *Trial*, p.150; NRS, AD15/27/1.
25 NRS, AD15/27/1.

On the 13 April Merrett borrowed money from Mrs Penn, claiming he needed to consult a famous detective in London about his mother's death. He also called on John Thomas of Abercorn Gardens for money, but without success. However, he did procure £15 from John Robertson, a solicitor of York Place. Along with James Scott and two 'respectable but foolish' girls, one under 16, Merrett took a late train to London. The girls' relations had them traced and returned. There had been no sex nor any attempts to seduce them. In all, their stay in London was of short duration, of which at least one night was spent in a hotel. Merrett sent a wire to the Rossleigh Motor Company, asking that they send him the motorcycle that he had partially paid for, down to him. As it was not fully paid for, they refused (later the Public Trustee paid up). He also asked them that money for the hotel bill be paid. Lacking money and girls, the two began their trip back to Edinburgh. It took them three days to reach Newark, presumably by hitchhiking. Then they took a lift in a car as far as Old Curmock, which took 9-10 hours, then they walked to Muirkirk and telephoned the police to send them a car. They finally returned to 31 Buckingham Terrace.[26]

The guardianship of the Penns ceased at the end of June and they left Edinburgh as the lease was now over. The university term ended too (on 25 June), and permanently for Merrett, who had not been a conscientious student. Blackburn advised the trustees that Merrett make a clean break from Edinburgh. He went to Ramsay Lodge, as arranged by Blackburn, on a yachting holiday; the second time that his interest turned to matters maritime, on the Clyde at Tighnabruaich (earlier he had had an inclination to join the Navy). The Public Trustee also demanded that he underwent a medical inspection. This was carried out by Dr John Orr of Strathearn Road in July. The latter concluded:

> *The lad is exceptionally developed physically for his age [seventeen] and looks at least over twenty years. He talks intelligently and confidently and is clear and lucid in his statements on general topics. He is sound in every bodily organ, and mentally he is perfectly sane.*[27]

---

26 Roughead, *Trial*, pp.150, 17-18, 197; NRS, AD15/27/1.
27 Ibid, *Trial*, p.18.

Evidence about Merrett's past actions was found in his favourite haunt, but it is not known when it was placed there. John Lawson, a youth employed at the Palais as car park attendant, recalled finding a bank book belonging to Mrs Merrett on the second top step inside the boiler room, the unlocked door of which was near to that of the cloak room. Evelyn Pearce, a cashier employed there, saw the bank book when it was handed to her. She intended to give it back to Merrett but never had the opportunity to do so, and handed it in to her manager.[28]

Merrett had relatively few dealings with authority for some time, but on 3 June he was asked to call at the Central Police Office. He was asked to write out his mother's name and then to write out her signature. He willingly carried out these requests without hesitation. The signatures he was asked to copy were those on his late mother's Boscombe bank cheques which were in the police's possession.[29]

By August Merrett was living at Hughenden Vicarage, about a mile to the north of High Wycombe in Buckinghamshire; as arranged by Blackburn. He was given tuition in order to pass the entry exams for Oxford or Cambridge; one of the two instructors was a Mr White from Oxford. The Vicar, the Rev. John Eldon Ellison, was the other. This, and his accommodation as a paying guest, was being paid for by the Public Trustee. But it was not a case of all work and no rest for him. He was a member of the Thames Valley Rugby Football Club and played badminton at Oakley Hall, often walking from the vicarage to High Wycombe, for games (rugby at this time was deemed very middle class compared to working class football). For the first, but not the last time, he re-invented his past for the benefit of his present. A fellow club member stated, he was 'introduced as a good player, as an orphan whose parents died young'.[30]

He was also of a highly sociable nature, as he had been in Edinburgh, and had quickly made a wide circle of friends. A local recalled, 'He is about six feet in height, and of fresh complexion. He walked with a stoop and wore plus fours and fancy stockings. He was a great favourite with the ladies'. Indeed, he was keeping company with a girl from Reading and was known as being fond of going to dances.[31]

This, then, was the young man who was found on 1 December by

28 Ibid, pp.199-200.
29 Ibid, p.97.
30 *Evening Telegraph*, 3 December 1926; *Dundee Courier*, 3 December 1926.
31 *Evening Telegraph*, 3 December 1926.

Superintendent George Kirby and PS George William Faithfull of the Buckinghamshire County Constabulary near to Benjamin Disraeli's tomb at Hughenden. He was reading at the time that they arrived to take him to the county police station in High Wycombe. Faithfull asked him to confirm his identity and announced he had a warrant for his arrest. Merrett merely said, 'I have nothing to say'. He was 'showing signs of emotion' when he was driven there in the back of a police car. He spent two days in the police cells at Chepping Wycombe Police Station until he was collected from thence by the Edinburgh Police on 3 December.[32]

On arrival at the Central Police Station, on the High Street, Merrett was shown into the charge office. Inspector Donald Rose was acting as lieutenant (in Scotland as in the USA, this was a post senior to that of Inspector) and read the charge to the accused youth. After cautioning him, he asked if he had anything to say and he replied 'No', paused and added 'I have nothing to say'. Then, Merrett, accompanied by a single detective in plain clothes, travelled to the Sherriff's court on George IV Bridge. The two were photographed by the press and pictures appeared in the newspapers. Other bystanders also observed them. At the court, whilst waiting his turn, he smoked a pipe and chatted to the detective, discussing his law studies at High Wycombe, amongst other matters. John Thomson, a solicitor, accompanied him to the court proceedings to meet the sheriff; later he continued his conversation with his solicitor.[33]

On the 9 December, Sheriff Substitute (ie Deputy Sheriff) Neish granted a warrant to imprison him. He was formally indicted on 14 January and the pleading diet was a week later, at Edinburgh Sheriff's Court before Sheriff Crole, when he pleaded not guilty to the two charges which had been presented to the Sheriff of the Lothians and Peebles on 27 November. These were twofold. One, that he had murdered his mother. Two, that he had presented 29 cheques on her bank account under her name, payable to himself, these cheques being forged. He was then formally committed for trial on 1 February. In the meantime he was placed in the newly built Saughton Prison in Edinburgh.[34]

Compared to his life in the previous year, this must have been a

---

32 *Evening Telegraph*, 3 December 1926.; NRS, AD15/27/1.
33 Roughead, *Trial*, p.200; *Edinburgh Evening Despatch*, 3 December 1927.
34 Roughead, *Trial*, pp.200, 19; *Edinburgh Evening News*, 21 January 1927.

shock to him; basic food, a restricted lifestyle and a limited choice in companions.

The case 'caused such a sensation not only in Edinburgh, but all over the country' as a leading Scottish newspaper observed. A large crowd had gathered in the public court on the day he was charged in order to catch a glimpse of him, but as it was heard in private, [they] were disappointed. Another newspaper gave their readers a description of the accused:

> Merrett is a big, powerfully built fellow, and was looking particularly fit and well groomed, and was wearing heavy, horn rimmed spectacles, a dark overcoat, and a pair of light Oxford bags and carried a crush felt hat in his hand. He took a keen interest in the proceedings which lasted only a few minutes, and answered in a firm voice, "Not Guilty, My Lord".[35]

A former friend was aggrieved with Merrett's impact on his own life to an extent that he sent him two telegrams whilst in prison. James Scott, on 27 January, told him that he wanted nothing more to do with him and that he had been the cause of his losing considerable time and money.[36]

Merrett's solicitors were Messrs Norman Macpherson and Dunlop. They called upon the Penns to give evidence. The outcome was stormy, with the solicitors claiming Mrs Penn was bad tempered and left. She recalled that her husband was insulted by being told by them that he was too good to live and that the Penns were of no use to the defence.[37]

Whilst in prison, a report was made of Merrett for the governor, Mr R.M. Dudgeon, partly by the prison's medical officer, Dr John Baird Cunningham of Edinburgh. It stated that his character and health were good and that this was a first offence. It was noted that his associates in Edinburgh were his 'classmates at the University', that his education was good and that he had been 'studying for entry into the diplomatic service'. However, much was not known. It was stated that his associates' characters were unknown as was whether he was industrious and of good behaviour. The governor concluded on 20 December, 'the accused is not of criminal habits or tendencies, nor an

---

35 *Sunday Post*, 23 January 1927; *Western Daily Press*, 4 December 1926.
36 NRS, AD15/27/18.
37 Roughead, *Trial*, pp.134-5.

associate of bad characters'. He did not recommend him for Borstal, but Dr Cunningham thought otherwise.[38]

The news of the arrest led to some contacting the authorities with their information. The manager of the Dunedin Palace gave the bank book of Mrs Merrett to the police. Dr Rosa agonised over what he should do about Mrs Sutherland's statement; after all she had been his patient and there was patient confidentiality to consider. He contacted his lawyers for advice and eventually spoke to both the lawyers for the defence and the prosecution. Merrett was now about to face the greatest test of his young life; to be tried for his life.[39]

---

38 NAS, JC26/1927/27; AD15/27/1.
39 Roughead, *Trial*, pp.200, 204.

5

The Trial of John Donald Merrett, 1927: Case for the Prosecution

Merrett's trial was relatively lengthy and received much publicity throughout the country; it was not only a murder trial where the accused's life was in the balance, but it was the relatively uncommon crime of matricide, had taken place in middle class environs, the accused was young and the crime had occurred in a major city. Roughead, who later edited the trial in the *Notable British Trials* series, had this to say about it:

> *It was a memorable time, that February week, in the High Court of Judiciary in the Parliament Square, Edinburgh, when at the instance of His Majesty's Advocate, John Donald Merrett stood at the bar indicted for the crimes of murder and uttering. No trial since that of Oscar Slater seventeen years before [Slater had been tried for the murder of Miss Marion Glichrist in Glasgow, had been found guilty and sentenced to life imprisonment; in 1927 he was released, a victim of a miscarriage of justice] had so engaged the public interest; and when the diet was called, the old Court-room, theatre of so many moving dramas, was crowded to its utmost limits... The richly robed presence on the Bench, holding with scrupulous hand the balance of justice; the brilliant and resourceful conduct of the defence; the figure in the dock, surprisingly mature, detached, indifferent, suggesting rather a bored spectator of some tedious business than a lad on trial for his life; these are impressions which*

none who then received them is likely to forget.[1]

The legal figures at the trial were notable men indeed, politically and legally. The presiding judge was the Lord Chief Justice, Scotland's foremost legal figure; the post was held between 1922 and 1933 by Robert Munro (1868-1955), Lord Alness. Hitherto he had been Secretary of State for Scotland in Lloyd George's government. He had been called to the Bar in 1893, had been Liberal MP for Wick Borough 1910-1918 and then for Roxburgh and Selkirk up to 1922. He had been Privy Councillor since 1913, the same year as being made Lord Advocate. However, he seems to have been involved in the continued miscarriage of justice over Oscar Slater, imprisoned for a crime he did not commit (Slater was eventually freed due to the campaigning by Roughead and Sir Arthur Conan Doyle).[2]

Leading the Counsel for the Crown, ie for the prosecution, was the Lord Advocate, the Right Honourable William Watson (1873-1948) KC; with him was the Right Honourable Lord Kinross, Advocate Depute. Watson had been born in Edinburgh, had become a KC in 1914, Advocate Depute in 1919. He was a Conservative, sitting as MP for South Lanarkshire from 1913-1918 and for Carlisle from 1924-1929. He had been Solicitor General for Scotland since 1922, when he also became Lord Advocate, and was also a Privy Councillor. He was deemed remarkably able:

> *His industry was such that he would generally get up a case beforehand, and come into the chamber much better prepared than most of his colleagues...opinions were masterpieces of concise and lucid statements. Every now and again he would coin a phrase, or sum up his view of the matter in hand in a pithy sentence, well calculated to abide in the memory.*[3]

The youngest of this trio of lawyer politicians was the Counsel for the panel (the accused), Mr Craigie M. Aitchison (1882-1941), KC. He became a barrister in 1907 and took silk in 1923. In 1924 he stood unsuccessfully as the Labour candidate for Hartlepool. He specialised in criminal cases and his repute stood high:

> *It is not too much to say that he was the greatest criminal advocate*

---

1 Roughead, *Trial*, pp.19-20.
2 ODNB online, 2004-2016.
3 ODNB 57, pp.682-3.

in Scotland of his time...His forensic eloquence, coupled with a pleasing voice and a gracious personality, was unmatched by any of his contemporaries.

It has been suggested that Merrett was only able to secure such talent because his father had associations with the Secret Service in South America; or so said 'informed gossip' according to one Major Hugh Pollard.[4] More probably; according to Roughead, the money for the defence costs came out of Chesney's trust fund. In fact, this is what Mr Thompson, acting for the Public Trustee, stated in 1928, and that these costs had substantially reduced the income available from the trust.[5] The capital sum available to him from his grandfather's will was £13,500.[6]

Supporting these luminaries were the aforementioned Lord Kinross for the prosecution and MacGregor Mitchell (1875-1938), for the defence. Mitchell had been an advocate since 1914 and KC since 1924. In 1923-1924 he had been Liberal MP for the Perth Division and was known as dealing with criminal cases[7]

Aitchison, had, of course, visited his client in prison in order to prepare the defence, but had not found him forthcoming or helpful. Roughead later learnt from Aitchison that when he saw him, the youth merely refused to give him any information whatsoever and said 'I am not guilty...it is up to you to get me off'.[8]

The prosecution needed to prove that Mrs Merrett was murdered, because the only suspect was the accused. Any evidence which pointed to that had, by necessity, to point to his guilt. The defence, of course, did not need to prove that she died by accident or by suicide, but had to cast sufficient doubt on the prosecution case, by making the alternative possibilities seem to be within the bounds of credibility, and so the jury would find him not guilty or at worst, a verdict of not proven.

Merrett travelled each day from Saughton Prison in a police van to the court. His arrival and departure were watched by crowds; perhaps a hundred people, both men and women, in small groups in the High Street and Parliament Square. He looked physically fit. His meals

---

4   ODNB 1, pp.528-9; Hastings, *The Other Mr Churchill*, p.115.
5   Roughead, *Classic Crimes*, p.447; *Daily Record*, 15 June 1928.
6   NRS, AD15/27/1.
7   *Who was Who, 1928-1940*, pp.757.
8   Whittington-Egan, *William Roughead's Chronicles of Murder* (1991), p.85.

were brought for him from a nearby restaurant and he put on weight whilst he was there. It was said that in court 'He has rather a striking appearance'. He wore a smart light grey suit and horn rimmed glasses and followed every word of the evidence. He had arrived in the dock of the court room, via a trapdoor leading to the cells at 10 am. Standing between two constables with drawn batons, he shook hands with his counsel and smiled at his friends in court. The trial was attended by many fashionably dressed women as well as lawyers and doctors who had a professional interest.[9]

Lord Kinross read out the indictment to the court. These were that Merrett was charged with the shooting of his mother which had led to her death and with presenting his mother's cheques to the value of £457 13s 6d. Merrett pleaded 'not guilty'. The jury of fifteen (including six women) were then sworn and were supplied with the indictment. Three shorthand writers were appointed to record what was said. Unlike cases in England, though, there is no opening speech for the Crown in Scotland on the grounds it could bias the jury when listening to the evidence then given. Instead, the trial proper commenced with the witnesses for the prosecution giving their evidence, guided by the prosecution counsel.[10]

Mrs Sutherland was the first witness to be called. She was taken through the statement she had given to constables Gibson and Watt, to the effect that she was in the kitchen when the fatal shot was fired and Merrett ran towards her, before they called the police. Aitchison then cross-examined her in order to undermine the value of her evidence. He had her agree that mother and son were on good terms and that the former was troubled over money issues prior to the shooting. He also made it clear to the court that Mrs Sutherland had given contradictory statements; telling Inspector Fleming and Dr Rosa that she had seen the gun fall from Mrs Merrett's hand – and thus that she died from her own hand – and then telling the constables a few days later that she had not seen this incident. He pressed the witness on these points and she appeared confused, making answers such as 'I think I said that I saw the lady falling, but I did not. I had got mixed up with other things' and 'I cannot rightly remember'. She inferred that

9 *Glasgow Herald*, 2 February 1927; *Sunday Post*, 6 February 1927; *Aberdeen Journal*, 2 February 1927; *Dundee Courier*, 2 February 1927; *Edinburgh Evening Despatch*, 2 February 1927.
10 Roughead, *Trial*, pp.49, 60; NRS, JC5/17.

Dr Rosa was incorrect about what she had told him.[11]

Former PC Middlemiss was the next witness. He told of the visit by himself and PC Izatt to the scene of the shooting. His memory was poor; he could not recall where he picked the gun from nor the position of the furniture in the room. He said he thought, at the time, it was a case of suicide. He stated he could not remember everything because he had handed in his report made at the time and so had not seen it since. PCs Izatt and Watt then gave their testimonies. Watt was asked whether a declaration was ever taken from Mrs Merrett and he replied, 'I cannot say' and as far as he was aware, none had been. Gibson said that neither he nor Watt pressed Mrs Sutherland on the question as to whether she saw Mrs Merrett falling from the chair.[12]

Inspector Fleming was in the witness box for a lengthy period during that first day of the trial. He discussed his investigation into the shooting, the statements he had taken and the evidence he had collected at the flat. He backed the suicide theory. However, he had to admit that he had not taken a deposition from the dying woman even though Dr Holcombe told him that her life was in the gravest of danger. When pressed by the judge on this, he claimed that he still believed that this was a case of suicide.[13]

Dr Bell had been the first surgeon to see Mrs Merrett, and was the last witness to be questioned that day. His evidence was important because he had stated that he had seen no powder blackening around Mrs Merrett's wound, so it was necessary for the defence to press him on this matter. Aitchison noted that the examination the doctor had made must have been 'just a very brief examination with a view to determining where to send patients?', to which Bell replied, 'That is so'. He was then made to agree that 'there had been very considerable bleeding'. Aitchison followed this up with 'Accordingly, you were not really in a good position to ascertain whether there was blackening or tattooing?' But here Bell stood firm:

> 'I satisfied myself that I could not find any. I looked for it.'
> 'If you did not remove the blood you could not see very well?'
> 'I did not remove the blood.'

---

11 Ibid, pp.61-76.
12 Ibid, pp.77-85
13 Ibid, pp.87-102.

> '*Do you mean in so far as the skin was not blood smeared or blood covered, you did not see any sign of blackening or tattooing?*'

Bell agreed that that was so. He added that Mrs Merrett was put into ward three, where attempted suicides were put. Aitchison had made his point. With that, the day's session ended at 4.15 pm as they were usually to do. All those present were ordered to attend on the next day. The jurors were housed in the Braid Hills Hotel on 134 Braid Road, in Morningside, south of the city centre. There they would be under supervision and secluded from those not involved in the trial. The hotel was to be their home for the next week.[14]

The second day of the trial was Wednesday, 2 February, beginning at 10.15 am. As ever, the court room was packed and there had been queues outside Parliament House before the court had even reassembled. The prosecution continued with their case. Dr Holcombe was the next witness presented; another important one as regards both the blackening (or not) around the wound, of statements made by Mrs Merrett and her mental state at the time. He began by being asked about the position and nature of the wound and said, when asked about the blackening, 'I could see parts of the ear, and I did not see tattooing or blackening'. He explained that he had washed the blood around the ear away and agreed that he still could not see any evidence of powder scorching. He then said that Mrs Merrett told him that Merrett had been standing beside her when the shot was fired. Aitchison had objected to Holcombe being asked about what a third party said, but after an exchange of discussion of precedents, the judge overruled his objection.[15]

Aitchison established that Mrs Merrett was still able to sign cheques when in hospital. He also made much of Dr Holcombe's cleaning the ear using a great deal of pressure to remove the blood there. Holcombe had to admit that he did not use a microscope or hand lens when examining the ear for signs of powder marks. Aitchison also wanted to establish whether Mrs Merrett was in a state of delirium and 'considerable mental disturbance'. The doctor said he was not an expert, but that he had seen no sign of it until after 25 March. Yet he could not exclude the possibility that the inflammation of the brain which led to the delirium had not been present for some time before

---

14 Roughead, *Trial*, pp.101-2; *Glasgow Herald*, 2 February 1927; NRS, JC5/17.
15 Ibid, pp.103-5; *The Scotsman*, 3 February 1927.

the obvious symptoms exhibited themselves. He was also asked how accurate his recollection was about Mrs Merrett's statement and confessed he had not written it down at the time and so was at the mercy of his memory ten months after the event. He agreed that head injuries often blocked out memories of events immediately leading up to the injury.[16]

Watson tried to rescue the credibility of his witness. He asked whether Mrs Penn had told the doctor that she did not believe her sister had committed suicide, 'She would not believe it at all' replied Holcombe. He replied that Mrs Merrett had been 'perfectly fit' to tell what had happened to her. In response to an intervention by the judge, he said that she seemed perfectly conscious and in full possession of her facilities.[17]

The nurses were next to be called. Principal was Elizabeth Grant, for Mrs Merrett had told her about her son being next to her as the shot seemed to have been fired. As with Dr Holcombe, Aitchison raised objections to such statements but as before the judge refused to uphold them. The nurse stated that her patient was absolutely clear when she made her statement. She also discussed the accused's visits to his mother and the visits of Mrs Hill and the Penns. She recalled a cheque being signed by Mrs Merrett on 25 March. She was asked if suicides, in her experience, often forget what they did in their attempt but she said not, nor did they appear to be surprised as to what had happened. She had to agree, though, that accidents to the head did result in patients' minds becoming blank.[18]

She was adamant on the subject of Mrs Merrett's memory concerning her alleged suicide attempt, 'Well, in my experience, she is the first one who had forgotten it, if she had forgotten it'. She said that people who attempted suicide were not reminded of the fact, but usually pointed it out themselves. She had never known of one who could not remember it. The issue of the nurse's memory as to conversations of nearly a year ago was flagged up, but she thought she could recall the main thrust of what had been said that directly affected the case. She could not say whether it was true that Merrett had been at the Palais dancing whilst his mother was in hospital. The judge then clarified that the nurse had made notes that she was now relying on for her

16 Ibid, pp.106-10.
17 Ibid, pp.111-12.
18 Ibid, pp.112-17.

evidence.[19]

Nurse Jean Innes was next. She verified that she had seen the patient on the day of her arrival and that she had not noticed any blackening about the wound. She recalled being present at the conversation between Mrs Merrett and Nurse Grant about what the former claimed happened on the fatal day. Aitchison queried her whether she was specifically looking for blackening about the wound and she replied, 'I did not look specially, but there were no signs of blackening'. Aitchison concluded by saying, 'All you can say is that you did not observe any signs?' She also had to admit that she could not exactly remember all the crucial conversation and that she had discussed it with her colleague on a later occasion. Yet she concluded on the question of her being mistaken as to Mrs Merrett's words, 'I might be, but I am almost sure of them'. After questioning from the judge she added that Mrs Merrett's speech was clear from 17-25 March.[20]

Mrs Hill was then examined. She talked of her friendship with Mrs Merrett, of her visit to Edinburgh to see her and what happened there, with Mrs Merrett referring to hearing a pistol shot near her ear. As with the others, she agreed that Mrs Merrett was quite lucid when she saw her. Aitchison tried to see if Mrs Hill would describe Mrs Merrett as a highly nervous character, but she did not do so. He asked her if Mrs Merrett spoke of fears that her estranged husband might be pressurising her for money, but Mrs Hill said not. The witness stated that mother and son were on the best of terms and that she never recalled Merrett having a gun. She also said that she had not recorded her conversations with the Merretts, so Aitchison asked, 'And, accordingly, are you speaking purely at a distance of ten and a half months from your recollection', which she agreed, and likewise to the question, 'you cannot be certain as to the exact words said either by you or Mrs Merrett'. He asked 'Did she at any time insinuate that her son had shot her?' Mrs Hill said 'No'. Watson asked if Merrett had volunteered his information about how the shooting had occurred or had she been questioned by her about it. The latter was the case. After some clarifications about her communications with the Penns, Mrs Hill stood down. During this evidence, Jane Wood, a juror, fell ill, so was allowed to leave the court for a few minutes, when the trial was suspended, but after an examination from Professor Littlejohn, she

19 Roughead, *Trial*, pp.117-21.
20 Ibid, pp.121-5.

returned to the court room.[21]

Mrs Penn was next to give her testimony; beginning with her late sister's history. She then agreed that there were no money worries (and implicitly no motive for suicide). She spoke of her meeting with Mrs Hill and her arrival at her sister's hospital bed. She recounted Mrs Merrett's remarks about hearing a pistol shot close by 'as if Donald had shot me' and that she was mentally sound at this point. There was some discussion by Aitchison that she and her husband were unsympathetic to Merrett's solicitors despite the fact that he was facing a capital charge. In fact, Mrs Penn became quite heated when he suggested that she had been bad tempered with the defence's solicitors, and that she was being told a lie. She also had to defend herself against the suggestion that there was animosity between her and her late sister, and that Mrs Merrett was careful and business like in her housekeeping.[22]

As with the other witnesses, Aitchison took her to task about the accuracy of her recollections of the statements she repeated from her sister. He said:

> 'So you are speaking purely from your recollection?'
> 'Her words are burnt into my mind'.

She also had to rebut the suggestion that she put words into her sister's mouth. She stressed that she had never changed her words on this point. It was suggested that she was hostile towards Merrett because he was heir to his grandfather's fortune and if he was removed, then Mrs Penn's son (William Henry Milner Penn, 1907-1990) would inherit the whole of a not inconsiderable sum when he came of age (not just half). Mrs Penn denied that she had expressed such sentiments at any stage. The next point of substance was whether accident or suicide was the cause of death. Mrs Penn stressed that there was no reason for her sister to have committed suicide. Aitchison brought up the fact that their brother was an inmate of an asylum, said to be in Manchester (Shropshire seems more likely as has been stated in chapter two). Was, Aitchison suggested, Mrs Merrett also afflicted with a hereditary strain of insanity? Mrs Penn replied, 'There is nothing inherited in my family whatsoever. He brought it on entirely

---

21 Ibid, pp.125-31; NRS, JC5/17.
22 Ibid, pp.131-6.

himself'. Aitchison then asked whether Mrs Penn had discussed the shooting with Mrs Sutherland, who had remained as servant at the flat whilst the Penns were in residence; she had not done so in any detail, nor had she talked at length with the nurses about it either. Finally Watson asked about the insanity of her brother and clarified that it was not due to family history.[23]

There was an unexpectedly dramatic scene during this day of the trial. The day ended perhaps a little prematurely because Mrs Penn collapsed during the cross-examination. She was the closest to the victim, save for Merrett, and so was the most emotionally affected by her death and thus the cross-examination by a, to her, hostile, interrogator, touching on many sensitive family matters, cannot have failed to have affected her. The court was thus adjourned.[24]

The third day of the trial was on Thursday, 3 February. After Mrs Penn's collapse of the previous day, she was returned to the witness box. The judge wanted to clear up the role of Mr Jenks and a few other matters. Jenks was stated as being Mrs Merrett's financial adviser and he had not spoken to her directly on his trip to Edinburgh. There was some discussion about Mrs Penn telling her sister that her son could not possibly have shot her, but that was only to 'comfort my sister, to keep her perfectly quiet...That was the sole reason'. She told the judge that her husband could give more details about Jenks.[25]

Penn was the next witness. Although rather younger than his wife, he was a little deaf and had to give his evidence with the aid of an ear-phone. Roughead observed, 'The comic relief which never fails to lighten the darkness of the most grave proceedings was here supplied by the appearance in the witness box of Mr Walter Penn...he was further handicapped by an irritable temper'. He spoke about their time in Edinburgh, at his sister-in-law's hospital bed and of discussions there and at the flat, including the statement by Merrett about saying he would confess if wished. Penn did not constrict his replies to the factual, but gave opinions, too, and had to be reprimanded by the judge about this. He stated that he had found the spent cartridge in the flat and made reflections on police incompetence. Oddly enough he was asked 'What sort of art do you go in for?' and he replied, 'Pictorial, anything I feel inclined for at the moment'. This led on to his memory

---

23 Roughead, *Trial*, pp.135-40.
24 *Dundee Courier*, 3 February 1927.
25 Roughead, *Trial*, pp.141-2.

and he claimed, 'On salient matters I very often think conditions make a vast deal of difference; there are things we could never forget in the world'. His hearing was also questioned, and he stated that he did not use his ear-phone when Merrett spoke to him yet could hear him well. Aitchison spoke to Penn at varying distances and it was only when they were close that Penn could hear him. On being asked about his nephew's 'confession', he replied, 'I consider it was just a childish way of brushing it on one side' and so did not treat it seriously.[26]

Another nurse, Elspeth Grant, took the stand. She stated that she had seen Mrs Merrett in the hospital and that she had talked clearly about a sound 'like a pistol or gun shot in my head' and 'Did Donald not do it; he is such a naughty boy'. She also raised the issue that Mrs Merrett was given morphine in the hospital to help dull the pain she was suffering. When asked if Mrs Merrett's remark about her son's culpability was raised, she replied, 'she said it quite seriously'. She could not recollect Mrs Penn stating 'That is impossible' when asked by her sister if Merrett was responsible.[27]

Betty Christie, now employed at The Locarno Club, Glasgow, spoke of her friendship with Merrett and his reactions after his mother's shooting. She thought he was upset about the incident and did not dance afterwards when he was at the club. She was finally asked, 'Did you just regard him as a big romping boy?' and she said that she did. Stott then told how Merrett purchased the gun at the shop in Princes Street and that it was a cheap Spanish make.[28]

Alan Macnaughton, an Edinburgh gunmaker, gave rather more information about guns. He admitted that he had made no tests as to how much blackening a gun of the type used would make but he was able to provide general information, that a considerable pull on the trigger would be needed to fire the gun, so an accidental handling of it would not result in a bullet firing from it. He also said, 'The blackening is caused by the heat of the burning powder and partly the consumed powder blown from the barrel. It is the want of complete consumption that causes the blackening'. He thought that at a short range a bullet from the gun would cause blackening on the victim but experiments would be needed to make sure. He was asked why pistols of this type were bought, and he replied:

26 Ibid, pp.32-3, 142-7.
27 Ibid, pp.147-9.
28 Ibid, pp.149-52.

'For self defence chiefly. They are not useful for rabbit shooting [the reason why Merrett said he bought it] or for killing any game. They are also not useful for target practice on account of the shortness of the barrel. It is a very difficult to take steady aim with them'.[29]

Aitchison then cross-examined him. Macnaughton declared that 'Some people purchase pistols of that type without really having any great idea of using them for anything'. He had to admit that guns were sometimes accidentally discharged, despite earlier saying that accidents with this type of gun were unlikely. It was put to him that the explosive in the gun was cordite not gunpowder and so the type of blackening produced might be lesser. Macnaughton could not confirm or deny whether this was the case as he had not carried out any experiments.[30]

Professor Littlejohn was a major figure in the prosecution's case, as he had carried out the post mortem on Mrs Merrett and subsequent pistol tests to determine blackening. He was an experienced and well-respected forensic scientist. He read out his previous reports in court, the first of which declared the death to have been suicide and the second which declared that it was almost certainly not, as have been detailed in previous chapters. He stated that gun tests had been carried out as recently as 30 January in the presence of Spilsbury and Churchill. He said it was very rare for women committing suicide to use a firearm and in the instance he recalled, he said that the woman who had done so was unlike Mrs Merrett. He added that an accidental discharge was extremely unlikely. He also pointed out that rubbing did not wholly obliterate blackening marks, so the fact that the hospital staff did not see any was proof that there was none in the first place.[31]

Aitchison had then to break Littlejohn's findings in the eyes of the jury. Littlejohn said that he thought suicide was inconceivable and Aitchison tried to have him admit that inconceivable did not equate with impossible. He also tried to suggest that if it could be proved that the discharge was a close one, i.e. fired from less than three inches, then suicide or accident were probable. Littlejohn agreed that if that could be proved, then his conclusion would be shaken.[32]

Aitchison had done his homework, which had involved studying

29 Roughead, *Trial*, pp.152-3.
30 Ibid, pp.153-4.
31 Ibid, pp.155-6.
32 Ibid, pp.157-8.

text books on forensic science. He cited Professor Dickson-Mann's book to the effect that the direction of a wound often enables an accurate diagnosis as to whether a shooting was the result of suicide or murder. Littlejohn agreed, but added that the book also stated 'Any suicide case should show evidence of a near discharge'. Littlejohn said the direction of the wound was about 120 degrees, but Aitchison suggested the barrel might have been at 90 but the person may have instinctively averted her head so as to result in a greater angle of entry. Littlejohn thought this unlikely. Aitchison then drew attention to Littlejohn's first report which gave suicide or accident as probable causes of shooting and Littlejohn adhered to these statements.[33]

The subject then passed to blackening on the skin caused by shooting. Professor Sydney Smith's *Text Book of Forensic Medicine* (1925) was cited, and to which Littlejohn had written the introduction. The book suggested that gun wounds on suicides would often result in an absence of blackening if the gun was an automatic charged with smokeless powder (no explosive is entirely smokeless, however). Littlejohn hesitated to reply then said he did not agree as he had had much experience and found that blackening still results. Littlejohn was then reminded that he had written of Smith's book that 'it shows an expert knowledge'. He stated that the book did say that in doubtful cases experiments must be made, and this he had done. Other references were made to passages in these books and Aitchison concluded, 'If experts differ, what are we to do in the matter?' and Littlejohn replied, 'I do not know'.[34]

There was also disagreement as to whether wiping the blackening away from skin was possible; Spilsbury's experiment in the case of bullets fired into dead skin suggested it would be, but this did not happen in Littlejohn's tests. The latter stated that only some of the blackening would be easily removed. His own book was then used against him, as he had stated that such could be removed in a certain example, but he stated that not all of the evidence of smoke would be removed. Such would have been the effect of Holcombe's cleaning the wound; some marks would be removed but others would remain. He also pointed out that suicides usually aim at the temple not the ear. He had to admit that this latter was not impossible but was extremely rare. Aitchison said it was a popular idea that behind the ear was

33 Ibid, pp.159-61.
34 Ibid, pp.161-5.

believed to have been the best place for suicides to shoot.[35]

Aitchison then led with hypotheses as to how Mrs Merrett might have accidentally shot herself, but Littlejohn thought that there were several points against such a theory. Eventually he admitted that it was possible. He was also asked about the level of brain damage that the shot would have caused. Littlejohn said few failed suicides forget what they have just tried to do, and few survive a shooting attempt. He was asked about the victim's mental state following the bullet wound to the head, but countered by stating he believed that Mrs Merrett's statements were reliable and not the result of delirium. He believed the evidence of the hospital staff who stated that up to 26 March, her statements were lucid, and so believable. Watson re-examined him and Littlejohn explained that the second report was different from the first because of his new knowledge of the absence of blackening meaning that the wound could not have been a near one and so was not suicidal. Aitchison then announced that he had another witness to introduce on his list and Watson did not oppose him on this.[36]

Professor John Glaister spoke next, reading out his reports and stating that a close discharge resulted in blackening and that rubbing would only remove some of it. Aitchison tried to suggest that in the absence of all the data, definitive conclusions could not be reached and Glaister tended to agree. Another example from Taylor's book was cited about a head wound from a case of admitted suicide in 1844. Glaister was cautious in his comments and answers. The fact that there was an upward entry did not mean Mrs Merrett's death was a suicide. Aitchison asked, 'Don't you agree the whole thing is in the region of conjecture, unless you were an eye witness to what actually happened?' Glaister agreed, 'It is problematical'. There was much questioning about blackening and the extent to which rubbing would remove it, but Glaister was adamant that rubbing would only take away part of it. Watson then suggested that the infirmary staff not seeing blackening was confirmation of Glaister's conclusions and then pointed out that the suicide example cited by Taylor was very unusual because it was rare for suicides to shoot themselves from behind. The court was then adjourned. It was decided, 'in consequence of the fatigue which the jury had already undergone and to which they may still be subjected', they would be allowed an 'airing in the

35 Roughead, pp.165-9.
36 Ibid, pp.170-6.

neighbourhood of Edinburgh this evening' and this was permitted on subsequent evenings.[37]

That day Roughead wrote to his American friend, Edmund Pearson of New York, giving him his thoughts about the unfolding drama, 'the best judicial drama since the Slater case...They are people of our own class'. He also suggested that 'in the event of Donald Merrett's being acquitted, [Pearson should] give him an introduction to Miss Lizbeth Borden: their conversation would be rich in curious reminiscences'. Miss Borden (1860-1927) was tried in America for hacking her parents to death one night in 1892 with an axe: she was acquitted but no one else was ever convicted of the double murder.[38]

The fourth day of the trial was on Friday, 4th February. On this day the focus of attention shifted from the first charge of murder to the second charge of uttering cheques knowing them to be forged. As in the previous day, it was a matter of experts holding forth. The first was Gerald Gurrin, who had often been employed by the police, banks and other institutions, where there were documents whose provenance was in question. He discussed the findings of his reports into the signatures of Merrett mother and son, as well as those which were questionable. He had found that 29 of the cheques had been forged and pointed out that these were far too similar to those genuinely made by Mrs Merrett. Enlargements were shown of these to the jury in order to illustrate the points he was making.[39]

Gurrin then stated that all 29 cheques which were forged were ones where payment was made to J.D. Merrett 'which [we] do not believe to have been made by Mrs Merrett'. However, he then said, 'there is nothing to enable me to form an opinion as to whether the 29 signatures...were written by J.D. Merrett'. After examining all the handwriting samples presented to him he concluded that the twenty nine cheques were written by Merrett. Photographs of these were shown to the jury.[40]

Taking a break from cross-examination, Aitchison had consigned today's cross-examination to Mitchell. He asked Gurrin if his evidence was based on his opinion, and that his opinion might not be shared by

---

37 Ibid, pp.177-81; NRS, JC5/17.
38 Whittington-Egan, *William Roughead's Chronicles of Murder* (1991).
39 Roughead, *Trial*, pp.182-5.
40 Ibid, pp.185-6; NRS, JC5/17.

all. He also inquired if differences in ink, pen and paper used would lead to differences in signatures. Gurrin replied that they might. There were also discussions about the differences in the shape of the letters. On the topic of the forged signatures being traced with ink, Gurrin had to state that he was not a chemist and had not subjected them to chemical analysis. Watson re-examined him to suggest that genuine signatures are usually different to one another rather than forgeries. The judge also intervened to ask whether there was any doubt that Mrs Merrett's signatures on the disputed cheques were forged and Gurrin said not, but that he was unable to connect Merrett with them.[41]

William Morrison Smith, an Edinburgh engraver of 30 years' experience in counterfeit handwriting, followed Gurrin. He, too, believed that Mrs Merrett's genuine signature had been traced to create the forgeries. He also said that there were variations in the genuine signatures. On asked if there were many variations between forged and genuine signatures, Smith discounted this because the forgeries had been clearly traced and the pen used was not writing fluently. Mitchell observed that Smith's evidence must be used with great caution and that miscarriages of justice had occurred due to the evidence of handwriting experts. Smith had not heard of this one case of three decades earlier when Adolf Beck was convicted of a crime he did not commit, partly because the handwriting of a cheque forged by a fraudster was identical to Beck's handwriting. Watson intervened to remind the jury that that had not been the same as mechanical copying of one signature with another.[42]

A number of the staff of the Clydesdale Bank of George Street, where Mrs Merrett had had an account, then gave evidence. They confirmed she had been overdrawn and letters from the manager had been sent to her informing her of the fact. Both Merretts had been seen in the bank, though Merrett came in alone on later occasions. None of them had deemed any of the cheques passed in favour of him as being suspicious at the time. They had all believed them to be perfectly genuine.[43]

The fifth day of the trial was on Saturday, 5th February, and it featured a large number of prosecution witnesses. Banking staff at Edinburgh

41 Roughead, *Trial*, pp.187-91.
42 Ibid, pp.191-3.
43 Ibid, pp.193-4.

and Boscombe explained Mrs Merrett's credit arrangements between the two banks. It was stated that a cheque book had gone missing and another one asked for. Robert Anderson explained how Mrs Merrett had rented the flat.[44]

Mrs Anderson (no relation of the above) recalled seeing Mrs Merrett shortly before her death and that she was in good spirits. Mrs Joan Sharp, the landlady at Palmerston Place, also stated that Mrs Merrett was 'cheerful and bright'. Emslie Lee, a trust officer, explained the source of her income. James Paton from the Rossleigh Motor Company testified that Merrett bought a motorcycle and later wanted to trade it in for a more expensive model, which he ultimately could not afford unassisted. PC William Davidson recalled Merrett's application for a firearms licence, allegedly to shoot animals and birds. George Scott stated that Merrett had told him about the shooting, claiming it was suicide or accident.[45]

John Lawson and Evelyn Pearce, two former employees of the Dunedin Palais, spoke of finding Mrs Merrett's bank book there, but could not remember when they had found it. Inspector Rose gave evidence of charging Merrett in December. The final prosecution witness was John Michael Geoghegan, an Edinburgh accountant, and he had examined Mrs Merrett's financial papers. He explained that she had kept careful records of her expenditure and cheques. He pointed out that the debated cheques were not recorded in her records, whereas the undisputed ones were. Those cheques in favour of her son were not recorded by Mrs Merrett. Those illicitly drawn on her Midland Bank account added up to £370 9s. Those on the Clydesdale Bank to £87 4s 6d and so the total stolen from her accounts added to £457 13s 6d. Geoghegan was not cross-examined; nor were the majority of these witnesses on that day. At some stage in the proceedings, Elizabeth Wilson, a juror, became unwell, and was allowed to be absent after the production of a medical certificate.[46]

It was now lunchtime on Saturday. The judge suggested that if the case could be wound up by the end of Monday, he would suggest that the court proceed through Saturday afternoon. However, if it was thought that this could not be done, he would recommend that the hearing ceased now. The jury agreed with him. The lawyers for the

44 Ibid, pp.195-6.
45 Ibid, pp.196-9.
46 Ibid, pp.199-202; NRS, JC5/17.

prosecution and defence discussed the matter, and whilst concluding that all the witnesses for the defence would be heard on Monday, that there would be insufficient time left for the summing up and charge to the jury. Therefore, at 1pm, the judge decided to adjourn the trial until Monday. He said he hoped that Monday would be the final day of the trial. The jury had to be kept segregated, so were treated to a ramble in the countryside and a motor drive. The judge also told them, 'I would strongly recommend you to abstain from discussing the case in any way among yourselves in the interval. You have only heard one side'.[47]

Merrett had been an observer throughout, but his behaviour had been noted by journalists. One stated, 'Throughout his nerve trying ordeal Merrett has displayed a complaisance and sangfroid which contrasted strongly with the emotionalism of jurywomen and witnesses'. However, sometimes he had reacted to what was being said. When Mrs Sutherland gave her evidence and quoted him as saying 'Rita, my mother has shot myself', she sobbed and Merrett watched her closely before withdrawing his gaze and bowing his head. When Fleming cited him as saying his mother scolded him for wasting money, 'These personal allusions seemed to affect his nerve'. However, he was unmoved by Mrs Penn's evident distress. Another noted that he remained composed throughout, 'appeared to be in a relatively cheerful mood', keeping an eye on proceedings, but occasional traces of strain were evident. He would sometimes talk to his counsel but rarely glanced at the crowded benches behind him.[48]

---

[47] *Western Morning News*, 4 February 1927; *Dundee Courier*, 7 February 1927; *Glasgow Herald*, 7 February 1927; *The Scotsman*, 7 February 1927.

[48] *Sunday Post*, 6 February 1927, *The Scotsman*, 8 February 1927.

6

The Trial of John Donald Merrett, 1927: Case for the Defence and Verdict

On Monday, 7th February, the trial was entering its last stages. It was the day when the evidence for the defence was finally given; as with the prosecution, there was no opening case for the defence made. The first two witnesses, Charles MacPherson, the city's public prosecutor, and Colonel Thom, spoke very briefly, stating that a charge had been made against Mrs Merrett and that that charge was suicide. The first important witness to come forward to cast doubt on whether she had been murdered was Dr Rosa, whom Mrs Sutherland had seen on the evening of the shooting, feeling unwell, but who had said that on that occasion the shot was fired when she was leaving the sitting room. Dr Rosa added his opinion, 'I took it that she saw Mrs Merrett falling'. As had Aitchison with the prosecution's witnesses, Watson had Rosa admit that he could not remember exactly what had been said at this distance of time and needless to say he had made no note of it.[1]

A potentially stronger witness was PS William Henderson. He stated that Mrs Sutherland had told him and Fleming on the day of the shooting, that she had not only seen Mrs Merrett falling from her chair, but that she had also seen 'a revolver falling from her hand'. Watson merely asked if he had heard Fleming having a conversation with Merrett; he had not. The judge had him state that she had been

---

1 Roughead, *Trial*, pp.203-6.

a little agitated but that the statement had been volunteered by her. He had no reason to doubt her accuracy. Further evidence in favour of the accused came from Elizabeth Hardie, with whom the Merretts had lodged in January 1926. She gave no evidence of any animosity between mother and son, who were, according to her, on 'intimate and affectionate terms'.[2]

The last three witnesses were all scientific experts and all were in the witness box at some length. The first was Professor George Robertson (1863-1932), Doctor of Medicine at Edinburgh University and an expert in mental health, having great practical experience dealing with officers suffering from shell shock due to the recent war. He had read the newspaper reports of the trial and had studied the temperature charts taken for Mrs Merrett. He had noted that her temperature had risen on 22 March (reaching 103 Fahrenheit at time of death) and had become feverish. He took it that she would have suffered mental as well as physical shock from the bullet wound.[3]

Robertson also retailed her physical injuries; probable damage to the brain and paralysis of one side of her body, which would also affect the brain or nervous system. He noted that medical doses of morphia had been rightly administered to dull the pain. Mental disturbance would have resulted, making her be in a state of 'altered consciousness'. The professor was able to state examples of cases where head injuries had resulted in memory loss and false recollections. Nor was it always possible for even an expert observer to know that the patient was in a state of altered consciousness. Changes of personality were other possible results. Intelligence was often reduced. No examination of Mrs Merrett's mental state had been undertaken when she had been in the hospital. The professor concluded, with serious doubts as to the validity of what Mrs Merrett had stated, 'I think that any statements she made should be received with the very greatest hesitation'. He added that she might well have been in a state of delirium prior to when it was first observed on 25 March.[4]

Watson then cross-examined him. He agreed that his knowledge of the actual case was limited; 'he had not read the post mortem report for instance, and he could not state whether Mrs Merrett was indeed suffering from 'altered consciousness'. Aitchison then tried

---

2 Roughead, *Trial*, pp.206-8.
3 Ibid, pp.208-9.
4 Ibid, pp.209-15.

to rescue the validity of his witness, discussing the effect of brain damage and the possibility that reasons for suicides are not always known. Robertson thought that Mrs Merrett might have forgotten her suicide attempt and those who saw her in hospital and who had given statements about what she had said, might not have realised that she was in a state of 'altered consciousness'.[5]

The penultimate witness was Robert Churchill, the gun expert. He began by making statements about the shooting experiments made by Spilsbury and himself. He said that pistol blackening did happen at short ranges but that it could be easily removed. Using the gun, he also demonstrated how it could have been used to inflict an ear wound without unnecessary straining. He also believed that she could have shot herself accidentally whilst tilting backwards in her chair. Being a short pistol, both theories were possible, large guns being used to shoot through the mouth.[6] Professor Smith later commented, 'Anybody firing a pistol at his own head is inclined to hold the barrel close to the skull – certainly no more than three inches away'.[7]

Churchill was cross-examined. He admitted that it was unusual for a woman to commit suicide by shooting, especially one unused to firearms as Mrs Merrett was. But it was not wholly unheard of. He cited an instance of a woman shooting herself whilst her husband was asleep in the same room. This did not exclude the possibility of suicide, therefore. Watson also had him admit that in their gun experiments, the actual gun had not been used and in only one of two instances had ammunition from the same shop being used.[8]

During the trial, a newspaper reporter asked Churchill if he believed Merrett was guilty and the dispassionate expert replied, 'I don't know. I am only interested in the firearms side of the case'. Churchill later said that he had never worked so hard on a case as he had on this one. Hoping to have some time in Edinburgh for social visits in the evening with his wife, Aitchison soon disabused him of such plans. He wrote, 'counsel for the defence was indefatigable. We had conferences each evening after dinner in which we went right through the transcript of the shorthand notes of the days' proceedings and prepared the next day's work as well'.[9]

5   Ibid, pp.215-20.
6   Ibid, pp.220-4.
7   Smith, *Mostly Murder* (1959), p.143.
8   Roughead, *Trial*, pp.224-6.

The final witness was the most important of all for the defence's case. This was the well known pathologist, Sir Bernard Spilsbury. A journalist noted 'A hush fell upon the court' when 'the eminent pathologist' appeared. He reeled off his many qualifications and experience. He had considered the site and direction of the wound and declared, 'there is nothing...which in my view is inconsistent either with suicide or with accident'. As with Churchill, he demonstrated such with the pistol that shooting to the head would not strain the firer. He agreed with Littlejohn's first report that stated that suicide or accident were likely. He did not believe that the lack of blackening was of importance, though he said that the experiments he and Churchill had undertaken had revealed some blackening at short ranges. Again, as with Churchill, he stated that rubbing would easily remove most traces of it. Taylor's textbook was cited as to the ease of removal of markings and Spilsbury naturally concurred with it. He also agreed that Mrs Merrett's statements were not to be entirely trusted because of the delirium resultant since, allegedly, 22 March. However Spilsbury was not an expert on mental health so his veracity on this subject can be doubted.[10]

Watson now needed to cast doubt on Spilsbury's statements. He questioned him on whether it was not more natural for a suicide to put the gun against their head. Spilsbury said that it was, but then that it was not unknown for the head to be moved away from the weapon, which might have happened. He also agreed that his experiments might have been better using the actual gun and ammunition from the same shop on both occasions. He did not differ in his propositions that accident or suicide were possible causes of death. Aitchison then concluded, 'My Lord, that is the case for the defence'.[11]

The accused did not speak in his defence as had been permissible since 1898. Robert Wood, on trial for murder in 1907, had done so and had done so very successfully indeed. He had been acquitted. Yet it was a risk; prosecuting counsel could make the accused look guilty if they appeared shifty or evasive. However the fact that he was not put in the witness box could not be mentioned by the prosecution as a suggestion that he had something to hide.

It was then time for the prosecution to address the jury with its

9 Hastings, *The Other Mr Churchill* (1963), p.113.
10 Roughead, *Trial*, pp.226-35; *Evening Telegraph*, 8 February 1927.
11 Roughead, *Trial*, pp.235-9.

case as to why they should find the accused guilty on both counts. Watson's case was that Mrs Merrett was leading a happy and contented life and had no reason to shoot herself, as stated by various witnesses. Mrs Merrett kept careful accounts, but these did not show the unauthorised withdrawals made on her son's behalf. Merrett had been spending well in excess of his ten shilling weekly allowance and this expenditure had been met by forging cheques from his mother's cheque books and cashing them. Gurrin's evidence was then cited. Mrs Merrett did not learn what had been happening until she received the letters from the bank on 17 March. Watson then asked that the court adjourn for the evening, which the judge allowed.[12] Possibly this interruption to his speech may have blunted its effectiveness.

The seventh day of the trial was on Tuesday, 8 February. Watson continued his address. He stated that Mrs Sutherland heard Mrs Merrett being shot, books falling in the lobby and then Merrett rushing in. Merrett's statement agreed that he went into the kitchen and so the statement about seeing the gun falling from Mrs Merrett's hand must be false. 'It is for you to judge whether the story now told by her is correct' he said. He said that Mrs Merrett's statements might be queried as noted by Robertson, but they were corroborated by the fact that she had been shot and that all her five statements were very similar to one another, lending weight to their veracity. Nor was there any evidence that she knew about the pistol. He repeated the statements made by Mrs Merrett to Bertha Hill, the Penns, the nurses and Dr Holcombe, about being shot whilst her son was standing besides her. He also made the point that six of the bullets bought by Merrett for his gun had been fired prior to the shooting of his mother. He wondered why Merrett had not rung for a doctor when his mother lay injured and said that his statement corroborated those of his mother in his proximity to her when the shot was fired. Furthermore, Merrett insisted his mother was worrying over money but no one else had made that point, even a lady who saw her the day before the tragedy. Nor did her last letter touch on money worries.[13]

As to the actual shooting, Watson admitted that nothing was impossible. But he pointed out the unlikelihood of a mother shooting herself whilst sitting in a room, quietly, writing a letter and with her

12 Ibid, pp.239-48.
13 Ibid, pp.249-58.

only son there. It was a question of probability. He added that all the shooting experiments showed that as there was no blackening at that range, backing up what the hospital staff had observed, and thus the shot was fired at a distance (ruling out suicide). He said that cheques were being signed after Mrs Merrett was in hospital, but she had only been known to sign one. The conclusions to be drawn from all this, Watson said, was that the jury find the accused guilty on both charges. He could submit no evidence that Mrs Merrett died by her own hand. Whereas her son had defrauded his mother by about £200 by 17 March, and had hoped he could keep avoiding discovery. He was desperate to stave off exposure. On that day he was standing by his mother, pistol in hand; then he pulled the trigger. His own statement was inconsistent and impossible to believe. Looking at these facts, Watson argued, must lead the jury to finding Merrett guilty.[14]

Aitchison then rose to give the address of the defence for the jury and spoke for a lengthier, but more compact, period, than had his opponent. Throughout his speech he encouraged them to give Merrett the benefit of the many doubts that he insisted were there. Presumption of innocence was a crucial tenet of Scottish law. As he had said throughout, the veracity of the prosecution witnesses must be questioned because of the distance of time, acting on memory. He urged them to show 'fair play' towards Merrett. The question was not why Mrs Merrett had died but whether the prosecution had proved conclusively that she was murdered and he cited a legal text book to support his case.[15]

He then challenged the evidence of Mrs Sutherland and Littlejohn who had changed their statements. He queried whether Merrett shot his mother by impulse and suggested Mrs Merrett equally might have shot herself on impulse. He stated that the sound of falling books suggested that Merrett was sitting at his books when the shot was fired and then knocked them over when he rose after the shooting. He reminded the jury that PS Henderson heard Mrs Sutherland claim she saw Mrs Merrett drop the gun. Dr Rosa's statement was brought up. The statements of prosecution witnesses were naturally dismissed as being unreliable. 'Do you think it right, in a case of this gravity, involving an issue of life and death, to place any reliance whatsoever upon the statements made by Mrs Merrett?' He also placed emphasis on the

14 Roughead, *Trial*, p.258-64.
15 Ibid, pp.264-7.

fact that the door of the room where the shooting occurred was open throughout, suggesting that this cast doubt on this being murder. The lack of a dying declaration from her was a police blunder for it might have cleared Merrett, though Professor Smith later thought 'In point of fact it would probably have hanged his client'. He claimed that Mrs Penn was hostile towards Merrett and Robertson's theory of altered consciousness further reduced the value of Mrs Merrett's remarks.[16]

He also defended Merrett's conduct in going to the dance hall when his mother lay in hospital because he wanted companionship in his lonely hour of need. Doubt was cast on the uttering of false cheques. The incorrect expert diagnosis of handwriting in the Adolf Beck case was discussed; and the resulting miscarriage of justice reiterated. It was also claimed that Mrs Merrett was not a good business woman and that she may have made errors with her cheques without always realising it.[17]

Forensic evidence from the defence's witnesses was then recalled. Aitchison made a big play on the fact that 'we have had the great and learned assistance of Sir Bernard Spilsbury... there is no name in Britain, there is no name in Europe, on medico-legal questions, on the same plane as the name of Sir Bernard Spilsbury'. His evidence just had to be believed, Aitchison emphasised. He also reminded them that suicide often results from unknown (to any but the victim) motives. Merrett's loyalty to his mother's memory was stated. The jury were flattered and there was a final appeal for a not guilty verdict:

> *Give him, by your verdict, a reputation up to which he will have to live for the rest of his life; and I will say this to you, as one who has been much and intimately in contact with him during these last few days – and it is my final word – send him out from this Court room this afternoon a free man with a clean bill, and, as far as I can judge, he will never dishonour your verdict.*[18]

It only remained for the judge to make his Charge to the Jury where he guided the jury through the main points of the case. After complimenting both the prosecution and defence, he reminded them of the gravity of the case – a capital one – and the rarity of matricide in Scotland. He then talked about the imprecision surrounding the

---

16 Ibid, pp.268-75; Smith, *Mostly Murder*, p.145.
17 Roughead, *Trial*, pp.276-87.
18 Ibid, pp.287-9.

case; the uncertainty of witnesses and lack of depositions taken, with the police's investigation being 'unsatisfactory, inconclusive and perfunctory' in their conduct, 'which was putting it mildly' claimed a later observer. How then did Mrs Merrett die? Accident, suicide or murder; and if the latter the culprit must be Merrett.[19]

The Crown, the judge said, was relying on witnesses such as Mrs Sutherland, on the reported statements of Mrs Merrett, the evidence of the police officers, the doctors and nurses at the Infirmary and the experiments made by Littlejohn and Glaister. The judge outlined the statements made by these, which pointed to murder, but encouraged a sceptical attitude towards them because they were contradictory and possibly confused due to the passage of time. The jury was also asked to consider the previous statement and behaviour of Merrett, as to whether this had any bearing on whether he was culpable of murder or not.[20]

He then passed to the second charge against the accused. They had to consider whether the Crown had proved the cheques to be forged and whether they had shown that Merrett passed them for payment knowing them to be forged. Even if this was the case it was not proof in itself that he was guilty of the first charge, that this was a motive for murder. He tended to suggest that the evidence of the Crown's handwriting experts should be taken seriously. As to whether Merrett presented them, he said that there should be no doubt. Where did the funds for Merrett's undoubted spending come from? The judge concluded that if there was reasonable doubt – not mere possibilities – that the Crown's case was not satisfactory, then Merrett must be found not guilty or not proven. If otherwise, they had to discharge their duty, however unpleasant, and find him guilty.[21]

The jury retired at 4.35 pm to discuss the verdict. We do not know what they said, of course, but there must have been some discussion and also some dissension. Merrett's calm has already been commented upon. It did not alter when the denouement approached. A reporter commented:

> *As the trial drew to is close, Merrett maintained the stoic calm which has characterised his demeanour all through the case. He showed some sign of restlessness during the morning, but later resumed*

19 Roughead, *Trial*, pp.289-91; Smith, *Mostly Murder*, p.145.
20 Ibid, pp.291-303.
21 Ibid, pp.303-8.

> *his patient bearing, sitting upright in the dock and following every word uttered. As the jury retired, he smiled at his escort as conveyed below.*[22]

They returned to the court at 5.30pm.

> *The accused exhibited the only sign of nervousness and concern that he had shown all through the protracted trial. His glance was steadily directed at the jury, and he seemed to be examining them one by one as if trying to read what was in their minds, while he also whispered a word to his police escort.*[23]

The Clerk of the Justiciary asked for their verdict and the chairman of the jury replied:

> *The verdict under the first charge is not proven, by a majority [10 to 5; the former number including all the women on the jury], and under the second charge, uttering, guilty, unanimously.*

Not proven is a verdict unique to Scottish law. It does not mean that the jury think the defendant is not guilty, only that they are not convinced that the prosecution has successfully made their case. The Defence had not been successful; nor had the prosecution. Sir Walter Scott called the verdict 'that bastard verdict' and Roughead referred to it as 'that indefensible and invidious finding' but many lawyers defend it.[24]

In the absence of Watson, Kinross moved that Merrett be sentenced on charge two, and when the judge asked Merrett if he had anything to say, he replied, as do most defendants who are found guilty, in the negative. The judge then pronounced:

> *John Donald Merrett, you have been found guilty, by a discriminating verdict of the jury, on the second charge only. The charge is serious in its quality – presenting cheques which the jury hold you knew to be forged. It is also serious in its extent, the amount involved being £457. I have before me a certificate from the Prison Commissioners to the effect that you are unsuitable for Borstal treatment. I have no option, therefore, but to sentence you to a term of imprisonment. In respect of your youth, I shall restrict that sentence to one of twelve months. That is the sentence of the Court.*

22 *Dundee Courier*, 9 Feb. 1927.
23 Ibid.
24 House, *Murder Not Proven?* (1984), pp.189-90.

He then thanked the jury for their services and the court rose.[25] A journalist reported of Merrett:

> *At the sound of his Lordship's voice, a tall lithe figure, clad in a smart grey suit, jumped to his feet and faced the judge. Merrett still unmoved, resumed his seat and after a few moments delay during which he smilingly acknowledged remarks made to him by agents acting in his defence, was escorted below without once glancing back into the body of the court, while a number of relatives and friends of his dead mother were seated.*[26]

Although there had only been a few people hanging around in the early afternoon, a large crowd gathered outside the City Chambers, near St. Giles Cathedral and the west entrance to Parliament Square, by three that afternoon, awaiting the verdict. These included young couples, mothers and nurses with prams or small toddlers, women with parcels and errand boys with their bicycles. Rumour and discussion abounded. They were discussing 'Will he get off?' and 'What will the verdict be?' Police were needed to keep the High Street open for traffic. On hearing the verdict, they surged ahead, cheering and waving. Merrett waved to two friends as he, escorted by a policeman, climbed into the police van on his way to prison, via the High Street. It seemed that the crowd wished him well.[27]

The possibility of lodging an appeal against the sentence was considered. It could be argued that the jury had been misdirected. They had been unable to exclude the possibility that he had forged the cheques, but had not been charged with forgery. Yet the plan was discounted.[28]

Roughead, in the detailed commentary on the trial, refers to the quality of the lawyers involved. He thought Watson's speech 'was in accordance to the best tradition of the Crown Office...fairness, moderation...even generosity...the Crown case was presented with force and clearness'. Yet he was let down by witnesses who changed their statements and a lamentable police investigation. Aitchison may have had a difficult task, too, but had performed very ably indeed, 'his address was a triumph of forensic oratory. Not a point

---

25 Roughead, *Trial*, pp.308-9.
26 *Dundee Courier*, 9 February 1927.
27 *Evening Telegraph*, 9 February 1927; *Edinburgh Evening Despatch*, 9 February 1927.
28 *Evening Telegraph*, 9 and 10 February 1927.

was missed, everything favourable to the accused was displayed in the strongest light...a model for young aspirants to the criminal bar'. Yet he disapproved of Aitchison's venom towards Mrs Penn as a deplorable necessity. Roughead also approved of the judge's charge 'logical, precise and even-handed', though he was supportive of the prosecution for the second charge but not the first. He also noted that despite Aitchison's eloquence, none of the jury believed Merrett to be 'not guilty'.[29]

Churchill placed the onus for the acquittal on Aitchison, 'in my opinion, the best cross-examiner I ever heard...he threw quick fire questions at one witness until he had conceded his point...counsel was the Scottish Marshall Hall, Muir and Norman Birkett rolled into one'.[30]

Smith apportioned the result due to 'The slackness of the police and the credit given to the misleading evidence of Spilsbury and Churchill'. Churchill's biographer argues against Smith's proposition. As he wrote, Spilsbury and Churchill were called in to say whether suicide was possible, not whether it had happened. Churchill thought that the prosecution was at fault, for arguing that suicide was impossible. He also thought that both men probably did not think Merrett was innocent. One journalist gave Spilsbury the credit, 'The weight of the expert witnesses means a very great deal. The authority of Sir Bernard Spilsbury is, of course, unchallenged in the general estimation...the prosecution case naturally crumbled'. One writer on the case stated 'The really fatal mistake [of the police] was not to fingerprint the pistol'. If the gun had shown Merrett's fingerprints then the case would have been proved against him; had it been clean of them, then the evidence would still have pointed towards him. Had the fingerprints been of his mother then that would have suggested his innocence unless one argues that he had been extremely quick witted and wiped his off and then pressed her fingers to the gun.[31]

Roughead, in his personal correspondence, had no doubt that 'He was certainly guilty'. He apportioned responsibility to 'the police made such a bungle of the business at the start that the Crown was heavily handicapped, and the young devil escaped'. In 1928 he referred to 'the

---

29 Roughead, *Trial*, pp.43-5.
30 Hastings, *The Other Mr Churchill*, p.124.
31 Hastings, *The Other Mr Churchill*, pp.113, 117, 125; Wilson, *Not Proven*, p.254; *Aberdeen Journal*, 9 February 1927.

boy who shot his mother last year and got off by the grace of God and of Craigie'. Finally there was the fact that 'Had the jury known how he treated his mother at the Infirmary they might have taken a different view. But what really saved his rascality young neck was that idiot servant with her two tales'.[32]

Journalists discussed the case. One said, 'Merrett may congratulate himself on the leniency with which he has been treated in respect of the less serious charge'. He commented that the trial had been unsensational and unexciting, which was unusual in a life and death case, which could be expected to be vivid. Much of the evidence on both sides had been 'wholly unsubstantial'. The conduct of the police had been 'inexplicable' and slack.[33] *The Scotsman* noted that there had been 'An unsatisfactory ending to a rather unsatisfactory case'.[34]

The question is whether Merrett was guilty or not of murder. In public, Roughead was sceptical as to his lack of guilt and finished his Introduction to the Trial which he edited for publication in the *Notable British Trials* series in 1929 with the following for the reader to consider:

> How did the accused propose to deal with the situation which his nefarious transactions had created? He had depleted his mother's bank accounts, dissipated her current income, despoiled her temporarily of livelihood. Detection, imminent and inevitable, confronted him. He could not have counted upon a timely accident, or foreseen her suicide on the discovery of his guilt. What was he going to do about it? How was the plot to end?[35]

Adam, in his study of mysterious deaths, published in 1931, was uncertain whether Mrs Merrett died accidentally, by suicide or by murder.[36] Neither could state in public the belief that Merrett was guilty for this would have constituted libel.

Apparently there was discussion along these lines in the following two decades and Roughead, in a book published in the year before his death, gives a chapter over to the case and states that Aitchison's hope that Merrett would thereafter leave a blameless life was misplaced, citing a later crime in 1928. He does not come to any conclusion

---

32 Whittington-Egan, *William Roughead's Chronicles of Murder* (1991), pp.65, 70, 85.
33 *Aberdeen Journal*, 9 February 1927.
34 Roughead, *Classic Crimes* (1951), p.447.
35 Roughead, *Trial*, p.45.
36 Adam, *Murder by Persons Unknown* (1931), p.83.

about the shooting, however.[37] A biography of Sir Bernard Spilsbury makes no comment.[38] After Merrett's death in 1954, opinion was universal that he had been guilty, due to later murders committed by the same man. Smith stated 'A worthless life was saved, and two innocent women were thereby condemned to die'. Hastings noted, 'It is perilously easy to be wise after the event that, on the facts of the case, one wonders that the jury were ever in doubt'.[39]

According to Massie, had the murder occurred in a less salubrious part of the city; in Canongate or Cowgate, for example, Merrett's story may well have been heard rather more sceptically and thus to his detriment. It is also worth noting that there was generally a more liberal attitude to juvenile offenders following 1918; the young Neville Heath was charged with numerous offences in the 1930s and was dealt with mildly, possibly in part due to his apparent good manners and class.[40]

So what did happen in the flat at 31 Buckingham Terrace on 17 March 1926? That Mrs Merrett was shot in the head in her sitting room with a small automatic pistol bought by her son at about 9.40 am when the flat's only other occupants were her son and Mrs Sutherland is undoubted. It has never been suggested that the latter was in any way involved. We shall examine the three hypotheses and see which seems most likely.

Could it have been an accident? The suggestion is that the gun was in the bureau as she was writing a letter. Could she have reached out for something in the bureau, assuming the gun was there and there is no certainty that it was, then, without seeing what it was and without knowing what it was, then have pulled the trigger, which would have needed some force, and by a horrible coincidence having pointed it at her head? It would also assume that the safety catch was off. It is not absolutely impossible, but it seems extremely improbable.

Then there is suicide. This presumes that she had the gun to hand – and there is no knowing that she did. It also presumes that she did so because of the letters just received from the bank that she was in financial difficulty. Yet there was no prior inference that she was upset and no suicide note. Her religious inclinations would not point to self

---

37 Roughead, *Classic Crimes*.
38 Browne and Tullett, *Bernard Spilsbury: His Life and Cases* (1951).
39 Hastings, *The Other Mr Churchill*, pp.113-14.
40 Massie, *Edinburgh* (1994), p.205.

murder. Would she have killed herself in the same room as her son? Had she been intent on suicide would she have not put the muzzle of the gun to her head in order to succeed? It is, of course, possible, but as with accident seems very unlikely.

Or was it murder? Her son had been defrauding his mother over the previous weeks in order to fund a lifestyle he could not have afforded otherwise. He had also bought a gun for no obvious reason (the one he gave was a lie). He was in the room at the time of the murder and his mother later recalled to several witnesses that he was standing by her just before the gun was fired. He had both motive and opportunity. By not having left the scene he was creating a good impression among the police; had he fled in panic then this would have suggested guilt.

The question arises, if this was murder, when did Merrett take the decision to do so? He had begun forging his mother's cheques in early February 1926 and bought the pistol a few days later. The question is: why did he make the purchase? Churchill suggested that a general reason for such was to give the buyer a feeling of power. This cannot be discounted. Partly it was to show off to people like Scott and Betty. Did he decide then that he might need to kill his mother? It seems unlikely that such an extreme step was so premeditated at such an early date. Possibly, as time went by and he continued to cash forged cheques, he may have felt that there might come a time when he might need to use it against his mother. But probably the final decision was not taken until the morning of the 17th when his mother may have made some reference to the bank's letters to her about her withdrawals. There cannot have been any heated exchange or Mrs Sutherland would have heard it and mentioned the same. Perhaps he realised what she had read and pre-empted her. The gun was probably bought, in part, as an insurance policy, lest he needed to use it to cover his tracks, and he seems to have practised firing it at some stage, perhaps in the Braids, so he knew how to use it, but the final decision to use it only took place on the morning itself.

If Merrett can be deemed a psychopath, then this behaviour would be fitting. Psychopaths tend to act impulsively, with little thought to the future, even their own, and with no consideration for others. He had that superficial charm and a self-belief in his own worth which are characteristics of this type.

If it was murder, for which Merrett was found not to be guilty, then it is arguable that this was a miscarriage of justice. Conventionally

The Trial of John Donald Merrett, 1927: Case for the Defence and Verdict

this term is used to define the situation when a defendant/s are found to be guilty and suffer the penalty for their crime/s, but at a later date the evidence used to convict has been found to be suspect and so the guilty verdict was applied improperly. However, writers have argued that if Merrett had been found guilty of murder, his youth would probably have saved him from the death penalty, though not necessarily as Derek Bentley found out to his cost in 1953. Had Merrett been reprieved after a guilty verdict he would have been given a gaol sentence and then have been released some time in the 1930s, perhaps. And then it would be anyone's guess as to what happened in his life next.

Yet it is surely the case that this is not the only type of miscarriage of justice. The phrase means that justice has not been correctly served in that an incorrect verdict of any type has been reached. If Merrett was guilty of murder then, in this case, justice did indeed miscarry in Edinburgh in February 1927. This had not only the immediate effect in that Merrett's guilt was found to have been not proven and thus failed to receive either the death penalty or, in the possibility of a reprieve, a lengthy term in gaol, but as the reader will discover, longer term effects when he continued his criminal career – spasmodically it must be said – and further victims suffered. The long-term results could not have been wholly foreseen in 1927, but without this verdict they could not have happened. For his later victims or their dependants, there would be no compensation.

There is another possibility and that came from the mouth of the only one who knew the truth: Merrett himself. Roughead once noted that he was the only one who knew the truth, but how truthful was he? Three decades after the trial, a girlfriend of Merrett's revealed that he had confessed to her what he alleged happened after she had been told by a third party that Merrett had killed his mother. According to her, he told her:

> *I did not murder her, Gerda. I had robbed her, I admit that. I had paid my gambling losses by forging her cheques. At last she began to suspect me. One day, searching my room for proof, she found a revolver I had bought...Next morning she accused me of stealing her money. I denied it. Suddenly she opened the drawer of her desk and pulled out the revolver and shouted at me: "Do you deny this, too?" That scared me. I ran towards her, shouting: "Be careful, Mother, its loaded". I tried to grab it out of her hand. We struggled. There was an explosion and she fell... I told the police that she had*

shot herself.[41]

The girlfriend commented, in 1957 about this story:

> *This is the story as Ches [Merrett] told it to me. Because of what happened later...most people now believe that Ronald Chesney did murder his mother in Edinburgh. But despite everything that others say about him, I believe that the story he told me that night is the truth. Is this because I loved him? I do not know. You who read my story must judge for yourselves.*[42]

The problem with this story is that it states that Mrs Merrett knew of her son's forgeries before 17 March and there is no evidence for this. It also suggests that Mrs Sutherland did not hear the shouting that led to the fatal moment. There is another contradiction in this story and his account to the police, for the latter stated that he was seated in his chair reading when the shot was fired. However, this account, in which he was involved in the shooting, may well be a step nearer the truth. Killers often give numerous stories about an incident and they become less untruthful as they proceed. The story was told because Merrett's current girlfriend had been told by his estranged wife that he had killed his mother and thus he had to produce a story that would be plausible to a sympathetic audience.

The author's opinion is that for some weeks Merrett had been leading a double life; outwardly polite to his mother in front of others, but secretly stealing from her. He may well have hated her to do so, as well as believing he needed the money to impress his peers (many students were very wealthy and probably he wished to ape them). However, when faced with disclosure on 17 March, he was probably too emotionally immature (he was aged only seventeen) to deal with the consequences of his behaviour in a more measured manner. Having a gun before him, he took what seemed to him at that moment the only feasible short-term solution open to him. Afterwards he did his best to cover his tracks. All this is hypothesis, but it does fit the facts and provides a possible explanation.

The reader will have to make up their own mind as to Merrett's guilt, though none writing after his death have ever doubted it. Clearly the jury at the trial were divided in their opinions as to his culpability. In this the prosecution were hampered by an incompetent police

---

41 *Woman's Sunday Mirror*, 6 October 1957.
42 Ibid.

investigation, by having Professor Littlejohn and Mrs Sutherland change their stories and by the length of time between shooting and trial. All this played into the hands of an extremely competent KC who, with a highly respected witness in the form of Sir Bernard Spilsbury, was able to cast enough doubt on the prosecution's case that his client was not found guilty of matricide. He had been an extremely fortunate young man.

The hypothesis has been advanced as to what would have happened had Merrett been found guilty of murder. He would have been sentenced to death by hanging. However this did not mean that he would have automatically died by the rope. There would certainly have been a judicial appeal and there might also have been a public appeal to the Home Secretary on the grounds of Merrett's youthfulness. It could well have been the case that he would have been reprieved and have been given a custodial sentence; certainly Harold Jones, found guilty of murder in Wales in the 1920s and in his early teens (below the age when he could have been executed) was sent to gaol for little over a decade.

Professor Smith, in private, told Littlejohn, 'That is not the last we'll hear of young Merrett'. It was a prophetic remark.[43]

---

43 Smith, *Mostly Murder*, p.145.

All images are from the author's collection unless otherwise stated

Bertha Merrett

John Donald Merrett as a boy

Malvern College, where John Merrett attended between 1924 and 1925

Merrett in 1927

31 Buckingham Terrace, Edinburgh today, and (right) in 1927

Sketch of the sitting room of 31 Buckingham Terrace

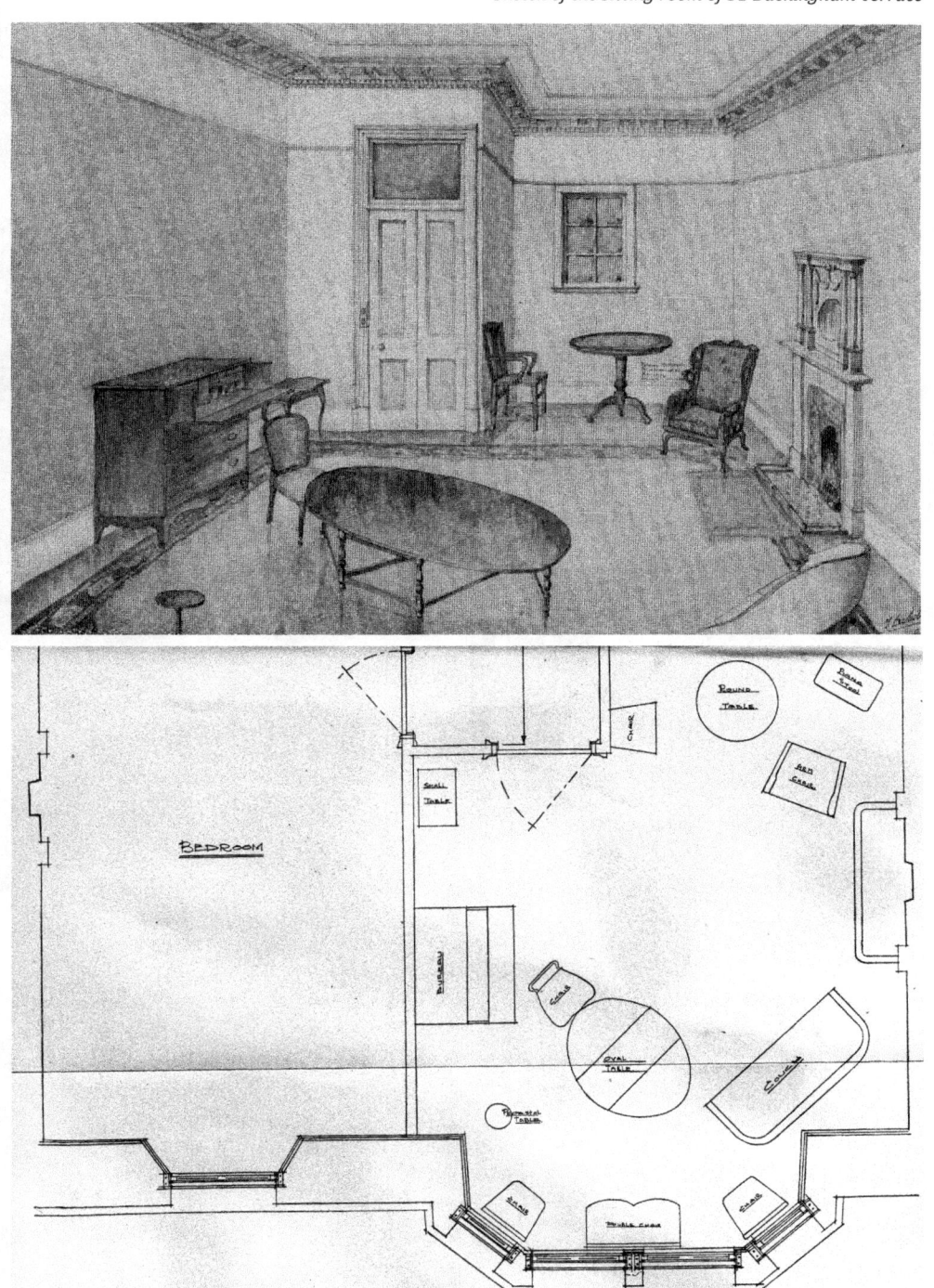

Plan of 31 Buckingham Terrace

Postcard showing Princes Street, Edinburgh, where Merrett purchased the pistol

*Bertha Merrett's headstone
at Piershill Cemetery, Edinburgh*

*Top: The automatic pistol used by Merrett
Bottom: The bueau from 31 Buckingham Terrace*

Case – before returning to Edinburgh. The ~~true~~ Xmas must visit vacation I believe ends on Jan 12th when I will be returning to Edinburgh till — would come to see if as soon as possible after that date – that we could arrange any further matters personally. I am sure I shall like the little Flat – & my boy will be most comfortable there with me – & much appreciate & like you allowing me to use your piano & it will be a great joy to me to be able to play once again on so good an instrument –. With kind regards

Yrs sincerely
Bertha Merrett

Above:
Bertha Merrett's handwriting
Right:
A forged signature

Left to right:
Counsel for the panel Craigie Aitchison,
Lord Chief Justice Lord Alness,
Lord Advocate the Right Honourable William Watson

High Court of Justiciary, Edinburgh

Ronald and Isobel Chesney

1939 Civil defence cards belonging to (left) Ronald Chesney and (right) Isobel Chesney

Ronald Chesney in naval uniform

Sonia Winnikes

Wandsworth Prison

Map of Montpelier Road, Ealing, 1950s

22 Montpelier Road in 1954

Footpath behind Montpelier Road

Left: The coffee pot used to attack Mrs Menzies
Below: The pistol used to shoot Chesney
© Mayor's Office for Policing and Crime
and Crown copyright, Metropolitan Police Service

2 St. Mary's Road, Ealing

German police officer points to site of Chesney's body, 1954

Ronald Chesney
Courtesy Adam Wood

7

Peace and War, 1928-1945

Merrett was released from prison in October 1927, having served a little more than half the sentence tariff; presumably he had behaved himself in an exemplary manner as many prisoners do, and thus earned time off for good behaviour. We have no knowledge of his experiences in prison, but it must have been shocking, even worse than when he was there awaiting trial, having to wear prison garb for the first time and continue with a basic diet. He had his fingerprints taken. Roughead, though, wrote favourably, of Saughton Prison, 'a sort of penal garden city, affording in its humane and hygienic regime the advantages of a rest cure, a criminous nursing home, and combining agreeably punishment with amusement'. Apparently whilst there the governor suggested that he go to Australia to a farm for young men who had gone wrong and wanted to start afresh; to learn farming but also to fish, hunt and shoot. Roughead thought that Merrett would have enjoyed the latter, but Merrett told the governor that this suggestion was 'Not for this lad'.[1]

There are two near contemporary accounts of what happened to Merrett on leaving prison. One is that he left Edinburgh and roamed around England, Wales and Scotland, in search of employment, travelling to Liverpool, London, Cardiff, Kent and Surrey. Occasionally he found casual employment and enjoyed brief spells of prosperity.

---

1   Massie, *Edinburgh* (1994), p.205; Whittington-Egan, *William Roughead's Chronicles of Murder* (1991), p.85.

He stayed for a weekend at a friend's house in Kingston upon Thames (someone he had known at school or university, presumably) and there he met the daughter of a friend of his host. This was Isobel Bonar. The other contemporary account, which is better known, and is usually the one repeated, is that he was befriended by a Mrs Mary Ann Bonar, who had known his mother in Edinburgh and we know she lived in the Lowlands (though she is not mentioned in the copious papers concerning the investigation into Mrs Merrett's death). Apparently she contacted him when he was in prison out of sympathy. He then travelled southward to stay with her at the end of 1927. Merrett subsequently told this account to a later girlfriend. Roughead noted this story, too. All that is certain is that he did meet the two women and was resident in Bexhill by early 1928, when they lived at 21 Jameson Road with the widowed Mrs Bonar who was working as a nurse.[2]

Mrs Mary Ann Bonar and her daughter Isobel Veronica Barbara Menzies McLearn Bonar were the two women destined to play key roles in Merrett's future. Little is known about their early lives. The former had been born Mary Ann McLearn on 25 January 1882 in Ayr, on the west coast of the Lowlands of Scotland. She was the fourth child of Richard and Isabella (nee Menzies); aged in 1891, respectively, 36 and 37-years-old and who had been married on 8 June 1874 in Ayr. Richard was employed in 1891 as a coal drummer and the family lived at 51 Wallace Road, Ayr. There were eight children who had survived infancy; Edward aged 15 and a carpenter, James (1876-1930) and a tailor, Alice (1878-1956), Jane (1880-1953), Fred aged eight, Hugh aged five and Isabella aged three. Also resident there was Richard's mother-in-law, the 80-year-old Margaret Menzies and a daughter of hers, Jane Menzies, aged 52. Although this was a working class household, they did have one domestic servant, the 18-year-old Mary Allan. The family were living in the same town in 1901, at Place W. Aury, and the daughters still at home were now working for a living; Mary was a shop baker's assistant and Jane was in domestic service. James was a ship's provisioner and Fred and Hugh were apprentices. Edward, Alice and Isabella no longer lived at home, and by this time their father had died. Their mother was designated as a housekeeper and seems to have had two boarders in order to bring in a little

2 Philips, *Murderer's Moon* (1956), pp.198-9; TNA, MEPO 2/9542; *The Weekly Record*, 16 and 23 June 1928; *Woman's Sunday Mirror*, 6 October 1957.

income. Mary soon left home and lived in Glasgow from 1903-1918. She later lived in Dumfries, Gateshead and Northumberland. She may have married a John Bonar, born in Glasgow in 1875, who had worked as a bookbinder, then an electrical engineer and later as a 'wireless operator' and was dead by 1928. Her only child was a daughter, born on 21 July 1911, but it is unknown where, and was brought up as a Catholic. It has been stated that they knew the Merretts in the mid 1920s and played bridge with Mrs Merrett, but this cannot be ascertained as fact.[3]

Not much is known about them. Mrs Bonar was deceptively frail. A neighbour once stated that she was, in later life, a 'Dresden China figure', very active and always did her own shopping. 'She gave the impression of being fragile and delicate. She always wore a red cardigan which set off her white hair and fresh complexion'.[4]

Another account speaks of her benevolence, 'She was not the type of woman who would make enemies. She was kind and pleasant and always ready to look after other people'. Apparently she had a small income of £220-330 per year, by the 1950s.[5] Yet she was no pushover. Her future grandson-in-law once quarrelled and hit his wife, she raised a chair above her head to strike him and he recalled, 'Lady Menzies [the name she later adopted] was a terribly strong woman'.[6] She was five feet three and a half inches high and 'rather heavily built'; her daughter was five feet eight and a half inches high. Nothing is known of her early life and education.[7] The two clearly took a shine to Merrett because in 1928 Mrs Bonar agreed to be guarantor on a hire purchase agreement for a motorcycle for Mr D.J. Chisney, the new name that Merrett had adopted for himself.[8]

A later girlfriend of Merrett's later said, 'They were immediately attracted to each other. Vera surrendered to him'. After he proposed to her, they travelled northwards on the motorcycle he bought. They were virtually penniless, though she had a few shillings. On 29 March 1928 after the briefest of courtships, John Donald Merrett, aged 19 and describing himself as a 'Mechanical Engineer' of 1 Bellahouston

---

3   TNA, MEPO 2/9542; McLeave, *Chesney: The Fabulous Murderer* (1954), pp.29-30; ancestry.co.uk
4   *Middlesex County Times*, 13 February 1954.
5   *Daily Mail*, 12 February 1954.
6   TNA, MEPO 2/9542.
7   LMA, COR/MW/184/162-163.
8   TNA, MEPO 2/9542.

Terrace, Gowan, Glasgow, married Isobel at Glasgow Registry Office. She was later described as 'a well educated and cultured woman', who always dressed well in tailored clothes and was fond of brightly coloured jumpers. She was tall and slim.[9]

After their marriage, Merrett apparently had a few very brief spells of employment. These enabled them to initially live in hotel and boarding house accommodation in the suburbs of Newcastle, Jesmond and Gosforth, and stating that they were Mr and Mrs John Chesney of Bexhill, Surrey (actually Sussex; presumably he changed his name because he wanted others to disassociate himself with the criminous Merrett). They were reduced to selling possessions to make ends meet. However before long, they were camping in a tent at Kenton just to the north of Newcastle. They had very little money, but Merrett thought of a scheme to make more. Visiting the branch of the National Provincial Bank in Gateshead, under the name of McCormick, and stating he had an annual income of £300 paid by the Public Trustee (which was correct), he opened an account by depositing either £1 or 25s. In return he received a cheque book containing 12 cheques. He tried to obtain money by using it in two shops, but presumably failed. Third time lucky, however. On Tuesday, 5 June, a woman, presumably Isobel, rang the Grand Hotel, opposite Newcastle Railway Station, to let them know that a room was needed there.[10]

They went to the city and visited Bainbridge's, a major department and drapery store on Eldon Square in the city centre. They then chose various goods; three shirts and collars, three ties and a pair of gloves, costing £3 7s 11d, ladies' underwear at £2 1s 9d, two pairs of silk stockings at £1 5s 1d and gloves for 8s 11d. These items were sent to Merrett's alleged address, the Grand Hotel, and were paid for by a cheque for £7 and signed 'J. MaCormick'. He needed an address that would inspire confidence in the shop and thus allow him these goods he desired. Merrett visited the hotel and was shown a bedroom, but when asked for a cash deposit was unable to give them one, so left, but not before he collected the parcel sent there by the shop.[11]

The two then went elsewhere. At some stage they obtained a green Austin car. Driving to a jewellers, they went inside the shop and

9   *Woman's Sunday Mirror*, 6 October 1957; TNA, MEPO 2/9542; *Daily Telegraph*, 13 February 1954.
10 *The Daily Record*, 15 June 1928; *The Weekly Record*, 16 June 1928.
11 *Newcastle Weekly Chronicle*, 9 June 1928; *Newcastle Evening Chronicle*, 7 June 1928; *The Daily Record*, 15 June 1928.

examined the goods to be found there. Eventually they selected a single stone diamond ring and offered to pay for it by cheque. This time, the shop assistant was cautious and told them that they could only have the ring after the cheque had been presented at a bank. Merrett said, 'I have a green Austin car outside'. This did not impress the assistant. Merrett changed tack and told him that he was attending a dance that night. Eventually he was allowed to take a one guinea ring and a cheque was given in payment. When this was presented at the bank on the following day it was not honoured. They also obtained a motor cycle on the 'pay out of income' method which, as with the cheques, did not require hard cash for goods offered.[12]

The cheque given to Bainbridge's was presumably taken to the bank on the following day and Robert Garland, shop superintendent, found that it was not honoured. He alerted the police and was able to give them a description of the wanted couple. On the following day, a detective by the name of Addison, stopped them on Elswick Road, a central street in the city. Merrett said that he was John Chesney of Bexhill, Surrey. There was the suggestion he had a well paid job to go to in Dundee, but whatever this was, it came to naught. He was then taken to the police station, where he was asked whether he had made the purchases in question. 'Yes, my wife and I have made a purchase at Bainbridge's and I hope the cheque has been honoured'. They were asked to produce evidence of marriage but could not do so. Merrett said Isobel was 19 and a ward in chancery, but she gave her real age (17).[13]

There is no other evidence that she was a ward in chancery, but if true, this meant that she was either an orphan or illegitimate, but had been appointed a judge as her guardian by the Chancery Court to safeguard an inheritance. Possibly her father was not Mrs Bonar's husband (though her marriage certificate gives him as her father). Her birth certificate has not been located under the surname Bonar (she does not seem to have been born in England or Scotland). Until she reached the age of 21 or on marriage she could not touch the capital of this estate. She was unable to marry before 21 without permission. Her fortune was probably a reason why Merrett was attracted to her – he was very short of money - and why, as we shall see, they had to elope to wed.

12 *Daily Record*, 15 June 1928; *Weekly Record*, 16 June 1928.
13 Ibid.

However, since her parents were, as far as is known, far from wealthy (mother from a working class background, father stated on her marriage certificate as a telegraphist) and may not have been married to one another, it is possible that she was not a ward in chancery and that journalists erred in 1928. There is no hard evidence other than this that she was a ward in chancery. Possibly she was a ward of court, someone under the protection of a court as her parents are deemed inadequate (or dead) for the purpose of looking after her.

The two were brought before Newcastle Magistrates' Court, Market Street, on 7 June, and were remanded for a week. Merrett told a detective that he had given a cheque to Bainbridge's and expressed to the shop that it should have been honoured. On 14 June 1928 the pair stood in the dock, charged with using fraud to obtain £7 10s worth of goods, using a book of cheques obtained from a bank in Gateshead, with him calling himself McCormick, as well as other frauds for goods costing £102 in total. He was described as a 'handsome, boyish looking Scots giant'. Thomas Hedley Smirk (1870-1932), a Newcastle solicitor, prosecuted. Mr John Charles Thompson, a Sunderland solicitor and representative of the Public Trustee, said that Isobel had never given any order for the goods illicitly obtained and it was deemed that she had acted under his influence and coercion so she was discharged. He was found guilty and given sentences of six months and three months, to run consecutively, and another of three months; thus nine in all, in Durham Prison. He was also sentenced to hard labour. When Isobel heard her husband's sentence she burst into tears and refused to be comforted by her mother, an aunt and some friends who were present in court. The court costs were paid by the Public Trustee. Merrett's gaol experiences are unknown and he was released on 28 January 1929; with six weeks remission being granted for good behaviour in the prison. On this day he and Isobel were married at the Catholic church of St. Cuthbert's in Durham as Isobel wanted a religious ceremony as well as just the brief civil service they had undergone in the previous year.[14]

Roughead noted Merrett's latest felony, almost gleefully, both in a book and in his private correspondence. Writing to Pearson he noted, 'This is the latest I have heard of him; but so promising and brought a boy will go further yet'. With his inheritance, 'which should permit of

---

14 TNA, MEPO 2/9542; *Dundee Courier*, 11 June 1928, and 17 February 1954; *Daily Record*, 15 June 1928; *Weekly Record*, 23 June 1928.

him enlarging the scope of his operations, he may alight to give the US the benefit of his new and more important works' and suggested that Pearson chronicle Merrett's potential future life of crime in America. Alas for Roughead, Merrett was to be almost unknown to the press until after the former's death. Roughead had also been commissioned to edit the 1927 trial for the Notable British Trials series, and his introduction, whilst it could not state that Merrett was guilty, certainly implied it.[15]

After this, Merrett appeared to leave his criminal career behind him, as on 17 August 1929 he came into the legacy from the grandfather he never knew (£1,996 8s 3d from his mother's will was not his until August 1933 when he was 25). From now on he was called Chesney and this name will be hereafter used. It is not certain how much money he was now possessed of. Traditionally this has been stated as being £50,000 (the amount in his grandfather's will). Yet the will clearly states that the residue was to be shared between all the children of the late William Milner's children, and so this had to be divided between Chesney and his cousin, William Penn (son of Annie and Walter Penn). This would therefore suggest the tidy sum of about £25,000. Yet Mr Thompson said in 1928 that the capital sum was between £6,000-8,000 (reduced from the £13,500 in about 1926-7) and given he was acting for the Public Trustees he was clearly in a position to know. Furthermore, given their reported financial scrapes in the 1930s this seems probable. The young man now began to consider what to do with his new found inherited wealth now he was an adult. He and his wife went to see the Public Trustee and also visited Ernest Goddard, a solicitor, for advice about their financial future. A deed was drawn up between Chesney and John Pybus, a Newcastle solicitor. It was decided that all his remaining inheritance should be settled upon his wife to give her an independent income for life, administered by trustees, though if she should pre-decease her husband the capital would revert to him. Curiously enough, though, this settlement was made on 30 January 1929; several months before he was legally entitled to do so. No one in Sussex knew of his former crimes. He forged a new identity for himself, in part by calling himself Ronald John Chesney and took to living at West Parade, Bexhill.[16] No one could then foresee the significance of this act.

15 Whittington-Egan, *William Roughead*, p.85.
16 Will of William Henry Milner; TNA, MEPO 2/9542; *Daily Record*, 15 June 1928.

Living on the south coast of England, Chesney as he now was, developed a hankering for the trappings of a naval life, as he had in 1925, when he desired a Royal Naval career, but now, in 1931, he could put it into effect, though nothing so demanding as an actual naval officer's job. He bought a 20 ton motor yacht called Rame, 39 feet long, 11.5 feet wide and with a draught of 6.4 feet. It was a wooden auxiliary cutter, with a paraffin motor and electric lighting. It had been built in Plymouth in 1926 and was bought from a Captain Goldsmith, DSO. He registered it at Plymouth in his own name only. By the following year it was owned by a Mr Turner of Hove.[17]

Chesney wanted a bigger boat and by 1932 had acquired one. This was the Amenartas (frequently alleged to have been bought in the late 1930s), a 54 ton yacht made of wood with a twin screw, two oil engines and electric lighting. It was 80.6 feet long, 12.2 feet wide and the draught was 5.5 feet. It had been built in New Jersey in 1918 and was bought from a Mr Ward of Newton Abbot. It was registered in both his and his wife's names. Yet, as with the Rame, they did not enjoy it long and Stanley Grant owned it by 1933.[18] Apparently Chesney, who also went by the name of Bennett, navigated the boat single-handedly from Fareham to Emsworth along the Hampshire coast.[19]

It is probable that these yachts were not acquired with hard cash but by hire purchase or a similar loan scheme and then had to be dispensed of to another after a few months when demands for money could no longer be resisted. As we shall note, despite a love of the high life, they had limited funds and so lived a very precarious financial existence. It seems likely that the income from the capital invested for his wife provided their only income and that was only sufficient for them to live a frugal lifestyle; the last thing they desired.

At Portsmouth he considered being a professional boxer, given his stature and schoolboy excellence at the art, and it was alleged he earned money in boxing booths near Portsmouth. Even more curiously he also tried to establish himself as a greengrocer in the suburbs. Neither of these two ventures came to anything and were soon abandoned. Yet one indicator of his character came from someone who knew his wife at this time and later reported, 'Chesney was at times rather cruel to his wife, forcing her at night in spite of her

---

17 *Lloyd's Register of Yachts*, 1931, pp.732, 423.
18 Ibid, 1932, pp.730, 114.
19 TNA, MEPO 2/9542.

struggles'. Marital rape was not a crime until 1991, but is suggestive as to character. The two were never to have children.[20]

The only information about their life on the south coast from about 1929-1931 comes from witnesses who reported it to a newspaper in 1954, so its accuracy can be questioned, though none of it seems out of character. One source gave a lengthy description of the pair:

> *They lived most extravagantly. Sometimes they appeared to have unlimited money and would pour it out, treating people in bars and spending recklessly. A week later they would be hard up. Their life was one of ups and downs financially.*
>
> *Both Chesney and his wife always drank short drinks. Chesney dominated any company he was in, and would throw back his head and roar with laughter when anything amused him. It was said that he once won the public school's boxing championship [as indeed he had]. He was a good talker and well informed on most things, but was apt to be boastful.*
>
> *At that time he was supposed to have an income from the Public Trustee [provided by his grandfather's will], but both he and his wife spent so extravagantly that they consistently ran up bills with tradesmen, and a number of county court judgements were secured against them by local shopkeepers.*
>
> *They lived the gay life. Mrs Chesney also had extravagant tastes, which she gratified lavishly. Always smartly dressed, she was a witty conversationalist and attractive, but drank heavily.*
>
> *Chesney was a buccaneer type, who was chased from address to address with bills.*[21]

Another witness concurred. He said that banks stopped lending him any money as his overdraft was substantial enough. He also tried to use cheques payable on non-existent balances.[22]

Apparently they lived in a flat on White Rock, Hastings and then at an address in St. Leonards, but the directories of the time do not list them, so they may have flitted from place to place and so not stayed long enough anywhere to appear in an official publication (perhaps to escape creditors). They were certainly known among those who patronised local restaurants and hotel bars. Chesney was the life

---

20 Ibid.
21 *Hastings and St. Leonards Observer*, 20 February 1954.
22 TNA, MEPO 2/9542.

and soul of any party, a jocular character, but was overbearing and if crossed had a quick temper. He had a smart red sports car and often drove it at high speeds along the coastal roads. He is said to have played rugby and one man recalled, 'he played a very strong game, often as full back' in the season of 1930/1. He was also alleged to have taken part in a boxing tournament on the pier. Both pursuits are probable for he had shown his expertise and interest in both in the 1920s.[23]

But there was also noted another side to his character. One person recalled, 'People always wondered where he got his money from as he never seemed to work and always had money to burn'. Another stated that he was 'a flash boy' and another that he was 'a wild type. You would not put anything past him. It was his make up. He was the type you would avoid if you could as you felt he would lead you in trouble. He was fond of big parties and never seemed to do any work'.[24]

Yet the Chesneys were not finished financially, for they lived at a small newly built villa, Fair Mile, Birdham Road, Appledram, near Chichester from about 1931-1935. They were not listed there in 1932-1934 and in 1932-1933 one Captain John Dunbrell was listed at the address. This suggests that they had to let it out not long after it was acquired. It is interesting to note that the Penns lived at nearby Bosham, and Chesney's cousin married in 1934 in Portsmouth but Chesney is not known to have attended, suggesting a family rift, presumably caused by the death of his mother.[25]

Meanwhile, Mrs Chesney's mother visited Plean Castle in Stirlingshire in about 1929. Apparently this was to inspect family records. The result was quite significant as was noted in the following year, 'Whilst they were there my brother-in-law acted as her host and showed her over the castle. Before they left they were in love with each other'. This was with Thomas Chalmers Menzies (1864-1939), a tinsmith and printer of Bishop Street, Glasgow and who had lived much of his life in England. However, he laid claim to the baronetcy of Menzies, following the death of David Prentice Menzies in 1927, his brother, stated as being the ninth baronet. The authentic eighth baronet, Sir Neil James Menzies, had died in 1910 and it was then thought the line, originating from 1665, was extinct. Apparently David

23 TNA, MEPO 2/9542.
24 Ibid.
25 *Chichester Directories.*

had revived the title by petition to the Clerk of Chancery.[26]

All this garnered much publicity for the wedding at Hanover Square Registry Office in London on 28 October 1930. The groom arrived punctually in a taxi from Warwick Place to find the place besieged by spectators. Apparently 'Sir Thomas wore full Highland dress and as chief of the Menzies clan he had three eagle feathers in his tam o'shanter'. He had to wait 25 minutes for his bride. She 'was dressed in a picture frock of blue satin with a hat to match and a heavy fur coat to which was fastened a sprig of lillies of the valley'. Mrs Chesney wore 'a beautiful gold tissue brocade coat and acted as bridesmaid'. As to the bride, 'she leaned on the arm of her son-in-law, Mr Ronald Chesney'. The civil ceremony was also attended by Mrs Bonar's sister, Alice McNeish.[27]

The wedding ceremony took about ten minutes and then there was a reception at the Grosvenor Hotel. There was a honeymoon in London before, allegedly, the newly weds went to Plean Castle. Many newspapers stated that Menzies had no right to the title he claimed. It was not listed in Debrett's or any other reference book for the peerage. Menzies had no truck with this, claiming that it was registered at Register House in Edinburgh and that he had no wish to submit to enquiries by solicitors going over pedigrees and charging vast sums.[28]

After some years the Chesneys left Appledram, and took a property titled Wilmhurst, on Gower Road, Weybridge, Surrey, in 1936, where Mrs Menzies lived with them; presumably her marriage to the so-called baronet was now at an end, though she retained the dubious title thereafter. Allegedly they split because he would not convert to Catholicism. She never saw any of her Scottish relatives after about 1934 and did not attend her late husband's funeral. Yet she clung to the title, stating in 1949, 'I am a titled lady through marriage. I do not want to give any particulars about my husband who has been dead for some years'. However by the end of 1936 they had left Weybridge behind. As ever, they were rolling stones.[29]

Little is known whether Chesney had any employment in these years. Yet he did briefly work in a profession more suited to his wealthy background, and described himself as a stockbroker, in 1937,

---

26 *Evening Telegraph*, 27 October 1930, 5 November 1930.
27 *Evening Telegraph*, 28 October 1930; Dundee Courier 29 October 1930.
28 *Western Daily Press*, 28 October 1930; *Evening Telegraph*, 28 October 1930.
29 Ancestry.com; *Daily Mail*, 12 February 1954; LMA, COR/MW/1949/140/01/244.

and perhaps in the previous year, too. On 28 September 1935 Chesney took over Johnston Morris and Company of 49/51 Broadstreet Avenue, in the City, and he is listed at this address in 1935-1936. Nothing is known of his employment, but he was over-stating his profession; he was not listed as a member of the London Stock Exchange. The probability is that he was employed under a broker, perhaps utilising his foreign language skills when dealing with foreign transactions.[30]

Chesney's hobby in the mid 1930s was certainly one fitting his wealth and social position; learning to fly, which was definitely not for the masses (the less well-off John George Haigh could only dream of this). He was a member of the Royal Aeronautical Club and earned his aviator's certificate on 12 July 1936. He learnt to fly at Sywell, an aerodrome established in 1932 between Northampton and Wellingborough and was a member of the Brooklands Flying Club Ltd. The plane he had learnt in was a de Havilland Moth, Gipsy I, of 85 hp. This was a biplane invented by Geoffrey de Havilland in 1927 and was one of the most popular sport aircraft in the 1930s.[31] Yet this outlet for his adventurous spirit was not enough, as we shall see.

Mrs Chesney was unable to have children. It was stated that this was because she had had a botched operation which led to her becoming infertile. They adopted, quite unofficially, Ann Elizabeth shortly after her birth on 13 June 1933, and a boy called John Nixon-Pearson (1927-2015) at the same time, who was about five on adoption.[32]

By the end of 1936 the Chesneys were becoming restless. Isobel later described the situation:

> *After years of growing desire to cruise round the world in our own boat, a lengthy illness and convalescence on my part gave my husband a excellent excuse to throw up work, shut up house and commence a long and hopeless search to find the ideal boat on a limited capital.*
>
> *It was a disheartening task, always on the verge of success, only to be met with obstacles. Great, therefore, was the day on which we were shown the ex-Bristol Channel pilot cutter Gladys May. She appeared over large for our single-handed requirements, but great assurance on the part of her owners as to her single-handed*

---

30 Tullett, *Portrait of a Bad Man* (1956), p.37; ancestry.com; *London Gazette*, 22 October 1935.
31 ancestry.com
32 TNA, MEPO 2/9542.

qualities, and a sneaking desire for the boat anyway, overcame our scruples, and, subject to survey, she was ours.[33]

Chesney and his wife, therefore, became the owners in 1936 of the *Gladys May*, buying it from Mr W.C. Couch and which was registered in Brixham. This was an auxiliary cutter, weighing 27 tonnes, and measuring 44.2 feet by 12.8 feet and seven feet draught. It was wooden, with a petrol motor. It had been built by Kitto and Sons in Porthleven in 1899. The equipment was very poor and in the next two weeks the couple made 'one mad rush' to make sure it had all the ocean cruising gear necessary.[34]

Chesney got the boat ready to set sail on 20 November 1936 and a crowd looked on. Yet, as his wife admitted, he was not a very experienced sailor:

Don had never cruised beyond the Channel, and his elementary navigation consisted of two months' study three years previously aboard an oil tanker. His intention was to take the yacht singlehanded across the Bay of Biscay to Gibraltar, where I and our infant daughter were to join him.[35]

The day was dull and visibility was poor. His loving wife had prepared a huge pot of broth for him to feed on his lone voyage. Yet Chesney's first attempt at dealing with the yacht was disastrous. He had never lowered the mainsail on a boat which had a gaff and when he did the gaff came down and hit him in the face, rendering him unconscious for ten minutes. Further mishaps occurred and 'A sore and battered crew and boat limped into Poole harbour that evening'. Chesney could not take the yacht by himself and yet lacked the cash to hire a professional. They drove down to Devon and 'picked up an excellent lad named Fry' who agreed to the wage offered. The yacht left Poole on the morning of 23 November, with Mrs Chesney watching it disappear into the mist.[36]

Chesney would often wake at 4.30 in the morning, but could not get the engine to work. Nevertheless, they steered the yacht along the west coast of France with favourable winds. It was not a voyage

---

33 Chesney, 'To Wide Horizons New', *Yachting Monthly*, vol. 66, no. 393 (January 1939), p.277.
34 Ibid; *Lloyd's Register of Yachts*, 1937, p.214.
35 Chesney, 'To Wide Horizons New', p.277.
36 Ibid, pp.277-9.

without danger; 'Don stood precariously on the edge of the bulwarks, most of the time under water, to clear the roller reefing'. Fry had to haul him back on board when he slipped. 'It was Don's first experience of dirty weather in a small ship, and he admits something at the pit of his tummy which was not seasickness!' However, shortly afterwards, he saw a tiny model boat sailing on the sea and 'his courage was reborn. He decided if so frail a craft could survive in such weather then *Gladys* could sail to the world's end and return to tell the tale. It was quite a cheery soul who gave over to Fry awhile later'.[37]

Another difficulty was that 'Don's navigation was very rusty and he could get no results from observations'. The two men worked together and at times the boat moved very quickly – eight knots at one stage. On another occasion a huge wave crashed on it when Chesney was on deck. Fry rushed up 'expecting the end of the world, but found nothing worse than a drenched and blasphemous Don whom he relieved to go and change'. In order to smooth the sea, Chesney filled up oil bags and cast them over the side. It was all exhausting work and there was a near miss with a steamer on one occasion and a tired Chesney collapsed into the yacht's chronometer gimbals, smashing them to pieces.[38]

At times they had to avoid being crushed by other vessels. On 29 November near Cape Finisterre they had to dodge a tramp which was actually a disguised Spanish destroyer. There were desperate struggles against the weather and water came aboard which needed pumping out for half an hour. By 3 December they were short of paraffin, coke and bread. This was rectified by purchases made at Cascais Bay, but water lapping around the saloon floor meant more pumping and 'considerable anxiety'. As fog rolled down the Tagus, there was no time to be spared in reaching Gibraltar.[39]

On the next two days the yacht ran before a string wind. Bilge pumping caused further anxiety, only relieved by passing Cape St. Vincent. A zeppelin was sighted overhead. High winds, a pump which ceased to work, a recalcitrant motor and the fact that the Cape Trafalgar light was not lit due to the Spanish Civil War all conspired to make this part of the journey more hazardous. Fortunately a favourable wind enabled *Gladys May* to glide into the Admiralty Harbour in Gibraltar

---

37 Chesney, 'To Wide Horizons New', p.279.
38 Ibid, p.280.
39 Ibid, pp.281-2.

on 10 December. Harbour officials came on board, as did invitations from the Royal Gibraltar Yacht Club.[40]

At ten in the morning of the following day the boat slipped into the Admiralty Dockyard. Chesney and Fry were greeted by an impressive ceremony from four representatives of four departments of the Navy. Labourers were called into repair the *Gladys May*, leading to a brief fire before work resumed. Scraping, painting and caulking followed. Fry left for England on 19 December. Two days later Mrs Chesney and her family arrived (after sailing from London on the *Oronsay* on 19 December) to find the yacht's interior to be 'in an unholy mess after the fire'. It was another six weeks before it was ship shape, though the Chesneys enjoyed 'many cocktail parties and dinners' with their new found acquaintances in Gibraltar and in making trips to nearby places. However, the engine still proved resistant to being made wholly serviceable.[41]

To date, Chesney's yachting had been extremely reckless to the point of foolhardiness. His experience of sailing hitherto had been limited and yet he had chosen to set sail into the open seas in November, rather than a month with gentler winds. He risked his life and that of his lad and was about to endanger the lives of his wife and family. He was, however, a born gambler and full of misplaced self confidence.

Finally, at six in the evening of 3 February 1937 the yacht set off for Oran, on the first leg of a voyage to Malta, another key naval base for the British Mediterranean Fleet. With Fry gone, Mrs Chesney took his place in the three hour watch routine. Her mother was cook, their adopted son was designated as potato peeler and the young Ann was stated as being the 'General Nuisance'. They also took their Scottish terrier with them, but he was later stolen by Arabs whilst on shore. The crew was depleted as Mrs Menzies soon succumbed to sea sickness, so Chesney and his wife did the cooking between watches.[42]

Apart from this, for the Chesneys the initial voyage was easy, with time for sun bathing in the thought that England was fogbound. There was consternation on 5 February when a boatful of Spaniards sailed towards them and a revolver was their sole means of defence. Fortunately the Spaniards were lost and merely wanted directions. They briefly harboured that night in Beni Saf harbour. They later put

---

40   Ibid, pp.282-3.
41   Ibid, p.283.
42   Ibid.

in at Oran and were entertained by the British Consul there.[43]

Chesney took the helm as his wife felt too ill at the time to do much but sunbathe, but she later recovered and shared this responsibility with her husband. As the sea was calm they sometimes slept on mattresses on deck. However, the weather turned for the worst and Chesney began to suffer from a series of poisoned fingers. His judgement was not always the best, for on sighting a large cruise ship bearing towards them, Mrs Chesney swerved to avoid it whilst her husband later complacently said, 'It's your right of way, hang on'.[44]

Better weather on another day led them to wear their pyjamas, whilst Chesney decided on a swim. Yet a puff of wind set the yacht moving quickly and 'he had to swim as never before, sweating and shouting instructions to me, the while swallowing water so fast I think he was trying to ground us. I managed to follow his frantic directions, threw him a line and continued sailing, towing a now placid Don merrily along'. There were pleasant times, buying fresh products from the local population when they were near the shores of Africa.[45]

There were further storms and the Chesneys worked together to secure the yacht. In the midst of one gale with the sea rising in hillocks, the new sail sheet parted with the foresail and 'Don went forward, and a battle was fought between man and maniac, and when he returned his hands were bleeding and nails torn, but the foresail was safely stowed'. Another mishap occurred just after the yacht left Tunisia for repairs – the two gallon cask of local wine which had been hardly sampled smashed.[46]

After making some good time, they passed Pantelleria Island. Dirty weather was then in the offing, and it was then that Chesney became very unwell. When he took his turn at watch, he seemed dazed and took some time to get his bearings. He complained of a headache. His wife could see that he was ill and took his temperature, which was 102 Fahrenheit. Mrs Menzies gave him quinine, aspirins and brandy, whilst Mrs Chesney took over his watch. The weather became rough and it was impossible, with Chesney's temperature, that he could do anything. They then rowed over him getting in the mainsail, which his wife could not do. She recalled, 'We had an awful battle over this,

43 Chesney, 'To Wide Horizons New', pp.283, 401.
44 Ibid, pp.402-3.
45 Ibid, pp.403-4.
46 Ibid, p.405.

and he insisted on coming on deck with his pyjamas to argue it out'. The fever was high and he felt weak, retired to bed and slept solidly for nine hours.[47]

Meanwhile the scared and tired Mrs Chesney had to cope alone and was unable to give much control to the yacht. Mrs Menzies could not help and she wondered if she had been wrong in dissuading Chesney to assist. He occasionally muttered 'How is she?' to which they replied, 'O.K.'. When dawn came, the sun shone and the wind dropped. Mrs Chesney realised that she had been asleep at her post for a time, but Malta was in sight and all crew members helped in smartening up *Gladys May*. By sunset they were off the Grand Harbour and eventually calmed the motor enough to allow the harbour pilot to board. Mrs Chesney finished her account of the journey thus:

> *Slowly, and with dignity, under the very nose of HMS Barham, the flag ship of the Mediterranean Fleet, we dropped anchor, and moored our stern to the quay. We had arrived.*[48]

The journey had shown that Chesney was a reasonably competent sailor but was far from being an excellent one as he lacked the experience. He was confident and brave. Yet he was also foolhardy and reckless in trying to initially sail singlehanded and in being complacent in emphasising the right of way at a dangerous moment. His wife wrote up a lengthy account of the voyage which was published in two sections in *Yachting Monthly* in early 1939. It reveals her to be a good story teller, witty and literate and well aware of the technical language of the sea and sailors. But it is also a poignant document when one realises what was to happen to her and her Don just over a decade later. There are few published accounts by someone who is later murdered concerning both themselves and their eventual murderer. Yet this is to run away with ourselves; tragedy lay in the future and the published account of the voyage shows the Chesneys working together as a husband and wife team.

The next two years of Chesney's life are not documented except in the books published shortly after his death. Their reliability is difficult to discern. The couple certainly continued their life overseas, because Chesney needed money (he may also have been hounded by creditors in Britain) and saw possibilities of acquiring it illegally; he

---

47 Ibid, pp.405-6.
48 Ibid, p.406.

was certainly in need of it. Chesney was a great one for gambling, but was not a success. Conrad Phillips recalled:

> We'd met in Monte Carlo just before the war. They used to call him "Unlucky Chesney" in the old days in the south of France. I didn't agree. I'd seen him play poker. He asked for trouble. Any gambler who tries to fill inside straights as he did isn't unlucky – he's just a moron... I remembered him well. He was huge, gorilla-like, six feet two inches tall and weighing twenty-two stones, with a longish narrow face, brooding dark baboon eyes, set too close together – a hulk of a man.[49]

All that is certain is that he lived a peripatetic lifestyle as his only known address in these years is that of the *Gladys May*. They apparently lived in Malta for two years. Apart from gambling at Monte Carlo, Nice and Cannes, Chesney also continued his criminal career to finance the former habit. After haunting bars for contacts, he is alleged to have taken consignments of arms from Tangier to supply General Franco's forces in Spain during the Civil War of 1936-1939. He is also alleged to have resumed his womanising ways at this time, too.[50]

Chesney's yacht was damaged in June 1938 and Mrs Chesney made a claim for insurance. With the outbreak of war in 1939, the *Gladys May* was left at Algiers with one John Johnstone. He had been entrusted by Chesney with caretaking it but had not received the £2 10s per week wages as promised by Chesney in the previous month, and it was possessed by Risgulla and Co., presumably for unpaid debts. Johnstone wrote to Mrs Chesney on 24 October asking for money but none arrived so he returned to England.[51]

The Chesneys and Mrs Menzies returned to England in August 1939. They were living at 2 St. Mary's Road in Ealing as war broke out. The reason why they moved to this address in this suburb in west London was undoubtedly because Mrs Menzies' widowed sister Alice was living there with her daughters, and had been since about 1935, practising as a midwife at that address. The couple were also desperately short of cash and so had little alternative. Indeed her elder daughter, Isobel McNeish, had married Raymond Sarant (1914-

---

49 Phillips, *Murderer's Moon*, pp.178-9.
50 *Lloyd's Register of Yachts*, 1937-1939, pp.730, 769, 796; Phillips, *Murderer's Moon*, pp.204-8; Tullett, *Portrait*, pp.41-50; TNA, MEPO 2/9542.
51 TNA, MEPO 2/9542; McLeave, *Chesney*, p.38.

1977) there in the summer of 1939.[52]

Mrs Menzies and her daughter opened the house in Ealing as a nursing home. They needed the money and her sister had moved out. They first took in three or four old people, but later had a dozen. They paid between 12 and 18 shillings a week, for food, lodgings and health care. In 1949 Mrs Menzies said, 'Myself and my daughter paid money out of our own private incomes to assist those people. It was regarded by me as something done in the war effort'. However they left Ealing in October 1940 because of the Blitz, but continued to rent the house for a further nine months.[53]

It is often stated that the Chesneys drove an ambulance in the Blitz, but this is untrue. On the day that Britain declared war on Germany, 3 September 1939, Mrs Chesney enrolled in the Ealing Civil Defence Force, number 9177 as an ambulance driver. It was noted that she was a 28-year-old housewife. Two days later, her husband did likewise and was number 9281. He was noted as having 'no occupation'. Mrs Menzies is merely noted as being involved in 'household duties'. Chesney's civil defence service did not last long as he was removed from the list on 1 March 1940 in order to take his medical examination for a rather more active part in the war. Mrs Chesney did not report for duty for her medical inspection on 29 January but was reinstated on 16 February. We do not know how active her service was, but Chesney was a temporary lieutenant in the Royal Navy months before the Blitz.[54] Fourteen years later a Royal Naval officer commented about Chesney, 'We wanted officers who could hit the enemy hard and often, and kill as many as possible. Chesney did just that'.[55]

Given his experience and interest in matters maritime it was no surprise that Chesney entered the Navy. The Royal Navy was Britain's senior military service and in 1939 it was the largest Navy in the world. It grew substantially during 1939-1945 both in personnel and ships in order to preserve food supplies to Britain and to support the land forces in the Mediterranean and the Far East as well as to defend home waters and attack enemy shipping. By 1945 there were 866,000 men and women in its ranks, though they had suffered over 50,000 fatalities and lost 1,525 ships.

52 *Kelly's Ealing Directories.*
53 LMA, COR/MW/1949/140/01/244.
54 Ealing Civil Defence record cards.
55 *Empire News*, 21 February 1954.

Chesney became a probationary temporary sub-lieutenant in the Royal Navy on 5 January 1940; the lowest rung on the ladder of commissioned ranks in the Senior Service. He had satisfied the selection board that he could handle yachts and small craft. Enquiries into his background failed to disclose anything controversial (after all his crimes had been committed under the name of John Donald Merrett). A later commander noted, 'Before the war this officer owned a 30 ton pilot cutter and cruised around the world, working the ship with no crew. He has an intimate knowledge of the Med. And speaks French as well as he speaks English. He has a working knowledge of Spanish'. He was a good candidate for a commission, for he was already a member of the Royal Naval Volunteer Reserve, a body of reservists established in 1903 to provide a pool of trained men for the expansion of the Royal Navy in times of war; Ian Fleming was also a member (as was his famous fictional creation, James Bond).[56] In 1940 Lieutenant Commander Mike Cumberledge recalled that Chesney took to wearing a gold earring at this time because of an old superstition that any one wearing one could not drown.[57]

He served on board a number of vessels. Initially he was in boats stationed in the Home Waters. In February 1940 he was on *HMS White Bear*, an armed yacht, and then on *HMS Nobles*, a harbour defence patrol craft, in the following month, stationed at Milford Haven as part of the Western approaches Command. On 3 April he was promoted to Temporary Lieutenant. In August he was on *HMS Osprey*, once a steamer converted for anti-submarine work, for a training course for anti-submarine activity and thereafter had a number of independent commands, firstly on a motor anti-submarine vessel (MASV), number 15. These 23 ton boats had an armament of eight machine guns. He had been based in Milford Haven in a defensive capacity. His superior was Commander Welman and his report about Chesney ran as follows:

> *A man of definite personality, possessed of fighting spirit to a marked degree, with common sense. Is possessed of above the average physical strength and fitness, and is particularly keen on Rugby Football and Boxing. Carries some of the defects of his qualities in being rather uncouth.*

---

56 *The Times*, 25 February 1954; RN Disclosures.
57 McLeave, *Chesney* (1956), p.42.

On the whole, Welman considered him to be a satisfactory officer, perhaps a little above average in certain qualities. He was not tipped for high command, though, with Rear Admiral Kekewich adding, 'I do not consider that this officer would make a good Senior Officer of a Flotilla'.[58]

Chesney remained at Portland in the Portsmouth Command for several months, on the base ship, *HMS Boscawen*. In March 1941 Chesney moved to another command, this time being in command of a motor gun boat (MGB) as MASVs 16-21 having been converted in 1940 to MGBs. He was in charge of boat 92, a heavier and faster boat than his previous command, and he stayed there until July 1941. Lieutenant Horne was less enthusiastic about Chesney than his predecessor had been, and stressed his perceived personality failings:

> *This officer is definitely keen on the Service and can be relied upon to do his best when at sea, but in harbour, he is inclined to get bored with the ordinary routine. He should try to realise the fact that wearing ear-rings with a beard and having a tendency to piratical language creates no particular feeling of "awesome respect" from ratings. Once he rids himself of the idea that he is a 'character' he would get even better results from his ship's company. He is keen on all games and is a moderate player. He has no leaning towards the arts and speaks or writes no foreign languages [in this Horne seems to have been incorrect], though he has travelled extensively. Generally, he is physically fit, though his tendency to corpulence goes hand in hand with his mental make-up.*

Although deeming him satisfactory and temperate, he was generally thought to be less than average in overall ability.[59]

There had been no motor gunboats in the Royal Navy until the beginning of World War Two when their numbers grew, firstly those converted from other vessels and then those built specifically for the task. They were described as the 'spitfires of the seas'. They would be armed with two guns, of between two and six pounders in calibre and with two heavy machine guns. The crew would be of two officers and ten ratings.[60]

In July Chesney was moved to the *HMS St. Christopher*, a base ship on the Western Approaches Command based at Fort William,

---

58 RN Disclosures; H.T. Lenton and J.J. Colledge, *Warships of World War II* (1964), p.507; TNA, ADM 208/1.
59 RN Disclosures.

then in August was part of the MGB Flotilla at Lowestoft in the Nore Command. Up to now, Chesney had only operated off the British Isles. For the next three months, Chesney led MGB 16, which was under repair for part of the time. In September he was moved again, to be on a lake patrol vessel near Belfast. He then spent some time in South Africa. He had travelled, 1st class, from Liverpool to Durban, South Africa on the Nestor on 29 November 1941, in order to take torpedo and signal courses. Afterwards he was posted to the *HMS Nile*, a base draft ship at Alexandria as part of the Mediterranean command.[61]

In February 1942 he was finally given an independent command; that of a 200 ton western desert schooner, the *Kheyr el Dine*, referred to as a sailing vessel. It had a speed of three knots and arrived at Alexandria in Egypt on 29 January, as part of the Western Desert Service. The Mediterranean was one of the theatres of naval operations which was of crucial significance during that stage of the war. Possibly Chesney was sent there because of his undoubted knowledge of the region. The Royal Navy there needed to help keep supplies running to the allied outpost of Malta and to the Eighth Army in North Africa, whilst thwarting supplies sent to their German enemies, the Afrika Korps under Field Marshal Erwin Rommel. Motor gunboats and motor torpedo boats were especially used for their speed to disrupt Axis shipping for Rommel's forces. In 1941-1942 the fortunes of war between Britain and her Axis foes fluctuated.

An insight into Chesney's life at this time is revealed in the following letter to his wife, written in 1942:

> *My own most dearly beloved,*
>
> *I have been really taking exercise today. I played squash this morning with the professional and didn't I sweat, then some holes of golf with Dougie, bridge and so to bed. Now four plus at bridge too. I am just waiting now for this Kheyr el Dine to come back to get away. Darling, I think of you all the time and love you so much. When I think it will be eighteen months before I see you, I can hardly bear it. I am going to try and be so nice for you when I come back. I hope you will still love me so much as I love you, because, dear heart, you are the whole world to me.*
>
> *I am enclosing a letter from B.A.O. which shows you how much I get*

---

60 Konstam, *British Motor Gun Boat 1939-1945* (2010), pp.4-5, 29.
61 Ibid; TNA, ADM 187/17; ADM 208/8-9

(damned little) and some photos. One as I am and two taken with my next bed neighbour while I was convalescing. Also the boat I sail and race and two photos I took of our sitting, not too good. I am having your allotment, as soon as the money arrives, remade as it was. But can you send me a little each month to help me out as it is pretty bloody being broke all the time, hence my gambling, with its usual results?

I got my official confirmation of my appointment tonight, so I will be at work by tomorrow or the day after. At last something to occupy me. I played squash again today, sailed and bridge, my usual war-winning effort. Bloody, isn't it? Good-night and God bless you, my own true love. I love you more every day, and only you. But despite this I have today acquired another sweetheart, however, it is really more for Sparker than you to be jealous.

Her name is Jane and she is a very pretty bull-terrier pup. I will take a photo of her and send it to you. I got her for nothing as nobody wanted her, and hope to be able to take her to sea with me when I go. She has already taken to lying on my bed as I write this. I am now discharged from hospital as fit though my ankle is as yet far from right and am just waiting to be told when to go off, so today I went sailing with Dougie and we won, then to the flicks and saw 'Affectionately Yours'. Damned funny. Goodnight and God bless you. Nothing must ever separate us. God bless you.

Donald.[62]

Chesney often wrote to his wife and his letters usually contain elements of self pity, maudlin affection for her and requests for money. In May 1942 one letter contained the phrase 'You are the most wonderful woman I know' and another, 'Darling I love you so terribly I weep sometimes for want of you, I do so adore you' (and at the same time asked for £10 be sent to cover his debts – his official papers made note of 'Unpaid Bills' twice in 1940). In another he told her 'I am so depressed without you here and no one really to talk to or help me with my worries'. However, he also wrote in a more optimistic tone at times, telling her that he and his crew would walk about the deck just in their trousers, would bathe at sea and that this was 'a pleasant way to win the war'.[63]

So far, Chesney's only physical worries had been a fracture on his

---

62 Phillips, *Murderer's Moon*, pp.209-10.
63 McLeave, *Chesney*, pp.44-6.

left ankle and three weeks laid up in May 1942. The next month was to see greater peril. The fortunes of the desert war were, as with the sand on which they were fought, ever shifting. At the battle of Gazala in May and June 1942, Rommel's Afrika Korps launched an offensive against Lieutenant General Ritchie's Allied forces. The former were victorious and swept onto the coast. During the allied retreat, Tobruk, which had withstood a lengthy siege in the previous year, had had its defences neglected, and lay exposed to a severe assault. On 20 June, the 15th and 21st Panzer divisions, supported by the Italian XX corps attacked from the south east. Defending Tobruk under Major General H.B. Klopper were the 2nd South African Division, the 11th Indian Brigade, the 32nd Army Tank Brigade and the 201st Guards Brigade. By 8am the anti-tank ditch had been breached and the tanks began moving against the key forts of Solero and Pilastrino. Ships in the harbour were being pounded by heavy artillery.

It was at this point in the fighting that there came Chesney's finest hour. Most writers recounting this part of Chesney's career almost descend into fiction, writing about Chesney going down, alone, with his ship, gun blazing and shooting his dog before surrendering to the Germans on shore.

Chesney gave his own account in the following year; less heroic, but still creditable. It was on 20 June, with the town under attack, and the boats in the harbour being subject to heavy shelling and dive bombing, that the boat was loading coal continually on the south side of the harbour. At five in the evening, Chesney was ordered to take his boat to a jetty on the north side of the harbour. Just as he was about to do so, 'some hundred odd troops' asked to be taken on board, so he let them do so. At a quarter to six they were across the harbour. German panzers were in sight so five rounds from the three pounder cannon were fired, to little effect, so he ceased.[64]

On reaching the jetty he inquired for orders, including what to do about the troops on board. They were disembarked. Meanwhile, stores of biscuit, water and bully beef were loaded aboard from the adjacent *HMS Aberdare*, a minesweeper. Chesney later remarked 'We were getting very heavily shelled' as panzers and 88mm guns were beginning to find the boat's range. However, only one shot hit them. The departure of an MTB (Motor Torpedo Boat) and *HMS Aberdare*, just after 8pm, convinced him to start to leave, 'as the shelling had

64 TNA, ADM 199/799.

now become serious, I also decided to do so'. This was not before the soldiers re-embarked, not finding anyone to issue other orders.[65]

Yet, with a speed of only 3 and a half knots and a boat crammed full of soldiers, it was slow going. A request to be towed by the Aberdare was refused. Yet they cleared the jetty only to see a motor launch sunk and one man in the water, obviously very badly hurt. Chesney went over the side to pick him up. As he did so, his own stationary vessel was hit, though not apparently badly and no one was injured. The boat was now underway again, but there was bad news. A soldier informed Chesney that the boat had been holed and speed was reduced to one knot.[66]

This was now the crisis. Chesney later wrote, 'I felt therefore, that the ship was no longer seaworthy and would certainly not convey the personnel any distance'. Lieutenant Martin Solomon, DSC, in command of a nearby MTB, drew near:

> *I saw Ches on my first run in, on the bridge, trying to coax every yard out of the schooner. She was being raked from stern to stern with everything the Germans had. A good quarter of the men must have died going through that Hell.*
>
> *At the start of my second run I saw the ship had been hit and drew alongside to take off about 100 of the men [about 85-90 soldiers and six of the crew, another witness stated]. I shouted at Ches to come aboard with them, but he just refused and no amount of pleading would shake him. When I looked back the Kheyr-el-Dine was just the stump of a broken mast and a few bubbles among the oil [it was registered as lost on 23 June; casualties unknown]. I thought Chesney had died there and in fact reported this when I got back to Alexandria.*[67]

Yet Solomon was mistaken. He had laid a smokescreen to effect the escape and in the confusion did not see all that had happened. After the panic-stricken men had left the beleaguered vessel by leaping on board the MTB, and threatening to sink it – all without Chesney's orders – Solomon's boat sheared off as fast as possible. He did not therefore see what had happened.[68]

The wounded were left behind, as were a few of the crew. These

---

65 Ibid.
66 Ibid.
67 McLeave, *Chesney*, p.52.

latter included stoker Culver, who, according to bosun Walsh, couldn't be moved from the engine room and he told Chesney this news. Chesney later wrote, 'I went below, and being considerably stronger than the rest of the crew, managed to drag him on deck'. Culver was unconscious and had a head wound. Another cause for concern was that the engine room's floor was half an inch deep in fuel oil.[69]

Just then an A Lighter (an armed barge) was nearby, but it was out of control and accidentally hit Chesney's boat. Chesney went to the cabin to fetch the boat's crucial papers and told his deputy, sub lieutenant Parsons, to abandon ship when the two boats could come adjacent to one another. The papers and first aid kit were thrown to the other boat and Chesney gave the order to 'Abandon Ship'. Then, with the help of Walsh and stoker Chase, he tried to lift the unconscious Culver aboard the adjacent vessel. Unfortunately the boat sheared off during this operation, overbalancing Chesney, Parsons and another crew member onto the A Lighter. Culver fell back onto the *Kheyr el Dine*.[70]

Going inside the boat, Chesney found its skipper, one Buck, in the wheelhouse. The steerings and telegraph had been shot away, hence the boat crashing into his. With the smoke laid down by Solomon's boat subsiding, Chesney could see his old boat, with four of the crew and one or two soldiers still there. He asked Buck to bring the boat over so as to take them off, but this was impossible because the Lighter was not under control. However, despite this, and under continued fire, Chesney and Parsons piloted it through the harbour boom. Yet on the following morning, the boat was spotted by an E Boat and Chesney and the others were forced to surrender.[71]

Yet it is possible that the *Kheyr el Dine* was not wholly *hors de combat* when Chesney abandoned it. Walsh and the others were able to beach it in a small cove on the south side of the harbour later that evening. At 10.30pm bowman Bird and others took the boat out. According to him it had had its bobstay broken by the A Lighter and there was a shell hole in the engine room but that was all. He deemed it seaworthy and could make 2 knots (Chesney and his coxswain later said it was unseaworthy). In any case, though, it was futile. At 2.30 am on the next day three E Boats attacked, took off the prisoners, and then blew

68 TNA, ADM 199/799.
69 Ibid.
70 Ibid.
71 Ibid.

up the vessel.[72]

On that day Tobruk surrendered. In all, 33,000 men and 2.2 million gallons of petrol had been lost to the enemy. It was the Eighth Army's greatest defeat and led Rommel to believe that he had ultimate victory in sight.

Solomon was not alone in his assumption about Chesney's fate. Yet, though he was stated as 'Missing on active service', it was also noted, 'No presumption of death has yet been made'. This did not prevent, on 17 August, a message appearing in the press in Egypt and elsewhere, that Chesney was missing on active service since June. His wife had posted the message and desired any information be sent to her at Colleton Hall.[73]

Chesney spent some months in an Italian prisoner of war camp, PG47, Modena. He was there on 10 November 1942 and penned a letter to his wife. As ever he stressed his love for her in the most cloying of terms; 'That is my one dream now, to be with you, my sweet, and never part from you'. Then he got to the crux of the matter, writing, 'Darling, I want you to pay out some money for me again as I have been doing a lot of buying.' He had bought pyjamas of £2 15s, socks for 15s, a suitcase for £15 and a rug for £5. He had also lost £5 playing cards.[74]

The POW Camp was one of three which initially catered primarily for New Zealand officers. Despite being a converted military barracks, it was a comfortable billet, which boasted its own symphony orchestra and regular concerts. Situated in one of the most fertile parts of the country, food and drink were plentiful. When Chesney arrived there were about 200 New Zealanders. When British and South African prisoners (about 1,000 in all) arrived, sports matches between each country were numerous; especially football, baseball and basketball. Despite all this, Chesney made three efforts to escape from the camp, but all were to be in vain. As a report later stated, he 'showed outstandingly high morale being a persistent escaper'. He was eventually repatriated on 30 March 1943 and was found fit for general service. He returned to Britain in *HMS Anne* on 20 June.[75]

He was back in service on 26 June, on various ships, including the

72 Ibid.
73 Ancestry.com
74 McLeave, *Chesney*, p.58.
75 RN Disclosures.

HMS Victory (a flagship of 21,164 tons), stationed at Portsmouth, then on the *HMS Skirmisher*, a base ship at Milford Haven, and then H*MS Prosepine*, a Naval Amphibious Base at Scapa as part of the Orkneys and Shetlands Command. In March 1944, Chesney was posted to *HMS Pleiades* for training in boat pool operations. Captain Lee-Morris was then his superior and he believed that Chesney was an above average officer, indeed, 'outstanding' being the word used. He commented:

> Whist he was serving under my command, I had little opportunity of observing his seagoing capabilities, but I consider that his record established that beyond question. As part of his training here, he took charge of a convoy of 12 small craft which were sent south to take part in the second front operation, and this task he carried out with the utmost efficiency and drive. I consider him a highly intelligent and able officer, who could be counted upon to execute any assignment with the greatest vigour, especially if it were of a dangerous or arduous nature. I have no hesitation in recommending him for promotion to Acting Temporary Lt. Cdr.[76]

The later part of Chesney's war was fairly uneventful as far as action was concerned. He was posted, on 29 May 1944, still as a lieutenant, to be second in command of *HMS Prudence*, a D/F Calibrating vessel, then at Barrow-in-Furness and Liverpool as part of the Western approaches Command and at Scapa as part of the Orkneys Command. In 1954 his former steward, Barry Crichton had the following recollections of him:

> He was a tremendous personality and a very strict disciplinarian. The crew did not like him for that, but he certainly made an impression on them the day he joined.
>
> He would eat 20 hard boiled eggs for breakfast just to show he could do it. And at 11 o'clock every morning I had to put down a pound of raw beef steak with the yolk of an egg poured over it. One of the junior officers tried it once and it made him sick, but Chesney just gobbled it down and looked hungry.

He even ate wine glasses and Crichton commented that it 'made me creep to hear him crunch the glass between his teeth. I asked him to stop it the day he cut his tongue'. When the captain left command, Chesney took over, being promoted to Lieutenant Commander on 30

---

76 RN Disclosures.

September 1944, and Crichton recalled, 'He behaved like a schoolboy. He danced round the wardroom shouting at the top of his voice, "More power, more money"', and began singing'.[77]

He left the Prudence by December 1944 and served on the *HMS Iron Duke* (a 25,000 ton battleship but now a depot ship at Scapa Flow), the *Victory*, a base ship, and the *HMS Odysseus*, a water boat, the latter from 26 March – 21 May 1945. All this was under the aegis of the Portsmouth Command and he was based in Portsmouth and then, with Odysseus, at Portland.[78]

Meanwhile his wife and mother-in-law had left Ealing and went to Whitsbury Cross, near Fordingbridge in Hampshire. They established a nursing home for a dozen elderly patients there, paying £7-8 per week. In 1942 they ran another at Colleton Hall in Devonshire. Whether they were running these competently is another question. The Rev. Heriot-Harris wanted to visit the patients but he was always turned down and he commented, 'There seemed to be something strange about the place'.[79] Chesney often visited his family when he was based in Portsmouth, for they were conveniently located.[80]

At the end of the war, Chesney was allotted five medals; the 1939-45, Atlantic, Africa, Italy and the War Medal, denoting that he had served overseas in the theatres of operation noted. He was not awarded any medals for particular gallantry or outstanding heroism, however. Although the medals could have been applied for from 1948, they never were. Whether this was an indication of modesty or lack of interest in wearing such or because he was too busy is impossible to discern.[81]

77 McLeave, *Chesney*, p.61.
78 TNA, ADM 208, 33-5.
79 McLeave, *Chesney*, pp.59-60.
80 TNA, MEPO 2/9542.
81 RN Disclosures.

8

Post War Years, 1945-1951

The end of the war did not result in Chesney's returning home to his wife and family as it did for many servicemen. He had little to return to in any case; and an austere Britain under a Labour government was scarcely appealing. But there was another way open to him, especially because his criminal habits of the previous decades were only dormant. Continental Europe was devastated after six years of conflict, especially after the fighting to liberate it in 1944-1945. Millions had been killed or had been displaced, survivors had lost loved ones, property and possessions. Central and Eastern Europe lay under the occupation of the four victorious allies. Nowhere was this more so than in defeated and devastated Germany which had not seen such destruction since the Thirty Years War of the seventeenth century. Three million German soldiers had been killed, with 1.8 million civilian dead, 3.6 million homes had been destroyed (20% of the total), 7.5 million were made homeless and a further 16.5 million were driven from their homes in the East after 1945; this little known ethnic cleansing led to 2.5 million deaths.[1]

The British zone of occupation was north-west Germany; the Rhineland, Westphalia and Lower Saxony; containing 23 million people. It was under the Chancellor of the Duchy of Lancaster and there was also a military governor, the first being Field Marshal Bernard Montgomery. The Central Control Commission was the

---

1   MacDonogh, *After the Reich* (2007), p.1.

administrative body who ruled the zone. This had a staff of 25,000 people, far more than in the American zone. The contrast between their accommodation and food and those of the conquered people was considerable. The British aim was to restore Germany as a trading nation and to denazify it. Their treatment of the Germans was less harsh than that of the other allies.[2]

There was also a vigorous black market in Germany as elsewhere in Europe. A cigarette was worth more than a 100 mark note. It could buy four ounces of bread or a suburban railway ticket. A packet of cigarettes was thus a major bribe. Soap and food were also highly prized items. Smuggling from the Russian zone to the west was also highly lucrative and dangerous.[3]

Chesney had enjoyed the war in his own way and now he wanted to be the winner by it in a way that would materially benefit his own pocket. He certainly was not about to look a gift horse in the mouth. And he was no stranger to smuggling. He could carry on where he had left off. Hamburg, as a major German port for ships to and from Britain, was an ideal location for a smuggler. Smuggling by servicemen of all ranks and of all nations was prevalent in the immediate aftermath of war; goods were ordered from one country and supplied from the other, suitably marked up, though tax free.

Chesney was ideally suited in both character and experience to exploit the new opportunities opened up to him by the circumstances of the post war world. The grim circumstances of the times were like manna from Heaven for one as he – and many others - and it is briefly worth outlining exactly why these years proved such a golden era for the smuggler. A historian of smuggling noted:

> *Immediately after the Second World War the Continent became a smugglers' paradise. Lorry loads of cigarettes, coffee and foodstuffs passed over the frontiers of Germany to the black market. In every country from the Mediterranean to the Baltic there was plenty of money, but an acute shortage of many essentials.*[4]

In more detail, legitimate commerce had become more difficult. In Britain purchase taxes were placed on non-essential goods if they were sold on the domestic market because of the need to export

2   Ibid, pp.250-68.
3   Ibid, pp.372-80.
4   Williams, *Contraband Cargoes* (1959), p.272-3.

goods to pay off war costs. Nylon stockings, for example, cost £4 per pair (the average weekly wage for many women). Many countries imposed tariffs, making imported goods more expensive. Consumers were therefore happy to pay lower prices for untaxed; ie smuggled goods. Furthermore, during 1946-1948 Britain had only one revenue cutter. So there were profits to be made from illegally entering the country and very little chance of being caught.[5]

Illegal trade between countries on the Continent was also rewarding, with Chesney allegedly making £3000 per week in 1946 as he had lorries drive from Brussels to Cologne and back. Cigarettes were sold in Germany for furs, jewellery and cameras. The amount of surplus military stores meant that they were easily stolen and sold to groups needing weaponry for their wars; such as that in Palestine.[6] The post war years therefore provided plenty of opportunities for the unscrupulous.

Chesney's activities at this time cannot be confirmed, but histories of the case written in the mid-1950s allege the following and though otherwise undocumented do not appear improbable. Chesney drove to Berlin with a German woman and a car load of cigarettes and coffee which he sold at a profit. He was also introduced to German racketeers. These contacts led to him having lorry loads of guns and ammunition smuggled across to Russia. He made considerable profits.[7]

A girlfriend of his made the following observation:

> *He was conducting a life of crime on a vast scale. Taking advantage of his position as a naval officer, he was climbing to complete control of a vast black market and smuggling organisation.*
>
> *Through his hands passed every kind of produce every kind of food, drink and clothing.*
>
> *Cigarettes – the most valuable currency of all in those days – disappeared in tens of thousands from the mess stores and were accounted for by false entries in his books, or even listed blatantly by him as stolen.*
>
> *The goods were sold for gold and silver and diamonds, and of these he was accumulating a treasure store.*
>
> *German civilians were roped in to help. Suddenly they found*

---

5 Phillipson, *Smuggling* (1973), pp.127-8.
6 Williams, *Contraband Cargoes*, p.273; Thomas, *Villains' Paradise* (2005), pp.49-52, 70.
7 McLeave, *Chesney: The Fabulous Murderer* (1954), pp.64-70.

themselves living in style in big country mansions to which the bluff, bearded Commander Chesney would come down for a weekend's shooting and between sport, inspect the stacks of goods smuggled in Red Cross wagons and ambulances.[8]

Officially, he was assigned as First Lieutenant and Executive Officer attached to *HMS Royal Katherine* from June 1945. He was well thought of by his superiors, despite his quirks. Commander Johnson, his senior from June to October later wrote that he was a:

Rather an exceptional Character. An Elizabethan by nature, born four hundred years after his time. His naval career has been spent in small ships such as LCTs, [landing crafts] MGBs, etc. for which work he is peculiarly adapted. His duties in ROYAL KATHERINE as Executive Officer are entirely foreign to his nature. In spite of that he has made a very good job of them. He is extremely loyal, very hard working and adaptable. He has done so well because he has not been too proud to ask when he does not know. He has great initiative and drive and energy, knows how to handle men and is very popular with them. A most likeable character who has made a great success of this change from buccaneering to orthodox navy. An expert linguist, speaking French fluently and German increasingly well.

Rear Admiral Hutton was also impressed, 'The above is a very good description of this unusual but interesting type of officer'.[9]

Chesney wrote to his wife shortly after the war's end (he wrote to her two or three times a week). One letter written on 10 October was certainly gushing:

Darling heart,

Never tell me I don't write to you twice a week – or even 3 times. Things are once more beginning to pursue the even tenor of their way, so I hope all will be well...Do keep your promise to write to me as you said you would, dear heart, because, despite all our disagreements on leave, I do love you so. God bless you, darling, goodnight, and all my love, now and for ever.

Donald.

He had also acquired two pet dogs.[10]

8   *Woman's Sunday Mirror*, 15 September 1957.
9   RN Disclosures.
10 McLeave, *Chesney*, pp.73-4.

This was an attempt to resolve the marital tensions, which were clearly at a high ebb. In these woes they were not alone. Separations caused by the war had led to an increase in divorces throughout Britain. Mrs Chesney did not reply to him as he wished (few of her letters survive) and so an angry epistle was composed.

> Naval Party 1738
> c/o B.F.M.O.
> Reading
> October 21st 1945
>
> My darling wife,
>
> Or don't you intend going on being my wife? I really am getting very, very cross with you. Still no letter, and have been back a fortnight, although it is some years since I was home with you. Miss – had come back and says that she hasn't heard a word from you, that you didn't either telephone or write. Am I to presume from that you don't intend to come out here and join me? It really is sickening of you, darling.
>
> I went to the Belsen trial on Thursday; quite interesting for half a day, but an absolute travesty of British justice which infuriated me. Most of the prisoners seem rather low-quality perverts. Kramer [Josef Kramer, 1906-1945, commandant of Bergen-Belsen, hanged 13 December 1945] looks clever, but bestial, and the sweet Irma [Irma Grese, 1923-1945, Warden at Bergen-Belsen and Auschwitz, hanged 13 December 1945] extremely clever and intelligent, not pretty, but very cruel.
>
> The prosecutor is good, very good, and takes complete charge of the court proceedings. On the other hand, the defence counsel, at least the one heard, seems to have been chosen for his complete lack of knowledge, ineptitude in the use of words, and a most engaging stammer.
>
> If these people are to be tried fairly, let it be done so, instead of making a fool of British justice. Personally, I think they should have been shot out of hand.
>
> We seem to be having a party every night, due to officers being released, almost daily. A terrible life.
>
> Do write, darling, and say what you are thinking and doing about us, because stupidly enough, I do still love you.
>
> Always your own,
> Donald.[11]

Despite, or because of his failing marriage, Chesney became the life and soul of parties held for the occupying forces. The Town Mayor of Stade recalled an officers' party in 1945 where Chesney 'ate glasses from the bar'. The man stated, 'I was astounded – never seen the trick done off the stage. But he did it at every party I gave'.[12]

Meanwhile, the neglected Mrs Chesney and her mother returned to Ealing in 1945 after having resided at Seaford, Sussex, during some of the war years. It was to be in Ealing that the denouement of the Chesney drama was to be violently resolved.

Ealing was a borough in Middlesex, seven miles to the west of central London. In 1951 it had a population of 187,000. Much of the borough was residential, with a large proportion of the employed population travelling to work in London and elsewhere. But there were also many industries, such as Hoovers and Glaxo, to the north of the borough along the Western Avenue (the A40). Transport links to London and elsewhere were many; by road there were trolley buses and motor buses for those without cars or bicycles; there were a number of underground links (Central, Piccadilly and District lines) as well as the trains along the newly formed British Rail's Western Region.

The hub of the borough was Ealing Broadway, which formed part of the Uxbridge Road. Here were the principal shops and the Town Hall. It was also here that the major transport routes ran. Around the north western edges of the borough there were new council housing estates being built in Northolt.

At this time, and in the following years, Ealing was at the zenith of its fame, both nationally and internationally. It had been the self styled 'Queen of the Suburbs' in its Edwardian heyday, but was perhaps less so by the 1930s, becoming part of the suburban sprawl of West London as population and housing continued to grow until both almost reached capacity. It was an attractive suburb, with a strong middle class element which employed domestic servants, but possessed less of the distinctive character than formerly.

However, in 1938 Michael Balcon took over as head of production at Ealing Film Studios on Ealing Green (not far from where the Chesneys had resided in 1939-1940). His wartime films such as *Nine Men* and *Went the Day Well?* helped project what Balcon saw as the

11 Phillips, *Murderer's Moon* (1956), pp.218-19.
12 *Sunday Despatch*, 21 February 1954.

British character throughout the world; usually that of community spirit and the triumph of the 'little man' over opposition, whether big business, bureaucracy or foreign foes. What put Ealing even more on the map were the Ealing Comedies of 1946-1955, including *Passport to Pimlico*, *The Lavender Hill Mob* and *The Ladykillers*, with stars such as Margaret Rutherford, Alec Guinness and Sid James.

Elsewhere in Ealing, there had been damage during the Second World War; 304 civilian deaths during the bombing of 1940-1945, with 353 people being seriously injured and 929 sustaining minor wounds. There had been 698 high explosive bombs, six mines, 32 oil bombs, 11 V1s, a V2 and thousands of incendiary bombs had been dropped on Ealing in this period.[13] Many houses and other property had also been destroyed. *The Ealing Official Guide* for 1950 noted:

> *Ealing is at present recovering from its war wounds. It suffered a good deal from the bombing and one flying bomb changed the appearance of the Broadway. Christ Church, one of the most beautiful buildings in the London Diocese, was badly damaged...Repairs, which will be long and costly, are proceeding. The proprietors of one of the big stores, which was also partly demolished, have laid out as a garden part of the site which was occupied before the bomb fell. St. Saviours church in the Grove...is still only a shell of its former self, but a rebuilding fund has been started.*[14]

The Railway Hotel on the High Street had been destroyed and Sanders, one of Ealing's big department stores, had been damaged, as had the film studios. Ealing Priory had been damaged by bombing, near to the new home of Mrs Chesney and Mrs Menzies.

Other social changes and government policy were affecting Ealing society. North Ealing was generally a stronghold of the middle class; detached houses built in the late nineteenth century, lived in by large families with servants. There was now less demand for such property. This had first become evident in the 1930s, with low rise flats being built, but was more so after 1945. Detached houses were being split into self contained flats for people on more moderate incomes. Servants were more difficult to obtain and so the running of detached houses was even more problematic. Ealing even had a Labour MP by 1945.

13 Upton, *Ealing at War, 1939-1945* (2005), p.65.
14 *Borough Guide to Ealing* (1950), p.10.

It was into this environment that, after the war, Mrs Menzies and her daughter sought another home and an income. They briefly resided at 40 Mount Park Road with Miss McNeish, who established a nursing home, St. Anthony's, there. They found suitable premises by the end of 1945. Montpelier Road was in north Ealing and the houses there had been built in the 1890s. North Ealing was on a gentle incline and the land rose from the Uxbridge Road in the town's centre. It was generally more socially exclusive than the lower middle class South and working class West Ealing. The north side of the road was consecutively numbered 27 to 19 from west to east, with 1-18 on the south side. The house they had was 22 Montpelier Road, close to Mount Park Road. It was a fifteen room detached house of three storeys on the north side of the road, with a driveway at the front and a lawn at the back. The house had been built in about 1896 for a Dr Pike and was then known as St. Cuthbert's; not acquiring its number until 1904. From 1928-1940 it was the residence of one Jacob Lerman and in 1939 it was valued at £3500. He left it during the war years and so it was lying empty by 1945.[15]

Shortly after the houses in Montpelier Road were built, they were at the zenith of their social pretensions. Most houses had names not numbers and were a mixture of detached and semi-detached, with one household per house. Residents included three doctors and a clergyman. Just to the west of the street was a renowned private school for girls, the Princess Helena College, established there in 1882, though after 1936 it lay abandoned in ruins. By the 1950s the street was less socially exclusive. This was because, in the 1930s, several of the houses had been sub-divided into flats and some even demolished to make way for the low rise block of flats called The Orchards, for fifteen small households. Garages were also built for many of these houses. Property in Montpelier Road had not been badly affected by bombing during the war, though a high explosive bomb exploded in the garden of number 23 on 11 October 1940.[16]

In 1954 number 22 was described thus:

> *The red brick, three storey building at no. 22 had once been a typical Ealing dwelling house...Outside it had the genteel appearance of houses built at the end of the last century, although the red brick*

15 *Kelly's Ealing Directories*; ELHC, Ealing Building Inspection Books.
16 Ibid.

was dulled, the sandstone facings of the windows weathered and flaking and the wisteria around the door drooping and dead.[17]

Another contemporary assessment was as follows:

It was suburbia at its best. Even the sparrows were huffy. No. 22, a solid three storied red-bricked Victorian house, was as unlike a scene of murder as anything could be [a far cry from the squalid tenement houses of Rillington Place]. Moreover, it was a home for old gentle folk, all of whom had lived for years in a backwater of life with nothing more exciting happening to them than occasional palpitations or a dream in which they saw themselves young and vigorous again.

This old detached house at the end of the road had a lift-up-your-hearts look about it, and with so much lavender and old lace around, it looked to me more like an old folks' party.[18]

The property had been taken over by Ealing Council on 26 October 1945 under Regulation 51 of the Defence Regulations of 1939 which enabled the council to requisition empty properties to house people made homeless by enemy action, 'for housing families inadequately housed'. Mrs Menzies applied to the council's surveyor, Charles William Seddon, to take the house for use as an old people's home and for accommodation for herself and her family. The Housing Management Sub Committee recommended that this motion be accepted on 14 December 1945 and on 4 January the Housing Committee approved it.[19]

It was allocated to them on 21 January 1946, but by some oversight the licence was not signed at that time. In return for it, they agreed to pay a weekly rent of 99s. On 21 February 1947 there was the suggestion that the licence be transferred to Mrs Chesney, but the committee refused to sanction this. Initially they offered to house six old people.[20]

It was not a registered home. There was no register kept of residents nor their next of kin. Most were sent there by the Central Aid Society of Bond Street, Ealing, a charitable organisation, though one of the inmates had been with them in Fordingbridge. Initially it was run by

17 McLeave, *Chesney*, p.7.
18 Phillips, *Murderer's Moon*, p.177.
19 ELHC, Civil Defence files, 178/84.
20 Ibid.

Mrs Chesney, her mother and the former's adopted daughter. Their adopted son lived there but went out to work elsewhere.[21]

On the ground floor were a large dining room, a kitchen, a sitting room, two toilets and steps down to the cellar. On the first floor were two front rooms for the proprietress and her family, a back room for three women and a front room for three men, and a bathroom. On the second floor was a large front room for four women, a small front room for three women and a back bedroom for two women. There was another bedroom with three beds. The bedrooms each had a basin with running water.[22]

In 1951 the county council considered the water closet and bathing facilities inadequate. Mrs Menzies wanted to build these at the back of the house as an addition. Lerman was opposed to this, for he considered that, with two bathrooms already, there was no need for another. He had other concerns with his property. He thought it was in a 'very bad state of repair' and after a visit was 'very disturbed at its appearance'. He was not happy that the council had allowed the current tenants too much liberty, 'it would seem that Lady Menzies has been given occupation of this house and in running some sort of business there'.[23]

A council inspector made the following report:

> *The cellar and whole house was in an extremely dusty condition, cobwebs were hanging from electric light flexes and the corners of the room, dust and dirt were in the corners of the stair treads and the rooms were generally untidy. Some of the beds were not covered with counterpanes and I noticed that the sheets were dirty.*

However, another official declared that the existence of a few cobwebs was no reason why it should be served a notice under the Public Health Act. As with all nursing homes it was subject to a bi-annual inspection by the Borough's Medical Officer of Health. However, potentially more serious flaws were made public in March 1949. The council also realised on 23 February 1949 that the licence of 1946 had not been signed, so this was rectified on 17 March and the weekly rent increased to £8 5s 11d.[24]

---

21 LMA, COR/MW/1949/140/01/244.
22 ELHC, Civil Defence files, 178/84.
23 Ibid.
24 Ibid.

However, that was not the most important event concerning 22 Montpelier Road at that time. On the morning of Saturday, 19 February 1949, at about nine, Ann Chesney made a shocking discovery and she at once alerted her mother. Mrs Chesney arrived at the bedroom of three elderly inmates and later recounted what she saw:

> When I went in I found that there was a strong smell of gas, and, with a quick look, I saw that Mr Blomfield and Mr Beard were dead... They were both in bed, and Mr Glass appeared to have been up and was sitting slumped over on the side of his own bed. He was still breathing. Gas was coming from the gas fire in the grate; the jets were not alight. After being seen by a doctor, Mr Glass was taken to Ealing Hospital [King Edward Memorial Hospital, Mattock Lane].[25]

However, Glass died in hospital on the following day. He was Alexander Glass, aged 85, a retired salesman; William John Blomfield was aged 83 and a retired electrical engineer and Mr Thomas Beard was aged 86, a retired railway labourer. Dr Teare carried out the post mortems. In all three cases, death was due to asphyxia from coal gas poisoning, the effects being delayed in the case of Glass. It was assumed that Glass had got up in the middle of the night, had tried to light the gas fire and then returned to bed without having succeeded, thus allowing the gas to escape into the room and filling it.[26]

A triple inquest was held at Ealing Town Hall on Tuesday, 22 February, being opened by Dr Harold George Broadbridge (1882-1971), Coroner for West Middlesex. Relatives of the three men gave evidence of their identity and Mrs Chesney gave hers. Teare gave the cause of death and then the inquest was adjourned to the following Monday, Broadbridge stating he would take the three inquests together as they seemed to have all died as a result of the same circumstances.[27]

The inquest was resumed as planned, though under the aegis of Dr Jacob Arthur Gorky of 40 Tachbrook Street, South Kensington, East Middlesex Deputy Coroner. Mary Menzies was the first witness to be called on this occasion. She outlined how the nursing home worked, nineteen old age pensioners paying whatever they could afford in return for full board, being looked after by herself and her daughter.

25 *Middlesex County Times*, 26 February 1949.
26 Ibid.
27 Ibid.

The three deceased had lived there for a year. The room included a gas fire and an electric radiator. The gas fire had not been used for some time and the tap was near to Mr Glass' bed. Then Ann gave her evidence of finding the men. Her mother told the court that the gas in the room had not been used for a year, but had been serviced by a gas company three months ago.[28]

Clarence Slater, service supervisor of the Gas Light and Coke Co., told the court that he had examined the gas fire. He had found that it was in a very poor condition. It could not be lit properly as the gas blew backwards as there had been an accumulation of carbon. 'I tried to light it a dozen times but it could not be lit properly' he explained. Dr Gorky began his summing up, praising Mrs Menzies' running the home 'as an act of great charity'. He then remarked that the three deceased seemed to be living on the best of terms. It was then that a fellow resident (whose identity is unknown) of the nursing home spoke up. She had been already muttering disagreement in the public gallery. She said, 'Lady Menzies said they were on friendly terms. They were fighting that night; it was a terrible night. They were underneath my room'. She also said that Mary Menzies had no right to the title she claimed.[29]

Inspector Frank Haynes of Ealing Police stepped into the witness box and said that what this woman was alleging was incorrect. The woman protested but was ordered to be silent and so she left. Dr Gorky said that she was in the wrong and reminded those assembled that the two other men died peacefully. He concluded:

> *I am satisfied that the fire was defective. It is quite conceivable that Mr Glass felt faint after inhaling a small amount of gas while trying to light the fire and had to sit down. He and his room-mates were then overcome. I discredit entirely the allegations of the lady I turned out of court.*

Therefore, a verdict of 'Accidental Death' was returned as cause of death. Sydney Blomfield, a relative of one of the deceased, contacted the local newspaper to record his feelings towards the proprietors of the nursing home:

> *We would wish publicly to thank Lady Menzies for her generosity and assistance to the aged, and assure her that we realise no*

---

28 Ibid, 5 March 1949.
29 Ibid; *Daily Telegraph*, 12 February 1954.

> *responsibility for the accident can be attributed to her in any way. We are grateful to her for having made the last years of these aged gentlemen as happy as it was possible for them to have been.*[30]

Mrs Chesney and her mother had got off very lightly indeed. Yet the county council was concerned about the way in which the home was being run, for in 1953 there were five inspections at the premises, far more than would be usual, though they concluded that there had been continuous improvement.[31]

However, one of the residents, from 1946-1954, one John Clark, recalled his time at the house in glowing terms. He remembered Mrs Menzies' first words of greeting to him thus, 'I want you to look on this as your home. I hope you'll be happy here'. Her future behaviour matched her first words, she 'looked after us like a mother. Her daughter, Vera Chesney, could on occasions be testy, but "Lady" Menzies was always even tempered and kind'. She brought up meals to guests who were unwell, brought them a morning cup of tea and checked that they were comfortable in bed at night. Each guest had a buzzer to summon her in the night if need be. Mrs Menzies was always upset when an old person died.[32]

It was a comfortable, easygoing life. Guests had to make their own entertainment and there was only the one wireless with only one station (and no television). Guests were left to their own devices and there were no rules. Food was fair and predictable, though there was no alcohol. Mrs Menzies often proffered advice, which was sometimes resented. Some accused her of profiteering, for they had to pay £2 per week for full board. The place 'wasn't always spotless' but 'had an air of faded gentility'. Clark liked it.[33]

Mrs Chesney was more of a mystery than her mother. She declared that she did not approve of alcohol and when one guest laced tea with rum she was told that she was trying to corrupt the others. She went out most nights but was never seen the worse for wear due to drink. When her mother was away in Scotland she remained in her room and the maid ran the place. Mrs Chesney was fond of make-up and chainsmoked. Sometimes she was smartly dressed, but Clark stated 'I

---

30 *Middlesex County Times*, 5 March 1949; *Daily Telegraph*, 12 February 1954.
31 *Middlesex County Times*, 20 March 1954.
32 *Illustrated...*, 24 April 1954.
33 Ibid.

think she was basically a kind person'.³⁴

The Chesneys' adopted daughter married Frederick Richard Trull (1924-1998) on 1 July 1950. He had served in the army from 1943-1947 and then worked as a houseman at Ealing Priory, not far from Montpelier Road. As said, the Chesneys were Catholic and it is probable that they met at the Priory and presumably married in the still not wholly repaired church. The reception was held in the back garden of number 22 and was attended by members of the clergy, army officers and residents of the home. They lived at various addresses in the district in the following years, settling at 16b Sutherland Road by 1954. They had two children, Veronica, born in 1951 and Christopher, two years later. John Nixon-Pearson married Miss Cecilia Symes in 1952 and by early 1954 they resided at 25 Gordon Road, Ealing, with Catherine, their first child. It is unknown whether Chesney attended either wedding; the local newspaper did not report them, and there is no reference that he did so.³⁵

Much had been happening in Chesney's life whilst he was separated from his wife. He was stationed at the naval base at Buxtehude, near Hamburg. A colleague recalled 'Whilst we were in Germany, it was common knowledge that Chesney was in some crooked business and the Army Special Investigation Bureau were interested in him'. In the year that the war ended, he met Barbara Schaller at Wilhelmshaven, where she was working as a teleprinter operator for the German Navy. Chesney was second in command of the naval unit who captured the headquarters where Barbara was employed. She later introduced him in Hamburg to her younger sister, Gerda, who had been born on 25 April 1927 in Saalfeld, Thuringia, in what had been, in 1945, recently proclaimed the Russian zone of Germany following its partition by the four victorious Allied Powers. She had eventually escaped the Soviet invaders, but was not unscathed as she said, 'I was roughly handled by Russian soldiers', which was a guarded way of saying that she was one of the very many German women raped by the victorious Soviet troops. After Chesney signed her work permit, she secured a job at the naval base as a stewardess, cleaning his rooms and seeing to his clothes which guaranteed adequate food, which not all Germans enjoyed at this time. She also became Chesney's housekeeper.³⁶

34 Ibid.
35 *Middlesex County Times*, 13 February 1954; TNA, MEPO 2/9542.
36 TNA, MEPO 2/9542; *Evening Standard*, 19 February 1954; *Sunday Pictorial*, 28 February 1954.

She later recalled seeing Chesney for the first time:

> *When I first set eyes on Chesney he frightened me. I saw a towering bearded figure in a glaring tartan shirt with an ear-ring in his left ear, two guns slung from his shoulder, two pistols in his belt, and a knife stuck in his knee boot. He was going hunting. Whenever he got angry his blue eyes would darken and his ears would stiffen.*[37]

Gerda later recalled, 'He was always decent and obliging to me and I learned to look up to him and in the course of time a liaison grew up between us'. She further explained:

> *After what the Russians had done to me I hated every man, but very soon I came under this strange New Zealander's spell. Although I was a servant, he treated me with the courtesy and attention due to a duchess. All through his years with me he stayed like this. Soon we fell in love and lived together in the barracks. In these years with him I never knew him to be unfaithful.*[38]

The romance between them began at a Christmas Eve party at the naval base. Gerda was tidying her hair in front of a mirror when Chesney appeared beside her. His hands hovered above her shoulders before touching her and despite her fears, 'Those hands big and strong though they were inexpressibly gentle and reassuring'. He complimented her on her looks, kissed and caressed her. They arranged to leave the party and go to his flat. Once there, he was kind and gentle towards her when they made love for the first time. He gave her a gold ankle chain and said, 'There! That is your chain. That means you are forever my slave and belong only to me'. She was not unwilling, however.[39]

It was a life of luxury for Gerda and Chesney. There was gold, diamonds and furs in abundance for the young woman who had had nothing in the previous year. Yet she also saw a childish side to her lover's character. He would lie back in the driving seat, manoeuvring the car with his knees whilst his arms were around her. Inevitably, on one occasion the car overturned and Gerda was hospitalised. As ever, Chesney avoided paying the price for his reckless behaviour.[40]

Chesney only spoke to Gerda a little about his estranged wife. He also

---

37 *Sunday Pictorial*, 28 February 1954.
38 Ibid.
39 *Woman's Weekly Mirror*, 15 September 1957.
40 Ibid.

referred to his mother. There are two accounts of how this happened. One, made by Gerda in 1954, ran as follows. A few months after they met, the pair were driving back in an open car one night after a poker party and Chesney decided to tell Gerda a version of an episode in his past. Apparently he was depressed, something which the moon often did for him, she said (a common belief in the 1950s was that the moon had a great influence, for the worse, on men's behaviour). Gerda recalled the incident:

> *Suddenly, he stopped the car, took me in his arms, and said, "Would you love me if I was a murderer?" Then he said, "I murdered my mother. It was my fault she died (as a variant his adopted daughter was told that he had shot her in New Zealand)". I was dumbfounded. At last I asked him, "How?" "I shot her," he said. He saw the horror on my face, then laughed and said quickly, "It isn't true. I just wanted to see if you really loved me".*
>
> *For some days he avoided my company. I became anxious. Then he explained that in 1926, when he was 17, he had gone to his mother whilst she sat writing a letter to her bank. He thought she was going to expose him as the forger of her cheques. On her desk was a pistol bought by him a few days before and left in his room. Ches told me that she picked up the gun and asked how he had come by it. "I tried to take it away from her," he said. "There was a struggle and the gun went off."*[41]

Gerda believed the story and later said, 'I believe the death of his mother haunted Ches all his life'. He clearly trusted her as much as he trusted anyone. The two then went to church for the first time together, Chesney telling her that he was a practising Catholic and that he gave a tenth of his income to the Church.[41] As we shall see, there is another account which dates this revelation to a later time and gives a more likely reason why he told her what allegedly happened.

On 17 April 1946 Chesney left the Navy but was not released until 28 July (his temporary commission expired on 27 April 1951). He was deemed to have done well, as Commander Liddell, who he served under from November 1945 to April 1946, wrote:

> *A strong and somewhat unusual personality and perhaps one more typical of the sixteenth and seventeenth centuries than the present day. Possesses lots of drive and initiative and the ability to get things*

---

41 *Sunday Pictorial*, 28 February 1954.

done. Rather too impulsive at times. Definitely an 'operational' type and I know of few officers I would rather have serving with me on active service. Has made a very good job of running the Germans here. Strong physique, good linguist.[42]

With the end of their time at Buxtehude, Chesney and Gerda moved on. They drove to Paris, via residence in a stately rectory in the German valley of the Weser, looked after by four servants. Chesney's scheme was not a wholly romantic one, but was also linked to his latest smuggling scheme. They finally drove to Paris, Chesney in his officer's uniform and Gerda described as his WREN assistant. Their car was a grand one, and had been stolen from the military authorities. It had once been used by Admiral Doenitz. They stayed in a cottage in the grounds of a chateau besides the Seine. Gerda was showered with jewels, clothing and every other material need she could want, as well as providing her with love. He also bought luxury goods in order to smuggle them into Germany and sell them on the Black Market. It was highly lucrative and Chesney made immense amounts of money. He also gave thanks for his good fortune at the church of Notre Dame de Lorette at Montmartre.[43]

It was in Paris that the two were arrested and escorted to Hamburg under guard. Whilst he was a prisoner on remand, Chesney managed to have someone cut the barbed wire which surrounded the prison. Gerda, who was not put under arrest, crawled through each night and stayed with him until five the next day. He would pass to her cigarettes he had acquired on the inside and then she would later sell these on the black market outside and bring Chesney the profits.[44]

When it came to trial, Chesney received his first conviction in almost two decades. At the Naval District Court Martial at Hamburg on 7-8 November 1946 he was charged on five counts. Firstly, with the theft of a car, with fraudulently obtaining a car, the theft of government petrol and acts prejudicial to naval discipline in not returning the car and for unauthorised use of it. The second charge was not proved, but the others were. He was given a four month gaol sentence. The Board found no reason to interfere with the sentence. Unfortunately the records of this trial no longer exist, for the only surviving records are of major offences or cases which set a precedent.[45]

42 RN Disclosures.
43 *Woman's Sunday Mirror*, 22 September 1957.
44 *Sunday Pictorial*, 28 February 1954.

He was incarcerated in Wormwood Scrubs Prison in west London from 10 November 1946 until 27 January 1947. He wrote to Gerda every week whilst he was there.[46]

Once he was out, he ditched his naval uniform and returned to Gerda in Paris. He told her he had seen his wife and she claimed that she might divorce him if he gave her a lot of money, or so he told her. They went to Belgium, with Gerda smuggled over the border. At the Majestic Hotel in Liege, Chesney gave her a British passport in the name of Emily Augusta Violet Strang, born in Havelock, New Zealand (a place he knew from his boyhood there) in 1922. At Liege, Chesney spent much time gambling, before returning to more high living in Paris. There was lots of conspicuous expenditure, but Chesney claimed he was receiving demands from his wife for more money. Chesney thought that the boat he had had in the 1930s would bring him luck and the *Gladys May* was in Algiers. The two went there.[47]

After the flight Chesney booked them into the smartest and most expensive hotel he could find, the Arletty, Chesney went in search of his old boat. He found it, but lacked the funds to buy it. He knew a wealthy gambler in the town and the pair of them went to his house in order that he might win enough money for the *Gladys May*. As ever, Chesney lost all his money. He then used Gerda's diamond necklace as collateral. It was then that he found that his opponent was cheating. Chesney drew his revolver, but was restrained by Gerda and so merely took all the money on the table, which was enough to buy his boat back. That done, they left Algiers.[48]

Allegedly they underwent a fake marriage ceremony there. Believing Chesney's assertion that the divorce papers were in the post and thus he was free to marry her, she consented to being wed. They were 'married' in Algiers on 25 April 1947, but when her sister was told of this, they could offer her no proof. She assumed this had happened, but had no fondness for Chesney, 'I didn't like him and was disgusted at what he had done to my sister'.[49]

With his boat, he could begin smuggling trips around the Mediterranean, whilst leaving Gerda in an expensive apartment in

---

45 RN Disclosures.
46 TNA, MEPO 2/9542; *Evening Standard*, 19 February 1954; *Sunday Pictorial*, 28 February 1954.
47 *Woman's Sunday Mirror*, 22 September 1957.
48 Ibid, 29 September 1957.

Paris, with enough money to live in luxury. Eventually, when he returned to her, he was ready for love and even took her to a church, 'and [according to Gerda] there, kneeling besides me in the golden glow of the candles, he solemnly pledged his life to me, swearing to love me until his last breath'. She also realised that she was carrying his child, which made him very happy, too.[50]

Chesney and Gerda later toured the French Riviera in a hired caravan, living off forged American dollars; $10,000 of which he lost gambling at Monte Carlo. Chesney met a former fellow convict there and soon he and Gerda were in Berne, smuggling forged bank notes. A few days later, Chesney completed the deal and brought back a fur coat for Gerda. She was happy, momentarily, but next day two detectives arrived at the hotel for him. He and Gerda swallowed the last of the forgeries before the detectives arrived. Their passports seemed in order and so the men left them. It was then that Gerda had her first miscarriage.[51]

Heartbroken both, they returned to Paris. However, other trouble was not far away for long. She had no official papers and was arrested by the military police and deported to Germany. Chesney had a worse time of it. He was hauled before the Paris Seine High Court on 24 November 1947. The charges were using a false name, fraudulent entry into France, smuggling and breaking the laws relating to aliens (a reference to Gerda, for he had supplied her with false papers). He received another four month sentence but in addition had to pay a fine of 150,000 francs. The sentence was reduced at the Paris Court of Appeal.[52]

Chesney became a professional smuggler in these years. An insight into this came from a man who had worked with him, who was known as Stanley and who later was stated to be an engineer living in Twickenham. He gave the following account in 1954:

> *I saw Chesney first in a bar in Paris. He had a great personality, a great beard and great ideas for making money by smuggling.*
>
> *I did two runs with Chesney, one from Cowes to Cherbourg and one from Cherbourg to Cowes.*

---

49 *Sunday Pictorial*, 28 February 1954.
50 *Woman's Sunday Mirror*, 29 September 1957.
51 Ibid.
52 TNA, MEPO 2/9542.

> We took 4 cwt of coffee beans to Cherbourg in 1947. With beans £2 a pound we netted about £900.
>
> We brought perfume back, bottle on bottle of it stacked in the bilges. It was worth about £1500.
>
> But we struck bad weather and the whole lot was broken. We made no money out of it.[53]

As with his running guns in Germany, contemporary accounts provide further (unverifiable) accounts of his smuggling activities at this time, and again they seem probable. This time he was based in the south of France, Spain, Italy, the Mediterranean and Tangier. He smuggled tobacco and drugs, leading to useful profits, often working with fellow ex-British officers. He also began smuggling ventures in northern Europe, too.[54]

Chesney returned to Gerda in Germany. They lived for a time in Ixelles, a suburb of Brussels and then in Ostend. They lived in rooms in the Hotel Miramar. Gerda suggested that Chesney gave up his criminal lifestyle. Apparently then, he flew into a rage. "What job will pay for all this?" he shouted at Gerda. "Do you think a clerk could buy you a dress like that?" Gerda said that she was not with him for material goods, but he insisted. "I don't think that's all you want," he shouted, dragging the dress off her shoulders. "But it's what I want. I want you to look the most beautiful woman in the world."[55]

It was at the Hotel Miramar that they had a surprise visit from Mrs Chesney. According to Gerda, 'Ches hurried across to her, showing in every muscle of his face the anger at her unexpected arrival in Ostend, "What brings you here, Vera?" he demanded fiercely'. She looked older than she was and was ill dressed. Gerda did not like her, 'His wife did not love him. She drank too much and was blackmailing him'. Chesney said he wanted a divorce but his wife refused. Apparently she threatened to denounce him to the authorities if he did not pay her; Gerda recalled, 'She was only after Chesney's money', but had been happy to briefly reside under the same room as the adulterous couple. Gerda thought that she was selfish and Mrs Chesney told the German girl about there being machine guns at her house in Ealing (there is no evidence that this was the case).[56]

53 *Sunday Despatch*, 21 February 1954.
54 McLeave, *Chesney*, pp.82-92.
55 *Woman's Sunday Mirror*, 29 September 1957.
56 Ibid, 6 October 1957.

Gerda thought that Mrs Chesney was not wholly unfriendly, but she dropped a bombshell when she said,

> Isn't it a bit dangerous having a child by a man like Ronald? There's an evil streak in him.

Gerda rebutted this on behalf of her lover. 'Not evil, Vera... He's reckless and foolish in many ways, but not evil. I know he's a gambler and a smuggler.'

> And murderer... Did you know that, Vera?... Yes, a murderer... Hasn't he told you about that yet? Then ask him about it Gerda. And ask him what he did to his own mother.[57]

Next day Mrs Chesney met her husband and they had a heated exchange when she demanded money from him. Chesney replied,

> How much do you want, Vera? How much do you want to leave me alone for good and give me my freedom?'

'Your freedom?' she sneered. 'That's something neither I nor any one else can ever give you. Freedom indeed: You lost that on the day your mother fell dying at your feet.'

Gerda wondered if Chesney would strike her, but he turned miserably away instead and said,

> 'You've no right to ask that.'

> 'No right? Do you mean I should not say that merely because they failed to find you guilty... because you escaped the hangman? Well, some of it will catch up with you sometime. Meanwhile I am your wife, Ronald and I need money.'

> 'How much this time?'

> 'I want £3,000... You can spend as much in a week the way you live... All on your woman.'[58]

Chesney paid up and she counted it out and left. But there was the other issue that she had raised: the death of Chesney's mother and his role in it. Neither spoke of it for a few days, until Chesney came back one night and decided to give Gerda his version of events. He began thus:

---

57 *Woman's Sunday Mirror*, 6 October 1957.
58 Ibid.

> You've got to trust me Gerda and believe in me... I have to tell you the whole story... something I hoped never to have to tell you... how my mother died.

Chesney then told her that his mother's death had been an accident, as has been related at the end of chapter six. Gerda also asked Chesney if he had ever been in love with his wife and he replied,

> I can't remember... That sounds stupid, but it's the truth. So much has happened since... But I tell you this, Gerda... I have never loved her or anyone else as I have loved you. You must believe that.

She did.[59]

Gerda was soon pregnant again, just as Chesney told her he must go to Palestine for an 'unofficial' job. She tried to persuade him not to, but he could not. Apparently he was involved with other men in shipping guns and explosives. The two went to Egypt and stayed in a first class hotel in Cairo. Chesney was certain that this venture would bring them a fortune. However it fell through and they had to leave quickly. Tragically, in their flight, Gerda fell over and suffered a second miscarriage. They limped back to Belgium, now very short of money.[60]

Worse was to follow. According to Gerda, Chesney had failed to pay up sufficiently and so his wife informed the British police about her husband's criminal activities and they told their Belgium counterparts. Chesney now had reverted to his birth name, was known as John Donald Merrett. They were at a hotel at Ostend again when he received another letter from his wife asking for money. Chesney was angry, screwed up the letter and said, 'I shall murder that woman, One day Vera will go too far!...Money!...That's all she wants and to think there is still more than £8,000 of mine tied up with her...She's worth a damned sight more to me dead than alive'. That day they went to Brussels, taking smuggled jewellery with them that he planned to sell.[61]

At the Hotel des Touristes, they were to receive a rude shock next morning at eight o'clock when two police officers arrived. Chesney tried to bluff and lie his way out, but to no avail. They were both arrested and on 25 March 1948 he was sentenced to a year and a fine of 500,000 francs by the 12th Chamber in Paris. Gerda received

59 Ibid.
60 Ibid.
61 Ibid, 13 October 1957.

a six month sentence, served at the Prison de Forest, 52 Avenue de la Jonction, Brussels, for having a forged passport and being in Belgium illegally. Yet Chesney only served a fraction of his tariff, for he must have been briefly at large in mid 1948. On 30 June of that year he was up before the 17th Chamber of Paris for an infraction of the Alien regulations. There was no custodial sentence this time, but a fine of 30,000 Francs was imposed.[62]

Chesney also wrote to the Surete Commissaire at this time:

> Dear Sir,
>
> I hear that you wanted to have a chat with me before I was rather hurriedly called to attend my affairs in Ostend. I don't think I shall be returning to France for some time and should like to square the debt I believe I owe you, but unfortunately have insufficient funds at the moment. If a business deal which I am in the process of putting through comes off you can rest assured that I will pay you with it. The other debt – the one I owe to society – I'm afraid I shall be unable to settle it as it makes too big a demand on my schedule.
>
> Yours faithfully
> John D. Milner.[63]

Gerda retained her feelings for Chesney after her release from prison in January 1949. She recalled, 'Chesney was full of the joy of living...He only needed very little for himself. I was well off with him and he looked after me very well indeed'. He had certainly given her a favourable view of his former life as well as telling her a downright lie. She reported that she knew of his standing trial for matricide, 'he was acquitted because he was innocent. He wrote a book about the case'. Yet she could no longer live with him following her deportation from Belgium, 'as I would only be one step away from prison if I did so'. She begged him to cease his smuggling career, but he refused.[64]

Chesney tried to arrange passage for Gerda to Israel in 1949, with the intention that he could then join her and they be married. On 10 April he asked his wartime friend Martin Solomon from Tobruk, to try to see if this was a possibility. It appears that it was not.[65]

Gerda then began to work in Cologne as a barmaid at the Cabaret Rote Muhle and at a night club called Café Tabu. The latter would have

---

62 TNA, MEPO 2/9542.
63 McLeave, *Chesney*, p.91.
64 *Sunday Pictorial*, 28 February 1954.
65 McLeave, *Chesney*, p.96.

important consequences for Chesney, but in the meantime he was in trouble with the law again. On 13 April 1949 he was fined 1,000 francs and given four months in prison for abetting an unspecified illegal activity at Tobruk and Brussels, but it would appear from later evidence that he served far less; indeed he was deported on 17 May.[66]

She wrote one last letter to her lover's wife.

> *Dear Vera,*
>
> *I find it very difficult to write to you because I knew from the very beginning that you would not pay any attention to it. I understand why you have not answered my previous mail because they were written exactly as I felt before I knew you.*
>
> *I also found there was a different understanding between the three of us after Ostend. In these last few days Ches has changed very much and I am afraid. He was very happy when we were together at Ostend. And he has told me that he still likes you, not as a woman, but like a sister. And if he can still help you whenever possible. I am afraid he has changed his mind now.*
>
> *It seems to me you never loved Ches, because if you did you would try to help him and get a divorce. I don't like to say this to you, but I feel it is better if I do.*
>
> *You know I am here for my passport, and after my trial I will be sent back to Germany, which means the Russian zone. I am not afraid for myself, but I am afraid for Ches because he will come with me wherever I am sent and that means hanging for both of us.*
>
> *Gerda.*[67]

Chesney also wrote, hoping for a divorce:

> *Dear Vera,*
>
> *I come before the court on Wednesday, 13th for sentence. I anticipate I shall get one or two months. Enclosed is a cutting of the Belgian police report. I have marked the passage referring to Lady Menzies. I am sorry you still take the attitude you do and that you won't tie yourself in knots to get the divorce.*
>
> *I first asked you for a divorce me in 1946, although you must have known a good three or four years ago that I did not intend to return to you. You can get a divorce for desertion. I have taken legal*

---

66 TNA, MEPO 2/9542.
67 Phillips, *Murderer's Moon*, p.227.
68 Phillips, *Murderer's Moon*, p.228.

advice on the subject, and were you to divorce me the object of the settlement would become void as we have no children.

Don[68]

Mrs Chesney wrote to her erring husband thus:

Dear Don,

It is a long time since I heard from you and it is becoming increasingly difficult to make ends meet. I can hardly remember when you last sent any money and soon I shall have to come across and see you although I have no wish to do so. I am sure it would be embarrassing both for you and myself to say nothing of the little girl friend who, I hear, is still with you. In your last letter you asked again for a divorce but, as I have told you many times, I cannot agree to it. It seems that our life together is over although I still cherish a little hope despite all that has happened in the past.

The children are well and often ask for you. Mother is as well as can be expected and sends her love. Please write very soon and try to help with the expenses for it is a great worry to me.

Take care of yourself,
Love, Vera.[69]

Yet on the subject of divorce was she adamant, writing in February 1949:

Dearest Don,

Of course I appreciate what you say. I know that you decided long ago things were finished between us. I can sympathise with you and your girlfriend, but after long talks with Mama and various friends. I have changed my mind about going through with this business. You know I am still very fond of you and will do anything to help you. I am only sorry it all had to happen this way. Still the same dull day after day chores to be done I suppose life must go on, even if we feel that it has stopped for us...Love, Vera.[70]

Divorce in Britain had been liberalised in 1937 with it being possible on grounds of cruelty, adultery and desertion. After 1945 divorce rates soared due to the upheaval of wartime. However, it was still frowned upon by the majority in the late 1940s and could damage an

69 Tullett, *Portrait*, p.127.
70 McLeave, *Chesney*, p.93.
71 Kynaston, *Austerity Britain*, 1945-1951 (2007), pp.206-7.

individual socially.[71]

Chesney appears to have been in Paris in early 1949 and the following episode shows aspects of his charming but dangerous personality as recounted in 1954 by Margaret Groom, then a 19-year-old redhead. She was on holiday with her parents allegedly in September, but as will be noted he was in gaol in England then. She went to the bar of the hotel they were staying in, for a sherry one evening. There was a large crowd there. She recalled, 'Dominating everyone was a giant of a man'. A waiter approached her with a drink and a request that she would join the large man. Feeling flattered, she accepted and met the man everyone called 'Ronnie'. She recalled, 'I fell in love with Chesney in a teenage girlish way. I thought him wonderful'. On seeing her parents later that evening she found they took a disapproving view on account of the difference in ages. But the night was not yet over.[72]

She slipped out of the hotel and went to his long, grey yacht, moored on the Seine. On board there were numerous young men and women, drinking. Margaret later stated:

> *Chesney gave me a drink in a small glass. "It is Pernod" he said. "It is nothing but aniseed. It is a girl's drink, my dear". I had several Pernods. Ronnie was wonderful. He was full of the most wonderful stories. He knew everything and everybody. He did not even try and kiss me. I felt I was seeing life. I said no more to my parents. I met him there next morning. After a short while he invited me back to the yacht. Something made me refuse.*[73]

The Groom family went to Ostend shortly afterwards and it was on the harbour that Chesney and Margaret were reunited. He explained that he was there on unspecified business, but claimed he had transport difficulties. In reality he was seeking a 'mule' to take contraband goods to Britain. He showed her a diamond in a canvas bag which had been in his pocket. 'You can have this' he said. Margaret declined, citing the impossibility of her taking it through customs. 'He roared with laughter. "I'll show you how"'.[74]

They met again that afternoon in a cafe. Although she said no to a drive with him to Brussels, she did agree to accompany him for a spin in his black saloon car. They stopped at a couple of places for drinks and, on re-entering the car, events took a more startling turn.

72 *Empire News*, 21 February 1954.
73 Ibid.
74 *Empire News*, 21 February 1954.

Margaret recalled:

> Then suddenly he became intense. He asked me to look behind to see if we were being followed. The car bounced forward at a terrific speed.
>
> Chesney crouched over the wheel, "They can't get me" he said, "let them try and catch me".
>
> I saw that the speedometer had crept up to the 80s. I felt like screaming. We hurtled through the night. Suddenly he braked and swung the car around into a lane and cruised along.
>
> He put an arm around my shoulder and laughed, "Nothing to worry about now, kid" he said. "Just some old friends of mine I didn't want to see. They never pay for a round".
>
> We drove into a town and left the car and walked down back streets. Then I made my worst mistake. I told him I was going back to England for a few days. He was sullen and angry.
>
> "You don't know what life is like, you silly –" he said. Suddenly he seized my arm and twisted me round. He clapped a hand over my mouth. I knew I was helpless in his grip, but I just had to fight.

Her struggles attached the attention of some passing men who ran to her aid. Margaret escaped as Chesney let her go to deal with them and she later realised she had had a lucky escape, reflecting, 'No woman was safe with such a man'.[75]

Chesney had only been in Britain for nine days before was up before the British courts for the first time in two decades on 26 May 1949 at the magistrates' court on Great Marlborough Street, Soho, London. Describing himself as 'a writer', he was charged with 'knowingly concerned in dealing with goods to wit, 222 pairs of nylon stockings with intent to defraud' at Bourton Street, W1. Nylon stockings at this time could command 15 shillings a pair, such were the restrictions on goods of all kinds due to severe rationing imposed by the post war government. He was found guilty and given the option of a fine of £25 and three months in prison or nine months in prison. Lacking money, he spent time in prison, being released on 25 January 1950, after having been given a remission of a few weeks.[76]

It was in the summer of 1950 that the last major figure made her debut in Chesney's life and she was very important as a catalyst for

---

75 Ibid.
76 LMA, PS/MSA/01/216; TNA, MEPO 2/9542.

his later actions. This was Sonia Sophie Winnikes, born in Duren in Germany on 4 March 1924, the daughter of a disabled war veteran and had two siblings. She had attended an elementary school in Duren and initially worked as a shop assistant in a handicraft business. The family moved across Germany in World War Two as allied bombing became increasingly heavy as the tide of war turned against Germany. They lived for a time in Erfurt, in the East, but moved again as the Soviet armies pushed into eastern Germany. Once back in Duren, now a devastated wreck after intense fighting of the previous autumn, she initially worked in her father's shop.[77]

After briefly working in several other jobs, she began employment in the Café Tabu, a night club in Cologne. She was one of the young women who worked behind the bar, serving drinks, but they also danced with the customers. There was no set tariff, but the girls expected tips. It was an all night job; she would arrive in the evening and return home in the early hours of the morning.[78]

Gerda (never mentioned by name by Sonia) also worked there and had talked to Sonia about him. It was not initially certain if the affair was finished. Sonia later recalled in a newspaper interview:

> *I had never met him until one night, an untidy, poorly dressed Englander came into the bar and asked for her [Gerda]. His shirt was frayed, his shoes dirty and worn, and generally he looked unkempt. I had an idea that he looked like a man who had just come out of prison...But this unhappy looking man did not appeal to me. For hours he stood in the bar over a single coffee and I realised that something had gone wrong with his romance. Two or three times after this he called at the Café Tabu and asked me to dance with him.*
>
> *At first I refused. Then early one morning over the wireless came the music of a lively foxtrot. Because I wanted to dance and I felt sorry for the woebegone figure leaning against the bar. I danced with him.*[79]

Sonia did not want to 'but in' between Chesney and Gerda, who was busily dancing with another man. (In fact, the two had already split.

---

77 *News of the World*, 28 February 1954; TNA, MEPO 2/9542.
78 *News of the World*, 28 February 1954.
79 *News of the World*, 28 February 1954.
80 Ibid.

Gerda remarked, 'I did not bear Sonia any grudges about this as I had already finished with Chesney. I knew he spent a great deal of money on Sonia.') She and Chesney saw more of one another. He smartened up his appearance and told Sonia that it was all over with Gerda.[80]

According to Gerda, Chesney did not like her working in the club. She agreed she would desist if he would stop smuggling. He initially agreed and then a few days later he proved he had not by bringing home smuggled coffee. Gerda decided to go back to work in the club, and both coaxing and threats failed to move her. The end was near.[81]

Chesney may have been deceitful, for Gerda later said that Chesney wanted her back. On one occasion, she claimed, 'He followed me and begged me to come back. After many such scenes, I said to him, "You always said you liked plump girls. Look at Sonia. She is nice". Another time, she found him lying on her bed in her hotel room in Cologne. 'You belong to me…You must come back,' he said, or so Gerda claimed in 1954. She refused and referred to Sonia. He went to the door and said, 'I am going to England'. That was the last time the two ever met; in the summer of 1953 she claimed 'I could no longer live without him' and in the following year admitted 'Giving Chesney to Sonia is the one thing in my life I regret'.[82]

Sonia still kept her distance, but one morning after work he offered to drive her home to Duren. They began meeting more often, mostly in cafes in the afternoons prior to her work shift. Every night he sent her an orchid and she began to feel sympathy for him. He told her more about his past; that his father had left his mother and himself when he was six and that his mother was dead. He told her that he had been in the Royal Navy, of his exploits as a frigate captain, his capture, of his being a prisoner of war in Italy and his escapes. He showed her a picture of his adopted daughter's marriage. She was never told that he had been on trial for the murder of his mother, however. Sonia recalled, 'I believed him then and I do not know any different now.' She noted, too, 'he was not sensible in spending money'.[83]

Their friendship deepened. As Sonia recalled, 'For nearly two months we continued to meet in the afternoons until eventually he became my lover.' Chesney did tell her about his wife, but that he had not seen her since 1945 (a lie), and that when he had been in charge

81 *Sunday Pictorial*, 28 February 1954.
82 *News of the World*, 28 February 1954; TNA, MEPO 2/9542.
83 *News of the World*, 28 February 1954.

of the camp at Buxtehude he had asked her to come to him but that she had refused. Sonia further stated, 'At first when he spoke of his wife he seemed very sad, but in the days that followed he spoke less and less of her'.[84]

Matters moved to another stage in late 1950 when Chesney asked her if she wanted to go with him to London. Sonia initially demurred, believing herself not to be wholly in love with Chesney. So he went alone. Once in London, Chesney found he could not bear to be apart from her. So he sent her a ticket so she could rejoin him. Sonia was convinced by his pleadings. They were reunited at Dover. They then went to 22 Montpelier Road, Ealing.[85]

Once there, they met Mrs Chesney and later Mrs Menzies, who came down from Scotland. Sonia recalled the situation, 'I might have been an old friend of both women so warmly was I greeted... Very soon Mrs Chesney and myself were bosom friends. "Please call me Vera," she said and addressed me as Sonia.' The two women even worked together in the home and Sonia was told by Chesney's wife that she had a 'boyfriend' of her own. It was all very pally. Chesney made cups of tea for the three women every morning and was always polite to his wife. Sonia and Mrs Menzies worked together, as Mrs Chesney was always a late riser. In the evenings they would sometimes all go out to a pub or to the cinema. Sonia stated, 'Mrs Chesney was a heavy drinker. In contrast Chesney drank very little. When he did drink at all he became tipsy very quickly'.[86]

According to John Clark, a resident at the home, Sonia 'was not beautiful, yet she was striking and she had an excellent figure.' What struck him equally was the relationship between Mrs Chesney and Sonia. 'Oddly enough Mrs Chesney seemed to get on very well with her. I used to see them arm in arm, and they regularly went shopping together.' It is possible that the two women were lonely and enjoyed each others' company for want of anything else.[87]

He was certainly a lively personality when he was at the Home. Clark recalled:

> *One day I saw an enormous man bounding down the stairs four at a time. He wore a ten-gallon hat, a vivid shirt and red trousers. He*

---

84 Ibid.
85 *Woman's Sunday Mirror*, 13 October 1957.
86 *News of the World*, 28 February 1954.
87 *Illustrated...*, 24 April 1954.

> was Ronald Chesney. He shouted to his wife to hurry up. She came down the stairs, and they went off in her car in high spirits.
>
> Sunshine House soon got to know Chesney after that. He came unexpectedly and left mysteriously. Once he stayed a month; another visit only lasted half an hour. But he electrified the place, bounding up and down stairs, chucking old dears under the chin, bringing up our early morning tea, serving meals in the living room...He came back, as breezy as ever. He wore a cloak, and stood at the bottom of the stairs, his arms outstretched, like some pirate home from the sea.

Clark knew he had a criminal record but clearly could not help being entranced by him.[88]

Chesney showed another side to his character whilst in Ealing. He stole his wife's motor car, a Ford HP8, leaving a note to say that he had merely borrowed it. In any case, as he wrote, it had been a present from himself to his wife and so he could not be charged with the theft. Because he was in debt to Sonia, Chesney felt he needed to make her a present of clothing. He went to Dora Leven's ladies' outfitters shop at 5 Central Buildings, Ealing Broadway. He had no money but demanded credit, saying that if it was not forthcoming, his wife would take her custom elsewhere. He took the goods but never paid a penny towards them.[89]

Another story which casts a light on Chesney's rather coarse character comes from this time. He was with friends in a restaurant in Jermyn Street in London in 1951. One of the women in the group complained of hunger. So Chesney picked up a chicken from the counter, tore it into two pieces and gave her half. He shouted to staff that he would buy it and then ate the rest himself.[90]

Eventually the four week permit which Sonia had been granted came to an end. She returned to Germany without Chesney. Sonia recalled, 'It was about this time that I fell fully and wholly in love with Chesney and began to regard him as the only man in the world for me'. Chesney soon returned and announced that he no longer wanted Sonia working in the café, perhaps because he did not like to think of her as dancing with other men. She did as requested and returned to work in her father's shop. The quid pro quo was that she demanded

88 Ibid.
89 TNA, MEPO 2/9542.
90 *Daily Telegraph*, 17 February 1954.

that he shave his beard, which she saw as being 'thick, coarse and untidy'. Yet Chesney had had his beard for sixteen years and regarded it as a link with his time in the Navy, but he reluctantly agreed and did as his lover requested.[91]

The question of divorce had not been wholly resisted or ignored by Mrs Chesney. She had made enquiries in 1945-1946 to Peacock and Goddard, but had baulked at the expense. On 24 February 1948 she had asked her solicitors about the possibility. In April Chesney approached them, too. The first stumbling block was that Mrs Chesney was concerned that divorce would result in the loss of her settlement rights (worth £6 per week for her). Matters stalled until Chesney's solicitors brought the matter up again in October, when they said he had agreed to provide evidence of his adultery, but were worried about the expense that bringing the necessary witnesses to England would entail. By April of the following year, Mrs Chesney decided not to proceed. In July 1949, Chesney's new solicitors asked again how matters stood. Mrs Chesney then said that it could go ahead but he would have to agree to pay all the expenses. It then ground to a halt because of his poverty.[92]

Chesney had suggested they split the settlement capital on a 50/50 basis, but she disagreed. Her other reasons for refusing were that as a Catholic she would be excommunicated if she consented to divorce. Then she said that she did not want to let a German woman have a British passport. Finally, when she had been ill a few years ago she promised God that if she recovered, she would not be divorced.[93]

Mrs Chesney was clearly under great strain. She took relief in drinking to excess from about 1949, drinking alone in her bedroom. She also had at least one male companion. This was former squadron leader Alvan Williams (1902-1967), whom she had met at Seaford in October 1945. He was a widower with one son. He knew of her drinking and was allegedly her only male friend. Williams had met Chesney occasionally and always got on with him. However, although Mrs Chesney never spoke of her husband being violent towards her, she mentioned that he asked her for money sometimes. She was, however, frightened of what he might do. Williams stated, 'She said

---

91 *News of the World*, 28 February 1954.
92 TNA, MEPO 2/9542.
93 Ibid.
94 TNA, MEPO 2/9542.

that if he got her there [abroad], she was frightened she might not return... "He might do me in or get me bumped off."[94]

Chesney and Sonia lived in Duren for a time. This town, near the borders of Belgium, Holland and West Germany, suited him well for another reason, for it was an ideal centre for any smuggling operations he would indulge in. When Chesney returned to London he wrote to her daily, asking that she come to him. After acquiring a permit, she did so and they stayed in Brighton together. Because of their limited funds they bought their food for her to cook the meals to eat at home. Chesney gave her £4 a week for housekeeping. After four weeks they returned together to Germany. They had another trip to England in March 1951. At first they stayed in an address in Clarges Street, Earl's Court in London and then, Chesney claiming he needed to travel to Spain, the two went to a hotel near Newhaven.[95]

Chesney's life was reasonably contented, but was also one of frustration. He had, as we shall soon see, plans for the longer term. It is not known for how long these had been formulating in his mind, but he was soon to relate it to others, in private, and this is an important signal as to what would ultimately lead to tragedy.

---

95 *News of the World*, 28 February 1954.

9

Countdown to Tragedy, 1951-1954

It was whilst Sonia and Chesney were on the coast that he reacquainted himself with Flying Officer Irwin Arthur Victor Maling (1898-1981) and made some portentious remarks to him which were to eventually lead to the doom of several individuals. Chesney had first run across him in 1949 in Ostend where he had persuaded the airman to ship his car over to England for him and sell it on his behalf, which he did for £165. As an engineer, Maling had surveyed a boat for Chesney at Tangier in January 1951, which he recommended as a purchase, but had to sail it to England for Chesney. However, the boat was damaged at Gibraltar when it broke its moorings.[1]

Maling was in business in Brighton and arranged that Chesney and Sonia stayed at a Mrs Schofield's guest house in Spring Street. The two stole from a gas meter and so had to leave. They later stayed at a flatlet on the Brighton seafront. Chesney and Maling spent some time together. The former told about how he needed money badly and that his wife had a trust settled upon her that he wanted. He indicated that he needed to dispose of his wife. Maling recalled, 'I told him that he should put all thoughts of doing away with his wife aside'. Chesney was not deterred and replied, 'If I think of a plan would you be prepared to furnish me with an alibi I would be prepared to pay £1,000'. In fact, on one occasion, after Chesney left him, Maling found an undated cheque

---

1   TNA, MEPO 2/9542.

from him for that amount, made payable to him, but Maling tore it up.[2]

It was at this time that his thoughts first seem to have turned towards the necessity that his wife be forcibly removed from the picture. She would not divorce him and so crucially release the settlement he had made for her in 1929. Therefore, to his mind, she had to die and that meant murder. But he had too healthy a regard for his own skin as to want to commit the deed himself. So he made a number of overtures to others.

On the following night the three of them were having drinks at the flatlet. Chesney left the other two at ten. He returned the next day and told Maling that he had tried to enter 22 Montpelier Road in secret but that something had gone wrong. He said that perhaps he could kill his wife by letting off gas taps in her bedroom, perhaps recalling the incident where the three old men had died by that method at that house in 1949.[3]

However, on 15 April at the Newhaven quayside Chesney and Sonia were in for a shock. Customs men confiscated their passports. They asked Chesney if he had any money on his person. He told them that he had only £3 in notes and £50 in travellers' cheques. They also took an interest in Chesney's car, where they found, hidden in a cavity under the spare wheel, a number of bags. In these were 112 pounds of coffee beans (a popular choice of goods for the smuggler; to be exchanged in Germany for goods not readily available in Britain). In one there was an envelope containing £100 in notes. Chesney told the men, 'I know I am on your black list, but I consider this most unfriendly'. He then tried to be more conciliatory, saying that he would play ball with them if they would allow him to clear his name. He said that he needed the goods to pay his travelling expenses as he meant to stay in Germany for six months and alleged that in a fortnight everything would be legal, concerning the movement of money and he was merely anticipating that.[4]

Sonia was taken away and subjected to the indignity of a strip search by female officers. She later wondered whether Chesney had asked her to accompany him because he cynically wanted her as cover and so would be less likely to be an object of suspicion. Chesney was then taken to a police station, where he was visited by Sonia and Mrs

2 TNA, MEPO 2/9542.
3 Ibid.
4 *Sussex Express and County Herald*, 27 April 1951.

Chesney.[5]

Whilst Chesney was awaiting trial, he wrote the following letter to his wife on 17 April:

> It was very sweet of you to come down and visit me yesterday, although I am afraid I was almost as domineering and demanding... I feel very, very lonely and friendless, and it seems funny that you, whom I have treated so very, very badly, should be my only friend, don't give up being my friend. Sonia is probably, as you say, only an infatuation, and even if I do marry her, I know whilst she may be everything to me, she will never be a friend to me, as you are and always have been... It seems to me that this time it is going to be tougher than all the others. May be I'm getting old.

Solomon also referred to the meeting between the Chesneys thus, 'When he was arrested for smuggling 100lbs of coffee he said what a fine wife she had been to him in his trouble'.[6]

On 24 April 1951 he faced two charges at Lewes Magistrates' Court with attempting to smuggle 112 pounds of coffee, which had been bought at a coffee shop on Ealing Broadway, and to take £98 out of the country. Chesney's choice of goods smuggled is easily explicable. Coffee was one of the most smuggled commodities at this time. The Exchange Controls Act of 1946 had created the offence of setting £75 (reduced to £50 in 1949) as the maximum that could be legally taken out of the country. Mr H.L. Willis, for Customs and Excise, stated that Chesney had wanted to take £98 more than was legal out of the country. He added that he had separated from his wife five years ago and had a long criminal record. Inspector L. Taylor stated that Chesney had committed many offences from 1926-1949 (the naval authorities sent them details of these and noted this new offence on his papers), detailed them and stated that he was also allegedly a gun smuggler in Egypt, France, Belgium and Germany. Chesney pleaded guilty, stating that he realised that he must be punished for his crime, but at the same time asked for leniency, stating mendaciously that his wife had kept him on the right side of the law from 1928-1946 and was willing to have him back. He was unable to pay a fine because his car and cash had been confiscated. The Chairman of the Court, Mr F. Bentham Stevens, described Chesney as being 'a professional

---

5   *News of the World*, 28 February 1954.
6   McLeave, *Chesney: The Fabulous Murderer* (1954), pp.111-12; *Daily Mail*, 18 February 1954.

smuggler' and had an extremely bad record. He was found guilty and sentenced to twelve months in prison and this was to be served in Wandsworth Prison in south London. He was described at this time as being 42-years-old, six feet high, with mid brown hair, born in New Zealand and being Church of England in religion (rather than the Catholicism he had espoused when he had been with Gerda). As in 1949 he described himself as a writer.[7]

Sonia had no scruples about her affair, 'I was indifferent to the fact that I was living with a married man in the role of husband and wife. For I knew I could not betray his wife because she too had a friend'. Yet Mrs Chesney spent time with Sonia after Chesney was arrested. They talked about divorce, but Mrs Chesney told her she no longer wanted one. Sonia recalled, 'She warned me against Chesney and told me I would have trouble with him'.[8]

At the same time, his mind was turning to another issue and he spoke to a considerably younger fellow convict by the name of Herbert John Boyd, who shared his cell for a time and was serving a twelve month stretch for shoplifting. Boyd recalled that they spent from the hours of 4pm to 8am in the cells every day. They talked of many things. The older man boasted of his exploits, smuggling gold coins into France and Belgium, that he had had a trust fund of £60,000 when 21 and how he had settled £9,000 of that on his wife. He also spoke of his desire to marry Sonia.[9]

However, as Boyd later recalled, 'One day he put a proposition to us that he would pay anyone a thousand pounds if his wife could be got rid of'. He and a fellow prisoner, Richard Pickersgill (serving nine months for theft) 'treated it as a joke'. Chesney persisted. Could Boyd drive a car? He could. Then, according to Boyd, 'He suggested it would be quite easy for me to run over his wife if I was driving a car, and I just laughed'. Chesney was 'white faced and with a strange look in his eyes he said he was deadly serious'. Boyd was taken aback, referring later to 'Britain where these sort of things just didn't happen'. Chesney also spoke to Pickersgill about his yachting trips, Sonia and Mrs Chesney. As Pickersgill was due to leave before him and Boyd, he gave him his wife's address before leaving.[10]

7   *Middlesex County Times*, 20 February 1954; *Sussex Express and County Herald*, 27 April 1951; LMA, ACC3444/PR/01/230.
8   TNA, MEPO 2/9542.
9   Ibid.
10 *News of the World*, 14 February 1954; TNA, MEPO 2/9542.

An older prisoner, Fred Burgess, sat next to Chesney while making mail bags in prison. As with Boyd, he was asked if he was a driver, but this time the answer was negative. Chesney then asked if he knew anyone who could drive and who would kill for £1000 (about two years' wages for a working man). Burgess recalled, 'I told him I did not want to know anything about it'. When talking about a crime known as 'the Cosy Corner Murder', Chesney remarked, 'I shall hang one of these days for murder'.[11] He added 'I shall probably murder my wife and mother-in-law. I hate them both'.[12]

Pickersgill left gaol on 19 December, Chesney on the 24th and Boyd on the 27th. Chesney met Boyd at the prison gates on his release. They went to 22 Montpelier Road and met Mrs Chesney there, who was not impressed and did not want an ex-convict dining at her house, even threatening to call the police. They left after breakfasting there, however. Chesney offered to help Boyd by finding him a job as a stage hand at a theatre. He then offered him £100 if he would go through a marriage ceremony with Sonia in order that she could claim British nationality, but he said no.[13]

The two met up several times in the next few weeks, when Chesney persisted in making offers to Boyd, who continually turned them down. On one occasion they met at 22 Nevern Place, Earl's Court and he was given the alternative of using a car or a gun to kill Mrs Chesney. Boyd replied, 'I still treated it as a joke and I told him I would not have anything to do with it'. Pickersgill remained in contact with Chesney and met him and Sonia in a café in January 1952. He met Chesney alone on the following day. Pickersgill recalled, 'He asked me if I wanted to make some money and I said that would depend on what it was'. Chesney said, 'it would be worth £2,000 to him for somebody to do his wife in' and money from the trust fund would cover the bill. Pickersgill recalled, 'I said there was nothing doing but he said think it over and meet me in the café tomorrow'.[14]

Pickersgill met up with Boyd. Boyd said that Pickergill told him that Chesney had given him £15-20 and a gun to be used to shoot Mrs Chesney. He was then told to go to Paris and meet a French ex-convict named Shevers. Boyd said, 'He must take you for a fool' and advised

11 TNA, MEPO 2/9542.
12 *Sunday Pictorial*, 21 February 1954.
13 Ibid.
14 Ibid.

Pickersgill to throw the gun into the Thames. Pickersgill met Chesney on the following day and asked for expenses. He was given £12. Pickersgill recalled, 'He said I could do it any way I wanted to, he just said I could run her down with a car or something like that'. Nothing happened, but when Boyd met Chesney at Holborn Tube station in late February he told him (again) that he was no longer interested.[15]

He told Boyd that he would ensure his financial future for him. But Boyd was not interested and so walked away. He did, apparently, consider informing the police, but thought that with his record, they would not believe him. He recalled that Chesney was known as 'Crasher Chesney'.[16]

When Chesney had been released from Wandsworth Prison on Christmas Eve, 1951, he had also telephoned Sonia, who was in Duren. They were together again in January 1952. He had briefly asked her to forget him, stating 'I am no use to you, darling'. Such a mood did not last long. Briefly they lived together, but, as always, Chesney was unable to give up his old ways for long. In May 1952 the couple were stopped on the Belgian border. Police found illicit coffee in the car and he was eventually incarcerated in a Belgian prison for seven weeks. Sonia, visiting him in prison, was unhappy and asked, 'Why do you do this? What can I do to stop you?' To this he replied, 'But what can I do to earn money for you?' He smiled. There were to be more mysterious trips made by Chesney and more stoppages by customs men.[17]

It is unclear if this spell in prison had dampened Chesney's criminal ardour. A shopkeeper in Dover recalled him entering his shop:

> *Mr Chesney was a flashily dressed individual, a real wide boy and said that he had just come out of prison. He seemed quite proud that he had done time for smuggling – I believe in smuggling money in and out of the country in cocoa tins. He also said he was engaged in arms smuggling and had also been caught carrying coffee across the border from Belgium to Germany. Chesney said he was going to carry on smuggling as he was not going to work.*

Yet Solomon claimed, 'When he came out he persuaded me he had abandoned the role of romantic swashbuckler. He changed his name officially from Chesney to Milner at that time to mark the change in

---

15 *Sunday Pictorial*, 21 February 1954.
16 *News of the World*, 14 February 1954.
17 *News of the World*, 28 February 1954.

his career'.[18]

Chesney had retained ownership of the *Gladys May* until 1949. The boat was then destroyed as it is no longer listed as being owned. It seems he was without a boat for some time. In 1952 he owned the *Antonina*, bought from a Mr W.A.L. White of Kensington. It was a wooden boat, with two oil engines and was twin screw. It was bigger than his old boat, weighing 153 tonnes, measuring 108.4 feet by 17.8 feet and had a draught of 9.5, so was larger than the *Gladys May*. It was more modern, too, having been built in 1940 in Lowestoft by Brooke Marine Co. Ltd and was registered at the Port of London. He retained it in the following year but it seems to have ceased to exist by 1954.[19]

He wrote to his wife again, date unknown, but probably early 1952:

> *Dear Vera,*
>
> *In the past we have had our quarrels, but I realise how good you have been to me and I should like to do some little thing to repay your kindnesses. It can't be too much fun for you leading the life you do at the moment, so what I suggest is that you come over here and join me for a fortnight. I have lots of friends, any of whom could put both of us up, and we could see some of the Rhineland. We might even make some money playing your system at the casino.*
>
> *I know Mama will probably advise against this and say you will have to pay for the holiday and settle my debts as well, but I have enough money for both of us and I should like to see you over here. Please let me know if you can make the trip and I shall get everything ready.*
>
> *Love,*
> *Don.*[20]

Chesney was looking for money wherever he could find it and had no scruples in his hunt. On 24 April 1952, Mrs Menzies' sister-in-law, Mrs Jane Bonar, complained that she had lent him £12 but had not been repaid. On 9 May of that year she complained further:

> *Don is a rotter and he has got money out of me trying to get him straight. That £100 in notes what was taken from him. I gave £100 in notes to him, thinking he was honourable then. I gave him a £50 cheque...keep away from him he has bled me alright.*[21]

18 *Daily Mail*, 17 and 18 February 1954.
19 *Lloyd's Register of Yachts, 1947-1953*.
20 Tullett, *Portrait of a Bad Man* (1956), p.163.
21 McLeave, *Chesney*, pp.116-17.

Mrs Bonar, who resided at Chester Lodge on Filsham Road, St. Leonard's, had not long to live and the following episode casts a poor light on the characters of Chesney's wife and mother-in-law. She is reputed to have run a nursing home in the nearby Brandsome Road, but the directories do not list the same. Although her sister and niece occasionally visited her, these visits appear to have ceased by 1953. This was despite Mrs Bonar becoming ill and asking a friend to write to them to request they see her. They did not do so. On 18 March 1953, Mrs Bonar died at St. Helen's Hospital, Hastings. When Mrs Menzies and Mrs Chesney visited her house, they found it full of people. The former became angry, 'How dare you not inform me of my sister's death?' She was then reminded that she had not troubled to respond to the imploring letters. Later the two of them searched the house for a will. It is unknown whether they found it, for the will left £352 9s 1d to Jane McMurray and Sarah Creamer. The latter two attended the funeral; it is not certain that Mrs Menzies and her daughter did so. Mrs Menzies' conduct there contrasts with the view of her described by a neighbour in 1954, 'She was a woman who did very much good for this borough – a really good woman', though what this was is unstated; possibly work associated with Ealing Priory is meant.[22]

Oddly enough, Chesney, calling himself Milner, opened negotiations in August of this year to rent his mother-in-law's late sister's house to run it as a nursing home. The deal fell through because his three references were found to be unsatisfactory.[23]

He had not given up on the idea of finding an assassin. In late 1952 Chesney was lodging at various addresses in Earl's Court (having been thrown out of one for being unable to pay the bill). He made the acquaintance of Joseph Greech, described as a 'dealer' in a pub, The Cumberland Hotel. Did Greech want £2,000? If so, he could earn it by driving at Mrs Chesney to kill her, and, preferably, her mother, too, for the death of the latter would result in insurance payments to Chesney. Greech assumed Chesney was jesting, 'In any case I knew he had no money'. Greech knew that Chesney bought and sold machine guns, exported cars and smuggled other goods. He thought that Chesney had pimped Sonia near to the pub. Chesney never alluded to his offer

---

22 *Hastings and St. Leonards Observer*, 28 March 1953, 20 February 1954; *Manchester Guardian*, 12 February 1954; ancestry.co.uk

23 Ibid.

again.²⁴

Chesney was in prison again in the autumn of 1952, this time at Verviers in Belgium, having apparently been given three months for smuggling. He shared a cell with Bollen Guillaume and Julian Hoat. He spoke to them about his smuggling career and the fact that he was separated from his wife, whom he claimed was an alcoholic. As with the convicts in English prisons, he told them he was looking for someone whom he could pay to kill his wife by driving at her. He boasted he had been accused of murder but was only given a sentence for swindling, and would not expand on the former offence. He gave Hoat his address and asked him to stay in touch. Neither man wished to assist him.²⁵

Whilst in gaol, Chesney wrote to his wife:

> *Dear Vera,*
>
> *Your refusal over all these years to divorce me until now, despite your promise made many years ago that you would, if I ever asked you, has caused us both a lot of suffering. It has condemned me to a life in prison while you too, through me I admit, have suffered a great deal through the loss of 'Henrietta' [her car]. I took her, I admit, in a fit of spleen after Sonia, who had come back to London, went back, not so much as for the material benefits she would bring.*
>
> *As for the carpets, they were mine anyway, and as you were not using them, I am, in the room I have in Germany. The only way I could see to get the money for the divorce, if am forced, was in recognised smuggling.*
>
> *I had saved £150 and sold the car when I was recognised in Belgium, after having been expelled in 1949, when caught with a lot of coffee. All my money, some of Sonia's, and the car, are gone. I have been in prison now for a couple of months and I don't know how much longer I have, but I would think it would be a good thing, when I am released, to get together and talk things over. I am now in a good way to being a bigger rotter than I normally was, unless I start a new life.*
>
> *I did not know about your letter, which you took so long in writing, until Sonia visited me the other day, and I must regretfully agree with all you wrote.*
>
> *Dear Vera, can you still believe that I am still fond of you and do not*

24 TNA, MEPO 2/9542.
25 Ibid.

want to part enemies. A divorce, yes, but can't we remain friends? Believe me, this existence of mine during the last few years has been Hell, even though I have deserved it.

Despite everything that has passed, I hope, and believe, that we can come to some arrangement whereby you will not be the loser. I hope so, and please try to remember it and do still remain my friend. I have no others, no one.

And all our years together do mean something. Please, please, do not be too hard on me.

Yours, Don.

P.S. Please write to me; but if you do, do it in the name of John Milner, in which I have been convicted.[26]

Another reason for the thefts was to ascertain if he was able to enter 22 Montpelier Road at night. This was probably not just for financial gain but to see whether such a feat was possible and that it could go undetected. It was.[27]

Chesney and Sonia made occasional visits to England in 1953. In January they met in Dover and then stayed together at 22 Nevern Street, Earl's Court (they stayed for three weeks but had to leave after only being able to pay two weeks' rent). Chesney went to meet Stephen Clarke, a solicitor in Hastings to discuss divorce again. Mrs Chesney had discussed the matter again, inconclusively, but Clarke was positive that the proceedings might begin. It was all a question of money, but as Chesney had none (he had to sell a gold wristlet at some stage in this period) it was stalemate yet again.[28]

Chesney needed another solution. He took a step which did not commit him to anything, but opened up possibilities for the future. In April 1953 Chesney reacquainted himself with Leslie Bernard Chown (1903-1988) a Chelsea photographer who he had been introduced to in the previous year (possibly by Ted Jackson, another photographer in Chelsea who later recalled Chesney telling him he would pay a man £100 to marry Sonia to give her a British passport). Chown had a criminal record and the police later thought, 'he knows more than he has said'. Two months later, on 27 June (Chesney was then living at 17 Earl's Court Square, part of the White House Hotel of numbers 15-19)

---

26 Phillips, *Murderer's Moon*, pp.230-1.
27 LMA, COR/MW/1954/184/01/163.
28 TNA, MEPO 2/9542.

Chown was surprised to receive in the post a passport in his name at his address on 124 Cheyne Walk. His passport had expired in 1944 and he had not renewed it since. The photograph in it was that of Chesney wearing horn rimmed glasses. He was shocked and confronted Chesney about it shortly afterwards, 'What the hell do you mean by this?' Chesney replied that 'My own passport is full of visas. I am getting too known – another passport would be useful'. One Dr Thorold M. Kellough (1895-1957) of 21 Holland Park had countersigned the two photographs which Chesney had sent together with a birth certificate and the fee of £1 10s 6d. Chown agreed to compound a felony, helped by Chesney agreeing to give him £25. Only £10 ever changed hands. Chown admitted, 'He had such an overbearing personality'. This new passport was used at least fourteen times to cross in and out of West Germany. Chesney now had four passports with this one (two in the name of Milner and one in the name of Chesney).[29]

Mrs Chown also met Chesney and later gave her impressions of him:

> He was very gay, a most entertaining personality. He spoke of women and drink and fun and of people he knew who were smugglers.
>
> He was a rolling stone himself and sometimes had plenty of money and sometimes almost none. The last time I saw him he was having to rely on money he won at bridge and at a card club he attended in Earl's Court (he also played cards at a bridge club in Ealing).
>
> Ours was a drifting association. He would drop in perhaps once or twice a year, then go on his way again.
>
> He sometimes used our house as an accommodation address and we would keep letters here for weeks, not knowing where to forward them.
>
> He looked what he was – the man of action, six feet tall he once weighed 22 stones, although he has now slimmed down to 16.
>
> He has a big nose – a real Cyrano de Bergerac nose. It fitted the style of the man (Maling thought it was slightly hooked, 'looks Jewish').[30]

Another contemporary assessment is as follows:

> He did not chuckle, but his laughter boomed out like a maroon. He was the modern version of a pirate Robin Hood. I always expected

---

[29] TNA, MEPO 2/9542; LMA, COR/MW/1954/184/01/163; *Sunday Despatch*, 21 February 1954.

[30] *Daily Mail*, 16 February 1954; LMA, COR/MW/1954/184/01/163.

him to greet me with something like "Avast, you scum".[31]

Chesney is not known to have had any political, intellectual or cultural interests. Nor did he drink much (many murderers are very abstemious). Sonia claimed he loved animals and that children loved him, and that he could be generous with gifts of furs and jewellery (he had been likewise with Gerda, too). He smoked cigars incessantly, had an enormous appetite for food and enjoyed playing bridge. He was also superstitious and had a white ivory charm in the shape of a pig. This was the symbol of St. Anthony (patron saint of things which are lost) and was his sole claim to any religious sentiment, except for occasional visits to church.[32]

Yet he was not a happy man. On 10 May he wrote a rather self pitying letter to his wife:

> *This life is slowly destroying my soul. There seems to be nothing I can do to earn money except by landing myself in prison in the process…I wish to God we could arrive at some understanding about the divorce and the money. We might both be able to make a fresh start.*[33]

Chesney was to spend one last spell in prison. He was arrested in the township of Vaals in south east Belgium on the 30 May 1953. Customs officers located the hiding place in his car for smuggled goods. On 2 June he was sentenced to a month in prison at Maestricht but served less than his given sentence.[34]

Once he was released he returned to England. Chesney decided to make out his will with his solicitors in St. Leonards on Sea. It provides insights into his feelings for both Sonia and his wife (and the lack of any feeing for Gerda). Written on 26 June it read:

> *This is the LAST Will of me JOHN DONALD MILNER formerly John Merrett – Chesney of 17 Earl's Court Square, London SW5.*
>
> 1. *I HEREBY REVOKE all wills and testamentary dispositions hithertofore made by me.*
> 2. *Subject to the payment of my debts funerals and testamentary expenses I GIVE all my property whatsoever and wheresoever*

---

31 *Daily Telegraph*, 17 February 1954.
32 TNA, MEPO 2/9542; *Sunday Despatch*, 21 February 1954.
33 McLeave, *Chesney*, p.122-3.
34 TNA, MEPO 2/9542.

to my friend Miss Sonja Sophie Winnikes in recognition of her many kindnesses to me extending over several years. AND I APPOINT her to be the sole executrix of this my will AND I DECLARE that I have not made any provision for my wife Isobel Veronica Chesney having regard to the treatment which I have received from her during our married life.[35]

Chesney was also involved in an import-export business, the Anglo-German Export Company. Eugene de Braic claimed that he financed Chesney in this. It has been claimed that this was merely a front for his criminal enterprises, in giving him an excuse to travel and to carry goods across frontiers. However, Solomon thought not. 'I can't believe his import-export business in Duren was merely a cloak for a different type of smuggling. I know he was exporting electric motors, handled general merchandise, agricultural equipment and Spanish mercury... he was always very short [of money].' Braic claimed Chesney obtained scrap and precious metals for him on the Ruhr for sale to Japanese and American clients.[36]

He was involved with others. He was a friend of one Souren, a Dutch businessman specialising in coffee roasting and dealt with a Mr Reissing, a manufacturer of cardboard in Buxtehude. These may have been criminal. The police believed he was associated with the 49-year-old Heinrich Mossmann, who was missing from Cologne on 15 October 1953. On 10 December his corpse was found in the Rhine. Mayer Cabot, also aged 49, was the chief suspect and was in police custody from November. At this time, Chesney lived in Eppendorfer Weg, Hamburg. Chesney's involvement in this matter was never cleared up.[37]

Yet he was also suffering from depression. In October 1953 Sonia claimed that she found him unconscious. He had swallowed an overdose of sleeping pills at her flat in Duren. He was taken to the local hospital and after some hours the doctors were able to save his life. She claimed that he had 'secret troubles'.[38]

In December 1953, Chesney wrote his last letter to his wife.

---

35 Will of John Donald Milner/Merrett.
36 *Daily Mail*, 18 February 1954; TNA, MEPO 2/9542.
37 TNA, MEPO 2/9542.
38 *Daily Mail*, 19 February 1954.

51 Josef Strasse
Duren, Germany
Monday

Dear Vera,

After seeing the picture before I left I couldn't help wishing on the crossing over. Once I left England the weather improved…I felt so homesick for Gladys especially as just as we came into the Hook a wizard 60-ft. ketch steamed up and down the canal under power. I wonder if those days will ever return.

Unfortunately, although I should like to follow Gregory Peck's way of life, there doesn't seem much opportunity of this, unless I revert to smuggling, and I really don't see much future in that – for me at any rate.

Sonia was not in the least surprised to see me when I knocked at the door at 2 a.m. She said that she was expecting me back and had a feeling that I should come, but a day late.

Despite what you thought, the money for the car was immediately forthcoming, although she did natter a bit and swear that it is for the last time. She does not, however, want me to come back to England straight away, and won't pay my fare, so I shall have to try and earn it. As I told you, there is no future in the contraband racket.

However, if I get a favourable answer to the letters I have written I shall try to persuade her out of it – but don't expect me back as soon as I said.

I'm still waiting for my permit to re-enter Belgium. I hope to get it on Tuesday or Wednesday, so I should get the car back the day after.

I don't think we've got anything more to discuss about the divorce. I know where I stand, if you don't change your mind, and I hope we shall be able to get cracking soon. It will be best for both of us I feel, anyway.

I was really touched and awfully grateful for the way you trusted me when I was at home last, especially after the way I have behaved to you. You know you are always still the only friend I have – even though I don't deserve it.

I'll let you know as soon as I can recover the car. I will, in any case, be glad to hear from you. I hope Bill is recovering from his flu and that you haven't managed to catch it.

Yours, Don.[39]

---

[39] Phillips, *Murderer's Moon*, pp.179-81.

Matters with Sonia were not wholly rosy either. She had her complaints, 'Chesney was not sure I would always remain with him. He was very jealous'. Chesney had to live with Sonia's parents and was legitimately employed in the textile industry in Duren. He did not get on well with her parents, though he occasionally helped out in their shop behind the counter. 'My father did not consider Chesney either likeable or pleasant. He did not like the fact that I associated with Chesney.'[40]

Despite all this, they enjoyed a happy Christmas in 1953, with her family and friends. The two went to a Catholic mass. They also spent time in Bad Neuenhar, gambling. Chesney rarely won and on this occasion lost about 300-600 marks, about 100 per day. Sonia had to bail him out and gave him 579 marks. In the first days of the New Year, Chesney declared he must return to England. He did so, leaving her with a red rose and a card full of endearments. Soon afterwards he rang her from Holland, claiming he had forgotten his cheque book, so returned for eight days. He then left again, again leaving her flowers and a message, 'These blossoms will die but my love will never die'. With his removal came a bombshell. A friend told Sonia that Chesney had been spending time with another young woman in Duren (probably Christa Romm, a slightly-built brunette who was also a 21-year-old kitchen maid). Sonia was shocked, 'To me this was the end of all my dreams'. He also stole 500 marks from her bank account, presumably by employing his old skills of forgery to good effect. On 7 January her bank account had stood at 2,000 marks; it was 1,500 on the 19th and back to 2,000 nine days later. She wrote an angry letter to him at his Earl's Court address. Chesney rang to apologise, blaming a 'sudden impulse' and that the girl 'meant nothing to him'. Sonia claimed 'I said I could never forgive him and never would'. Chesney wrote another begging letter.[41]

Their relationship had had its share of crises. As Sonia stated, 'Again and again he assured me that as soon as he got a divorce he would marry me. When we quarrelled it was usually because I asked him how long it would be before our marriage could take place...Our quarrels never lasted very long. He was a wonderful lover and he could charm away my doubts when he used to say, "Don't worry, Sonia. One day we will be married and you will be Mrs Chesney". All the same things did

---

40 TNA, MEPO 2/9542.
41 *News of the World*, 28 February 1954; TNA, MEPO 2/9542; LMA, COR/MW/184/163.

not seem to work out the way we wanted and we had many quarrels. Yet we were always reconciled'. He had also talked about committing suicide and had once tried to do so.[42]

Chesney was accustomed to leaving a trail of debts in his wake. The Hotel Royal at Cologne claimed he owed them 202 marks. Dr Jan Daems of Ostend claimed he had treated him but Chesney absconded prior to payment. Mr A. Prange of Hamburg sold an Opel car to Chesney for 4,000 marks, though Chesney claimed it was a gift from Gerda's father. No payment was ever made.[43]

Meanwhile, in January 1954 Mrs Menzies asked the council to lend her money in order to buy the house. Her daughter was interviewed on 15 January and was told that her mother could not be granted a loan due to her age, but was told that they might do so if her husband could be joint guarantor. She said that that would not be possible, but said she would discuss it with her mother. Nothing transpired of this.[44]

Chesney had failed to persuade anyone to kill his wife. But he still wanted the money he had settled on her. His smuggling ventures seem to have come to an end, partly because Churchill's Conservative government of 1951-1955 was abolishing rationing, reducing purchase tax, lowering import duties and reducing the number of restrictions imposed by their predecessors and so removing at a stroke the necessity for black markets to exist. There were more luxury goods legitimately sold in the shops. The number of revenue patrol boats was increased after 1949. The economic recovery of West Germany and the customs union of the Benelux countries also conspired against the smuggler.[45]

His employment in Duren was probably too much hard work for limited gain. Lacking scruples (and an assassin), he decided to murder his wife himself. But he needed to make sure he would not be identified as her killer, despite having a strong motive to kill her. He needed to make preparations first, but at least had a passport in another man's name.

He was to have another brush with the law before his trip to England. On 13 January 1954 customs officers made a provisional arrest of him in Aachen on suspicion of smuggling. However, presumably nothing

---

42 *News of the World*, 21 February 1954.
43 TNA, MEPO 2/9542.
44 Ibid.
45 Phillipson, *Smuggling*, pp.130, 136; Williams, *Contraband Cargoes*, p.273.

could be proved for he was released after questioning. He took solace in Christa's arms in a house in Aachen and also a hotel in Bonn.[46]

Chesney visited England again on 19 January 1954 and stayed at the hotel at 17 Earl's Court Square, arriving by car. Three days later he was at Jackson's house, which he was using as a poste restante address, receiving daily letters from both Sonia and Christa. Chesney told Jackson that his wife had withdrawn her divorce offer, 'I hate her. How can I get rid of her?' Did he know anyone who could cause her to be 'bumped off...by accident'. On the 23rd he tried to see his wife at number 22 but failed. On the following day he visited 40 Mount Park Road and talked to Miss McNeish. Later Chesney contacted his wife and asked for items at her house which he said were his; including ammunition. She told him there were none. Miss McNeish recalled that Chesney:

> told me on the 24th January 1954, that he had finished with Sonia and had returned to this country and was going to settle down. He also mentioned that he had a new girlfriend and that he was going into partnership with a friend in the Chelsea area, and they were going to open up a photographic business and specialise in wedding photographs.

She was unimpressed, 'Each time I have seen him or heard about him he was just going to commence some new venture, but nothing was seen to emanate'. He also jested to her that he had 100 tablets on him so that he could end his life if need be and was vitriolic against Mrs Menzies, stating, 'she should have been dead years ago'. On the same day he visited his adopted son and his family.[47]

Eventually he did visit number 22. Miss Thorpe later recalled that towards the end of January, she was working in the kitchen one Saturday morning and at about 11, opened the front door to a man she had never seen before. He was aged about 47, was five feet eleven inches high, with broad build, moustached, wearing an overcoat and smoking a pipe. He asked for 'Mrs Chesney' and she replied that 'She is in bed, sir'. The caller evidently needed additional conformation for he then asked, 'Isn't she up yet?' Miss Thorpe replied, 'No, she's ill.' The man walked past her and went upstairs. Mrs Menzies later appeared and told the servant 'That is Mr Chesney'.[48]

46 TNA, MEPO 2/9542.
47 TNA, MEPO 2/9542; *Sunday Despatch*, 21 February 1954.
48 TNA, MEPO 2/9542.

The Chesneys then had dinner in her room. That was the only time Miss Thorpe saw Chesney but she was told more about him by his wife only two or three days later. She told her that he was a rotter, that he had stolen two carpets from the house one night time in the past and had also taken her motor car. When asked why she did not divorce him, she said that it cost too much, and was not worth it because she had no wish to remarry.[49]

Chesney also took time to meet others in London. One was Chown, on about 20 January. He told Chown about stealing money from Sonia, and that he had found another mistress, Christa Romm (he was 'quite mad about her' and wrote from England to ask her to join him there). He told him he wanted to sell a black 1933 Packard car. Initially he tried to sell it to Harold Massey, a dealer in Ealing who he had previously done business with, and made his need for money come across all too clearly claiming he wanted £60. It was refused. So he had it auctioned at Paddington on 2 February. There it was sold to a Cliff Davis of Goldhawk Road, Hammersmith, for £45.[50]

At this time he corresponded with Christa Romm, writing:

> *Someone has told Sonia about us. She has written so in a letter...I have replied that she should pay no attention to it. But kid, you must not say much to [indecipherable name] and Maria. I don't trust them. I don't want anything to prevent you coming to me...I am happy to hear that at least someone loves me although I am not good enough for you. Yours, Ches.*[51]

Later that day he turned up again at Chown's, this time when Chown was at 43 Oakley Street. He told him that the car had sold for £30. Chown suggested that Chesney apologise to Sonia and make up with her. Chesney had been using Chown's address as a post restante address and received mail from both Sonia and Christa (addressed from the former 'Mein Leiber Ches'). The two men talked about a joint photographic business. But other conversation was odd and Chesney became increasingly bombastic. Chown recalled, 'Chesney was a wild sort of talker and sometimes spoke of holding up a bank in Germany and shooting the cashiers, he said it was his bank. I thought it sheer nonsense'. Other talk was on a similar theme, 'He was always talking

---

49 TNA, MEPO 2/9542.
50 TNA, MEPO 2/9542; *Daily Mail*, 13 February 1954.
51 *Sunday Pictorial*, 21 February 1954.

of crime like a maniac schoolboy' and said that his wife was 'worth more dead than alive'. Prophetically, 'He also said that he had quite made up his mind never to go back to prison, as he could not stand the mental strain of it'. He talked to a Mrs Sherwood in Chelsea and she recalled him as being depressed and suicidal. 'I knew Chesney was broke. He nearly always was. I never knew him to be plush.'[52]

Chesney was a noticeable figure in Ealing. The local newspaper stated:

> *Chesney, with his distinctive figure, was known in Ealing. He always wore an ear-ring in his right ear and was usually accompanied by a boxer dog. People who knew him by sight say that he spoke but little. He had not been seen during the past few months.*

It was later said that he wore very colourful shirts, green cord trousers, and old duffel coat and gold bangles on his arms.

An Ealing taxi driver recalled:

> *I always found him quiet and he was not a free tipper. But he did look rather like the wild man from Borneo with his huge build black beard and duffel coat thrown over his shoulders. Mostly I took him to the house rented by his adopted daughter.*

Mrs Trull was certainly fond of him, referring to him as 'Daddy Don', who was 'full of the joy of living'. She also said, 'My father was very good to me when he came home'.[53] Yet it is highly likely that before leaving Ealing he made sure that he was able to enter number 22 without attracting the attention of its residents.

On 2 February he made a last visit to Jackson. He told him that he was returning to Sonia in Germany and was quite cynical as to his motive, which was 'to get more money out of her'. He also talked about Christa, 'She will come over just the same', despite her presumed earlier refusal. Jackson thought 'Both girls seemed to be desperately in love with him'. Unless this is all mere bragging on Chesney's part it does reveal that this middle-aged man had great charm to have secured the affections of two far younger women.[54]

Chesney returned from England on 4 February. Two days previously he had pawned a watch to buy a lucky charm to bolster his courage.

---

52 TNA, MEPO 2/9542.
53 *Middlesex County Times*, 20 February 1954; *Daily Telegraph*, 17 February 1954; *Sun Herald*, 21 February 1954; TNA, MEPO 2/9542.
54 *Sunday Despatch*, 21 February 1954.

Peter Timberlake, an immigration officer at Harwich, recalled Chesney making himself as noticeable as possible. This included accidentally knocking over a WPC near to the passport desk and remarking, 'I must not knock you police women about'. Timberlake knew he was a smuggler and had him searched by Guy Lazenby, a customs officer. They found an automatic pistol on him, but as he had a firearms certificate to show them this was not a problem for him. He was asked how much currency he was taking out of the country and he replied, only £5 'worse luck'. Chesney complained about such treatment, alleging it was only because he was on the 'Customs Blacklist' and had already 'done time'. Using a passport in the name of Milner, he eventually took the MV Koningin Emma, a day boat, to the Hook of Holland.[55]

Chesney returned to Duren. He told Sonia that he had met his wife and though drunk, she had been kindly towards him. Yet the two rowed at the Dom Hotel and Sonia was frightened when he began to wave his gun about in their room, so fled. They were soon reconciled, however. He and Sonia spent 6-9 February in the Frifo hotel, 5-7 Lange Leidsedwarsstraat, Amsterdam, under the name of Milner. On the morning after their arrival they had breakfast in bed and had dinner in their room, too, at 5.30pm that day. They ate chicken soup and bami. Jacoba van Westerloo was the maid who brought the latter to their room. She remembered seeing Sonia in bed and asked her, 'Are you ill?' Sonia asked Chesney, 'What is ill?' and he replied 'sick'. Sonia then told the maid, 'Yes I am'. It was not only Sonia who was unwell for on the following day when the two ate in the restaurant, Jacoba remembered 'I noticed that Milner looked very "down" and Winnikes was trying to cheer him up'. These were turbulent times, with a great deal of quarrelling over the money he had stolen from her and his affair with Fraulein Romm. On the 8th they went for an evening stroll. He then told her that he had some work to do in England. The two went to the railway station so she could catch the train at 6am on 9 February. That afternoon Chesney telegrammed her to say 'Fog impossible. Yet another day. I love you'.[56]

On 7 February, Williams, now living in Hendon since 1953, and running a shop, had another evening out with Mrs Chesney. They saw

---

55 TNA, MEPO 2/9542.
56 *News of the World*, 21 February 1954; *Manchester Guardian*, 20 February 1954; LMA, COR/MW/1954/181/163.

a film at the Hendon Gaumont Cinema. He recalled, 'She was quite normal and happy; she was her usual self'. They last saw one another at five to ten that night.[57]

Chesney had no sooner returned to the Continent than he wanted to return to England. At half past three on the afternoon of 6 February he had bought a ticket at the KLM passenger desk at Amsterdam to travel by aeroplane to London on 8th February and to return on the following day at eight in the morning. Yet on the day of travel he changed his ticket to travel on the 9th and to return the next day; then he changed his tickets for the final time; to travel on the 10th and return on the 11th. Chesney was nervous (and no wonder; he was about to undertake a dangerous venture); on the morning of his travel, he was seen to be 'very nervously walking up and down the hotel'. Whilst breakfasting at 11.15 and reading a newspaper, he kept looking through the window at the street, before leaving at half past. He took the KLM 137 flight on the 10th and arrived at London airport at 7pm. All this was in the name of Chown, of course.[58]

The plan seems to have been for Chesney to enter Britain as Chown, go to 22 Montpelier Road and secretly enter by the back without anyone being aware of it. He would then kill his wife whilst making it look accidental (he was well aware of her drinking), then leave the country and then claim his settlement money. There might be suspicion against him as the gainer by his wife's 'accidental' death but there would be no evidence to link him to it and in any case he was last in the country several days previously. A solid alibi. The death of his mother in 1926 had not been planned yet he profited; this time murder would be planned and he would escape scot fee without even a trial. It was a cold-blooded and ruthless scheme, but typical of the man.

Meanwhile, the inhabitants of 22 Montpelier Road had no indication about their impending fate. On Tuesday, 10 February, at about ten in the morning the telephone rang. Mrs Menzies and her daughter spent about half an hour answering it. It was not known what the conversation concerned nor who rung. Clark recalled Mrs Menzies dusting his room and reminiscing about her time with her daughter and her son-in-law sailing in the Mediterranean on the Gladys May. She remarked, 'But for Vera, he'd be dead. I wonder how he'll show her

57 TNA, MEPO 2/9452.
58 Ibid.

gratitude'. Although Clark did not ask what this meant, presumably this was a reference to an early attempt of suicide by Chesney. Later that day Mrs Chesney was seen by Miss Thorpe making tea at about a quarter to four, and afterwards she visited Miss McNeish at number 40. She left in the early evening to buy a newspaper and then to visit the Palladium Cinema on Ealing Broadway. Mrs Menzies made tea for Mrs Trull. She had come round and had been given £1 5s towards her exam fees at Acton College. Miss McNeish was there, too, and talked about moving her nursing home to the nearby 65 Castlebar Road. Mrs Trull left at 8.15pm. Miss Thorpe went to bed at ten and heard Mrs Chesney (who had returned after the film at 9.30pm) saying goodnight to someone upstairs, then coughing. The back door was bolted at 10 pm and so was the front door. These precautions had been taken since Chesney stole his wife's car in 1951.[59]

On arrival at Heathrow Airport, Miss Ann Slattery, a receptionist, handed Chesney a health form, because of a smallpox outbreak in Holland. He was soon on the coach to London. A fellow passenger recalled 'He was very big built man with a large nose and thick horn rimmed glasses'. He asked to be let off the coach en route to its one stopping point at Sloane Street in south Kensington. This was refused. When the coach arrived, it is probable that Chesney took a District Line train, possibly from South Kensington or Sloane Square tube station westwards to the end of the line at Ealing Broadway and then walked the fifteen minutes north from there to Montpelier Road. He probably crossed Haven Green and walked up Mount Park Road, passing St. Andrew's Presbyterian church and then St. Peter's. However, this route would have taken him past Mrs McNeish's house and since he had to be unrecognised he may have taken a longer route, perhaps via Castlebar Road and then swinging eastwards and walking close to the still not rebuilt St. Benedict's Priory.[60]

All he needed to do now was to enter the house once the inhabitants were all asleep, kill his wife whilst making it appear to have been an accident and then return the way he had come. No one of his name had entered the country and no one would investigate what would appear to have been an accidental death. He could then claim the settlement money and marry whom he pleased. He was on the brink of success.

59 TNA, MEPO 2/9542; *Illustrated...*, 24 April 1954.
60 Ibid.

10
Denouement, 1954-1955

There were no living witnesses to what happened next at the house, but the following report by Superintendent Daws seems plausible:

> *It appears evident that Chesney, having travelled from Amsterdam as Chown, entered the premises at 22 Montpelier Road by way of the French windows on the ground floor back room. He ascended to his wife's bedroom, where she was under the influence of drink, and forcibly took her to the bathroom (evidenced by the post mortem bruises on the elbows) where he drowned her. He then put soap on her hair intending to stage a death by accident whilst she was under the influence of drink.*
>
> *Having murdered his wife, Chesney was descending the stairs when he was confronted in the hall by Mrs Menzies, who, as we know, had been attending various patients. She, of course, knew Chesney and he therefore had no alternative but to kill her. He struck her with his fists (evidenced by the bruises on his right hand and arm and on Mrs Menzies' face) and knocked her to the floor. She got up and ran into the front room where a terrific struggle took place. He found he could not subdue her with blows from the coffee pot – Mrs Menzies' skull was very thick – so having overpowered her on the settee he tied the ligature round her neck and killed her in that way.*
>
> *After committing the murders it was essential that Chesney should gain sufficient time to return to Holland as planned on the 8am plane on 11th February 1954, to establish his alibi he was at the Hotel Frefo between 6th and 12th February. He therefore concealed*

> the body of Mrs Menzies in the back room under the chair covers etc., a room he knew was little used – and then tidied the front room so that no evidence of the terrific struggle was apparent.
>
> When he had done this Chesney went upstairs, tidied his wife's bed (evidenced by the blood smears on the sheets) turned out the light (the clock stopped at 10 minutes past one), went to the bedroom, locked the door, took the key down to the ground floor front room, and left it on the tray. He knew that the old people resident in the house used the bathroom and were sometimes in it for long periods on end, and this would lead to delay in the discovery of his wife's body.
>
> He then left by the back door, having replaced the French windows in their normal position, made his way to London Airport, and left under the alias of Chown on the 8am plane for Amsterdam.[1]

After leaving he probably took the night bus, number 289, from Ealing to London and then another to Heathrow. Not wanting to be recognised he could hardly take a taxi and the trains had stopped running. He then took the KLM Flight 118 which left Heathrow at eight in the morning of 11 February. Because of fog, the aeroplane was re-directed and so did not land at Amsterdam airport but at Dusseldorf, at about 11.35 am. Chesney had lunch at the airport and then arrived back at his hotel in Amsterdam between 2 and 4pm; the hotel proprietor recalled, 'He appeared to be very nervous on his return'. He ate a meal of bami. In the early evening, he sent a telegram to Sonia. He needed to know if she still loved him, a sure indicator that his anxious state of mind demanded reassurance. She said that she did. They met on the following morning in Cologne, but could not go to her home because her father forbade him. So they spent the weekend at Bergisch-Gladbach, 40 miles from Duren. He told her that he did not go to England as planned as he wanted to see her again. She noticed that his right fist was swollen and he told her he 'knocked it on a taxi'.[2]

On the Saturday, Chesney wrote a letter to Jackson, revealing his plans for the future:

> Things are now once again ok with the girlfriend, Sonia, I mean. The other one I let drop (unless you can use her). Sonia has agreed

---

1   TNA, MEPO 2/9542.
2   Ibid; *Aberdeen Evening Express*, 20 February 1954.

to finance our photographic venture and will come over with me in about two days. I hope our arrangement still stands and I thought the payment will probably have to be in instalments. Tell Jill when you see her that things are ok with us again. She told me as well as you that they would be.

He was still confident and optimistic for the future. Sonia recalled, 'We were very happy together and gaily he walked from the station at Cologne towards the Dom Hotel'. On Monday, 15 February they passed a newsstand and saw copies of the previous day's English newspapers on sale. One was the popular tabloid Sunday newspaper, the *News of the World*. This was allegedly Chesney's favourite. He saw that the headline was about an interview with Herbert John Boyd alleging that he had been offered money to kill Mrs Chesney. Sonia recalled, 'He seemed genuinely surprised when he saw that front page last Sunday' and after buying a copy he told her 'I must go back to England at once'. 'He was very excited and nervous,' she recalled.[3]

The *News of the World* front page headline article, headed 'I was offered £1,000 to kill', was the story of Herbert Boyd's being in prison and being offered that sum to kill Mrs Chesney. The article did not state or hint that the man was Chesney. To have done so would have been taking a grave risk with the law by creating prejudice against Chesney prior to a possible trial (*The Daily Mirror* had been heavily fined and its editor gaoled in 1949 for printing a very suggestive article about John George Haigh being a vampire killer and so newspapers were cautious). The only reference to Chesney was at the end of the article, stating he was the husband of the murdered woman and had served in the war as a naval officer, known as Crasher Chesney. Yet to a guilty man this would have seemed proof enough that he was a suspect.[4]

Chesney needed more than emotional support; as ever he needed cash. Sonia agreed to lend him most of her savings, nearly 1,000 marks, about £35 in English money. On 12 February her savings stood at 1,800, 200 less than on 28 January and now they were down to 800 marks. Apparently, 'He begged me to go with him to London, but I decided against the idea. We had a long discussion during which he spoke of our trip to Holland and impressed on me that he could not possibly be suspected because we were in Holland just before the murder was committed'. He certainly seems to have convinced

3   *News of the World*, 28 February 1954; TNA, MEPO 2/9542.
4   *News of the World*, 14 February 1954.

her, for she stated, 'But I cannot and never will believe that he was a murderer. I am sure he loved me and desperately wanted to marry me and give me British nationality but I cannot believe he would have murdered for my sake'.[5] They said their goodbyes at the railway station at three in the afternoon. He had told her that he would take the train to Aachen, then to Ostend and then to Harwich.[6]

But he did not do as he said he would. Returning to England to face the music would have been difficult, so he chose the path of least resistance. Instead he took Kurt Huls' taxi to Cologne (he was an in-law of Sonia).

Later that day, Chesney was outside the Opera House, Cologne, and at about half past three he hailed the taxi belonging to the young Willi Hambach to drive him to the Hotel Am Bok in Bergisch-Gladbach, which was near the town hall. He was heavily laden with various cases, including a lady's handbag, a brief case, a trunk and two travelling bags. All this luggage was deposited in the luggage room of the railway station. Chesney then asked to be taken to the Dutch border via Duren, to collect a 'woman' (Sonia) at eight that night. Meanwhile he went to the Café Reichard to look for her.[7]

That afternoon, a telephone call was put through from Cologne to the offices of Meancer, Idle and Brocketts, solicitors, of 28 Grand Parade, St. Leonards, where Stephen Clarke, solicitor, worked, and by whom Chesney had drawn up his will in the previous year. His call was then transferred to Clarke's home address at Sedlescombe Road South, telling him that he had read in the newspapers about his wife's death, and thought that they suggested that he was responsible. He asked Clarke for advice. The solicitor said that much would depend on how far Chesney was involved, and was told that he was not at all concerned in the affair. Clarke had read the same newspaper article and thought that it implicated him. Chesney countered, 'That is all cock'.[8]

Then Clarke advised him to return to England, but warned him about saying anything to the police without legal representation, because he had had previous convictions. Chesney explained that he was not in England at the time of the murder and that Boyd had swindled him

5 *News of the World*, 21 February 1954; LMA, COR/MW/1954/184/163.
6 *News of the World*, 21 February 1954.
7 TNA, MEPO 2/9542.
8 LMA, COR/MW/1954/184/163.

previously. He asked that Clarke contact the Public Trustee about the settlement funds. Clarke said he would need to be forwarded the proper authority from Chesney to do this. Chesney then said that he would see the police in Clarke's company on Wednesday or Thursday and that he would ring him on Tuesday at the same time to let him know when he would be arriving.[9]

Shortly afterwards, Clarke contacted the Hastings police. He arranged for Inspector Longhurst to visit him at six that evening. He did so and was given a letter for the chief constable of the county, explaining that Chesney would be soon returning to England and under what conditions he would speak to the police. He told Longhurst that Chesney 'has nothing to conceal'.[10]

After speaking to Clarke, Chesney tried ringing Sonia several times but was rebuffed 'Why can't you leave me alone? I don't want to be disturbed'. In search of emotional support, he made another telephone call and Gerda recalled, 'Then one February night, my telephone rang. "Gerda!" It sounded almost as if he was sobbing. "What's wrong, Ches?" He spoke in a low, urgent voice, "Gerda, darling, listen to me. Whatever happens, you must know this…you are the one I love". "Ches, where are you?" I asked. "Come here". "I can't do that". "But I must see you, Ches, I must. Please". There was a silence, then he said, "I'm in the telephone box at the Opera House. I'll wait for you". Gerda rushed to meet Chesney, and was about to cross the road that separated them, but then a police officer appeared and Chesney was gone.[11]

Doubtless even more despondent, at eight Chesney was met by the taxi at the Opera House as arranged and from there they went to the railway station to collect the luggage and then travelled back to Duren, 35 miles away. The first port of call was Mrs Sommer's house (she was Sonia's married sister). Hambach recalled, 'He told me he did not dare show his face at the Winnikes home or even in the vicinity otherwise they would beat him'. Chesney remained in the taxi while Hambach called at the house, to be told by Mrs Sommer that her sister was not there and they should try at her father's house.[12]

Given his relations with her parents, this was not what Chesney wanted to hear, but having no option, they drove there. As before,

9   Ibid.
10 Ibid.
11 *Woman's Sunday Mirror*, 13 October 1957.
12 *News Chronicle*, 19 February 1954; TNA, MEPO 2/9542.

Chesney's nerve was lacking and so he asked Hambach to call at the two storey house. Herr Winnikes had clearly read the newspaper reports which alluded to Chesney and the killings in Ealing, for he asked him if he was a journalist. He said no, but requested that Chesney see his daughter in private. Sonia arrived and asked Hambach to enter the house, but her father would not leave her alone in the room. Hambach, realising that he would not budge, said the matter was of no importance, as he had been told to secure an interview with Sonia alone. He left and took the taxi around the corner because Chesney did not want it parked outside the house.[13]

Chesney learnt that Sonia would not budge from where she was. So he wrote her a letter and asked Hambach to deliver it to her personally. The man went back, but was confronted by her father, so returned to Chesney and handed it back to him. Their mission having become futile, they drove to the café Birkesdorf in Duren. There they drank beer, ate sandwiches and played cards. Chesney had not given up the hope of seeing her. He resolved to knock on her window, hoping that she would then climb out and thus be reunited with him. The two men drove back and he knocked several times, all to no avail. It was now a quarter to twelve.[14]

Chesney had failed to see his beloved. Admitting defeat, he got back into the taxi and asked to be driven to Cologne railway station. He deposited his luggage there at about half past twelve. He paid the driver and told him he would see him again at Duren at noon. Hambach recalled that on the way back Chesney was uncommunicative, 'he seemed very depressed because he had not met Miss Winnikes'. It is quite possible that he was the last person to speak to Chesney or even the last to see him alive. Chesney took a little used path which was not far from a settlement of British employees of the High Commission.[15]

He also wrote two last letters. One was to Clarke. It read:

> *After our telephone conversation of this afternoon, I enclose a letter to the Public Trustee, asking him to transfer the funds from the Chesney Settlement trust, M32111, to your firm. On receipt, please arrange to transfer the total amount, less £3,000, which I would like you to retain for me, to Miss Sonia Winneckes.*

---

13 *News Chronicle*, 19 February 1954; TNA, MEPO 2/9542.
14 Ibid.
15 Ibid.

> With regard to my wife's death I need hardly tell you that I am innocent, but that, with my past record, things will probably be sticky for me. However, I must let the police make their inquiries, and I shall be over this week.
>
> John Milner.[16]

To the Public Trustee, he wrote (on headed note paper of the Anglo-Germanic Export Company of importers and exporters):

> Dear Sir,
>
> As a result of Mrs Chesney's death, the settlement fund is now free, there being no issue of the marriage.
>
> Please release the papers, funds concerned to my solicitors, Messrs Meancer, Idle & Brockett of St. Leonards-on-Sea, Sussex.
>
> John D. Merrett
> Ronald J. Chesney
> John Milner[17]

He wrote another letter to his solicitors:

> 16 February
>
> Dear Clarke,
>
> Since writing to you yesterday, I have given the matter of my future much thought and I realise, that although innocent, I haven't the chance of the proverbial snowball in Hades of getting out of this mess.
>
> I have seen so much of prisons I have no wish to return there even for a day and the prospect of being hanged appeals to me even less.
>
> I assure you that the way I shall have taken to get out of it all may seem cowardly – but it nevertheless does require some courage. I know, too, it will probably be taken to indicate my guilt. This is, however, not the case. I can only hope that the police eventually do find the doer of the deed.
>
> I wish only to make sure that Miss Sonia Winneckes gets everything to which I am heir, and which falls due to me, ie the settlement money, some £10,000 and the carpets, silver and chest of drawers at 22 Montpelier Road, Ealing.
>
> Please get in touch with her when you receive this letter and act for her in her best interests.

16 Tullett, *Portrait of a Bad Man* (1956), p.191.
17 Ibid.

Despite all appearances to the contrary, I am in full possession of all my senses and do what I do after careful consideration.

Whether as a deed of gift while living or as a will when dead, please see that Miss Winneckes receives everything of which I die possessed.

Yours truly
JOHN MILNER[18]

He also wrote a last letter to Sonia:

Darling, my darling,

Here is all the money that is left. Unfortunately, I have got rid of a lot of it, as you will see. But in spite of the fact that you have told me that you love me, you would not come to the telephone or out to see me when I sent the taxi-driver for you.

I wanted to look into your eyes again and hold you close. You know I am not guilty, and how difficult it was for both of us when I read that in the papers.

In view of what lies behind me, and in view of the fact that I didn't see you this evening, I am sending everything. I have spoken to my solicitor and you will get the money, about 20,000 marks.

Forget me and find another. You must be happy. Tonight, at about 11.30pm, I knocked at your window, but I suppose your father locked you in. Just when I wanted to see you once again he wouldn't let me.

When you get this letter I will no longer be alive. I die with your face before my eyes.

Oh, Sonia, my darling, without you I cannot live. I can see you will not come back to me. Your father's influence is too strong.

I ask you once again to forgive me for the pain I have caused you. During the time have known you I have loved only you.

As I die, I love you more than ever. Adieu, my darling, adieu.

Ches.[19]

Chesney clearly believed that he had run out of options. Although he had killed his wife as planned, he had not succeeded in making it appear as an accident because he had had to kill his despised mother-in-law, which had not been part of his plan. This death could not

---

18 Tullett, *Portrait of a Bad Man* (1956), p.194.
19 Phillips, *Murderer's Moon* (1956), pp.233-4.

conceivably appear as being the result of an accident and so it cast serious doubt on whether the other had been. As with most murderers, he was eager to read what newspaper reports of the crime had to say about them (both Neville Heath and John Haigh devoured reports of their own crimes). These convinced him that the police believed he was culpable and would be on his track. He had no wish to serve another prison sentence and still less to be hanged for murder. Nor had he any chance of obtaining the money he desired by the murder. Sonia was unobtainable. He had no one to turn to, no source of solace. He had little money and so no place to run. Yet he did have his colt automatic revolver and that was reliable.

On the morning of 16 February, Kriminal Kommissar Erwin Kunn of the Cologne Police was informed of a discovery made by a retired postman in a stretch of woodland 25 yards from the Military Ring Strasse and 150 yards from Durenerstrasse on the north side of the city towards Ehrenfeld. He went to the scene and later made the following report:

> *There I saw the body of a man since identified as John Donald Milner/Chesney/Merrett. The body was on its back. The right arm was stretched out level with the shoulder. The left arm was lying alongside the torso with the hand about level with the upper thigh. He was dressed in an overcoat of grey/white colour, three buttons of this coat were done up. The lower part of the coat was thrown back on both sides up to the level of the upper thigh. The body lay with the buttocks upon the rear part of the waistcoat.*
>
> *The pistol lay on the right leg of the body and had been fired, but there was no trace of blood on it. A hat was lying a few inches from the left of the body, and the inner part of it showed splashes of blood and parts of the skull driven outwards. On the left near part of the hat was a hole about 1cm in size.*
>
> *Milner/Chesney was wearing grey leather gloves. There was splashes of blood on the left trouser leg from the knees upwards to the level of the outer end of the upper thigh, some of which was as big as a farthing. To the left and right of the buttons of the coat there were splashes of blood which had partly run off. Some of these splashes were about the size of a shilling. There was also blood on the face.*
>
> *In addition to the overcoat Milner/Chesney was wearing a steel blue suit with a peacock serge pattern, and knitted waist coat and shirt with red and white stripes, a red tie and a grey woollen scarf.*

> There were numerous spots of blood on the collar of the shirt and the rear part of the woollen scarf, caused by the blood flowing from the mouth. This was clearly a case of suicide.
>
> Examination of the pistol showed it contained a spent cartridge, but the magazine was empty...in my opinion, death had taken place about seven or eight hours earlier.[20]

On Chesney's person and in his luggage were clothing, but there were other items, too. These included 11 indecent sketches, a cardboard file with papers concerning The Anglo-German Export Company, a copy of the *News of the World* for the 14th, pipes and cigar cases. More sinister were the two white towels, both soiled with blood. The only cash was 10.8 deutschmarks; a far cry from the 600 which Hambach claimed he had seen him with on the previous day. There was also a note,

> Everything I possess belongs to Miss Sonia Winnikes, 51 Josef Strasse, Duren. Signed John Donald Milner.[21]

His corpse was taken to a hospital in Cologne where it was viewed by both Gerda and Sonia, whose visits coincided and they briefly gazed at one another. An attendant recalled the former: 'She seemed very devoted to Chesney, and said she was a close friend of him. She was attractive, quietly spoken and she made a good impression'.[22]

A death certificate was issued by the British Consul General at Dusseldorf, following information given by the German police.[23] He was buried on 22 February in a graveyard near Cologne in a plain deal coffin in a service lacking any religious rites, because no catholic priest would officiate over the grave of a suicide. The funeral car went by a circuitous route to avoid the press. The sole mourner was the faithful Gerda (now studying in Cologne), accompanied by her mother, and who had paid for the coffin and marker (his family did not, unsurprisingly perhaps, claim the body).[24] She later said, 'A few days ago I pawned almost all my valuables to save Chesney from a pauper's grave'. She had 1,000 red carnations on his coffin and had snowdrops and violets, his favourite flowers, apparently, placed inside

20 TNA, MEPO 2/9542.
21 LMA, COR/MW/1954/184/163.
22 *Empire News*, 21 February 1954; *News Chronicle*, 20 February 1954.
23 *The Times*, 27 October 1955.
24 *Aberdeen Evening Express*, 23 February 1954.

the coffin. She was glad that Sonia was not present at the burial.[25] She loved him still, recalling in 1957, 'I heard the soil falling on the coffin. That melancholy sound still chokes in my ears. It reminds me that I still owe one last service to the man I loved. One day I shall ask permission to take his remains from alien soil and leave them in the place he loved perhaps more than anything in the world...more than money, more than women, perhaps even more than me...the sea'.[26] Sonia put daffodils on Chesney's grave.[27]

Not everyone believed that this was a case of suicide. Gerda said, 'He was very fond of living and I do not believe that he has committed suicide. It is quite possible that he has changed so much in character during this period that he might, after all, have committed suicide'. A German convict thought likewise, believing he had been killed by the assassin he had employed to murder his wife and mother-in-law, and reported it to the authorities. Bollen Guillaume, who had once shared a cell with him remarked, 'I cannot believe in the suicide of Chesney because he appeared to me as a man who enjoyed life too much to try and end it by his own hand'.[28] The evidence suggests otherwise. Chesney had made at least two previous suicide attempts and quite clearly suffered from depression when matters were not going his way. He did not want to return to prison. His murder plan had failed in that he was not unsuspected. He had written letters that clearly point to what he was about to do.

The German police informed their British counterparts of developments. On Wednesday, 17 February, Daws and DS Frederick Chadburn, who spoke German, travelled on the night boat to Ostend, arriving in Cologne early on the following day. They interviewed both Sonia (who later went into hiding) and Gerda, as well as spending time with their German counterparts, including being shown Chesney's corpse and clothing at the mortuary of the University forensic laboratory. Dr Lobber severed Chesney's forearms for them to return to England with, for they provided valuable evidence. They inspected the luggage which Chesney had with him shortly before his death. Apart from clothing, there was a return half of a ticket from London to Cologne issued at Liverpool Street Station, luggage

25 *Sunday Pictorial*, 27 February 1954.
26 *Woman's Sunday Mirror*, 13 October 1957.
27 *News of the World*, 28 February 1954.
28 TNA, MEPO 2/9542.

labels of a Dutch shipping line and a card for crossing the German border. There were also two address books, one including the name of Maling and the other the name, address and telephone of Dr Kellough, recommender for his passport. They found his passport on him, in the name of Milner, and his Colt .38 automatic. They returned to England on 20 February.[29]

In the meantime, Dr Lewis Nickolls at the police laboratory had been busy. He had made a number of discoveries. There were bloodstains and hairs on Mrs Menzies' slippers. Two of the hairs belonged to Chesney. His hairs were also found on Mrs Chesney's pink cardigan. Although bloodstains on Chesney's shoes had been wiped off, it was evident that they had been there. Hairs from the dogs at Montpelier Road were found on Chesney's clothing. His trousers had bloodstains which were not his own. Teare examined the severed arms and fingerprinted them. Under his fingernails were woollen fibres which were similar to those of Mrs Chesney's cardigan.[30]

Not all believed Chesney was a murderer. Solomon claimed, 'In all our many talks he never spoke of his wife with hatred. He continued to visit her and her mother and they seemed on good terms'. It was not only old friends who thought thus. There was, in public, a denial that Chesney was responsible for the murders. Certainly the *Middlesex County Times* gave that impression. It stated:

> There was no evidence to connect Chesney with the murders, nor was there anything to show that he was in the country when the crimes were committed. Chesney is known to have been in England at the end of last month but to have left via Harwich on February 4.

The newspaper then summarised his life and gave the best possible viewpoint:

> Whatever else he was, or was not, Chesney was a colourful figure. He moved across life like a bad character in a melodrama. In his time he played many parts – among them forger, war time naval officer, smuggler, poseur.
>
> It has been suggested that he may have been responsible for the Perfect Crime. If so, he still dared not risk an encounter with the police.
>
> He preferred to take the easier way out, admitting in his last note

---

29 *Middlesex County Times*, 20 February 1954, 27 March 1954; TNA, MEPO 2/9542.
30 TNA, MEPO 2/9542.

> to his glamorous German girl-friend, "After all that lies behind me I have no chance".

Whether in fact he did have a chance must now remain a mere matter for conjecture. It would seem that he not only had a chance but a reasonably good one. For the case against him – if any – at the time of his sudden departure from this life could not be considered an overwhelming one – certainly not strong enough to justify the issuing of a warrant for his arrest even if he had remained in this country.

But his own inglorious past frightened him. He would not take the risk of returning to England to "assist the police in their enquiries" into the double murder.

He at least should have known that however evil a man's past life, it must not be disclosed in the English Courts of Justice until that man has been found guilty of yet another crime.

But, conscience makes cowards of us all. Thus he wrote to his German friend, "I am ending everything".[31]

Gerda also had very fond memories of her former lover. In a newspaper interview shortly after, she said:

> Ronald Chesney belonged to me. He loved no other woman as he loved me – certainly not Sonia Winneckes, to whom they are saying he left his money. Chesney would trust no one as he trusted me. Although he was a black marketer, a forger, maybe a murderer, I alone can cherish a memory of the side of him that was clean and good.
>
> If Chesney had come back to me instead of to Sonia when he was in trouble at the end, we would have fled with him to my parents in the Russian zone of Germany. Even if he had murdered his wife and mother-in-law, I would never have allowed anyone to take him from me.
>
> But I had given him up because I wanted him to end this life of crookedness – not because I thought it was wrong, but because it was always landing him or myself in prison. I could not bear the continual separations...
>
> Ever since I left him I have been searching for someone like Ches. I never found him. I never will.[32]

---

31 *Middlesex County Times*, 20 February 1954; *Evening Standard*, 18 February 1954.
32 *Sunday Pictorial*, 27 February 1954.

Three years later, she added:

> He was a criminal. He did unspeakable things in his lust for money, leading me into adventures that were perilous and sometimes sordid. But even so, I still remember him as a man who often showed me loyalty and tenderness, and one often lit the dark demands of his passionate love with sudden rays of appealing gentleness and almost bewildering generosity.[33]

At the time this was written, the journalists were unaware of the forensic evidence that had been unearthed by doctors Teare and Nickolls. They were unaware of the witnesses who had seen Chesney enter and leave the country and had seen him near to the scene of the murders. Had Chesney stood trial, there seems little doubt that the same decision which was to have been reached at the inquest would not have been reached, though it would have been a more prolonged business as Chesney's QC would have tried to throw as much doubt as possible on the Crown's case. It is unlikely, though, that they would have succeeded.

A double inquest was opened at Ealing Town Hall on Monday, 15 February. Dr Broadbridge, the Coroner for West Middlesex, who had presided over the inquest about the deaths at 22 Montpelier Road only five years previously, ordered the postponement of the funerals for further enquiries to be made. At the inquest, Miss McNeish, dressed in deep mourning clothes, gave identification of the two deceased. She was accompanied by her mother and a detective from Ealing Police Station. Teare gave the causes of death. The whole proceeding lasted five minutes before being adjourned until 23 February, which in its turn was adjourned until 22 March.[34] The St. Benedict's Parish Magazine for March 1954 noted the deaths of the two unfortunate women, who were parishioners at Ealing Priory and that there was not a requiem mass held, though the local newspaper said otherwise.[35]

Meanwhile, preparations for the double burial proceeded; the undertaker from Ealing visited Hastings Borough Cemetery in the last week of February to find an appropriate site. He found one in the Catholic part of the cemetery overlooking the Coghurst Valley. The coffin containing the recently interred Jane Bonar was taken from a

---

33 *Woman's Sunday Mirror*, 15 September 1957.
34 *Middlesex County Times*, 20 February 1954.
35 *St. Benedict's Parish Magazine*, March 1954.

nearby plot and put into the hole reserved for the bodies of her sister and niece. The burial was scheduled for Friday, 5 March at noon, and photographers and journalists gathered.[36]

They had to wait in the windswept cemetery for an hour for the cortege of a hearse and two cars from Ealing to pass through the cemetery gates. There were about a dozen mourners, which almost certainly included Miss McNeish and Mrs Trull. Father Terence Scanlan, of the church of St. Thomas of Canterbury of St. Leonard's, performed the last rites in a service lasting a quarter of an hour. He blessed the grave, the coffins were lowered, sprinkled with holy water, and the female mourners then dropped bunches of flowers into the grave. There were eleven floral wreaths, including one of tulips and daffodils from Tom Barratt, Daws and the Ealing CID. A marble headstone now marked the place where the three are buried at grave reference O B F3.[37] The stone no longer stands.

On Tuesday, 22 March, at the Queen's Hall at Ealing Town Hall, the inquest proper began. The public gallery was packed with spectators, most of whom were female. Crowds assembled of up to 300 people outside the town hall while the proceeding was in progress. All of which was very common during such procedures at the time. Solicitors appeared, representing the police, the relatives of the victim and finally on behalf of Sonia. The inquest was to determine how the victims met their deaths and who was responsible.[38]

The coroner opened the inquest by giving the customary warning that the eleven man jury should forget anything they had previously read about the case, for it had been reported in numerous newspapers in the past weeks. Miss McNeish was the first witness to appear. She explained about the marriage settlement and the concern Mrs Chesney had about being worth more to her husband dead than alive. She described the discovery of the corpses. She stated that Chesney wished to divorce his wife in order to marry Sonia. Letters from Chesney to his wife were produced and extracts read out in order to show Chesney's desire for divorce; firstly to marry Gerda and then Sonia. It was also said that Chesney believed that his mother-in-law had once informed the police about his smuggling activities, which

36 *Hastings and St. Leonards Observer*, 6 March 1954.
37 Ibid.
38 *Middlesex County Times*, 27 March 1954.

had angered him.[39]

Miss Thorpe spoke next, about finding the corpses. Mrs Trull said that her adopted mother feared her husband might arrange to have her killed in an 'accident' so as to gain her money and freedom to remarry. Dr Teare said that Mrs Chesney had been asphyxiated by drowning and her mother by strangulation. Colour photographs (used for the first time in a murder enquiry) of scratchmarks on Chesney's arms caused by a fight a few days before his death were shown to the jury. Dr Nickolls explained that the forensic evidence found on clothing and under his fingernails clearly linked Chesney to the murders. He was cross-examined by Clarke, who was representing his late client:

> 'Can you say whether the head hairs were Chesney's?'
> 'No.'
> 'Is it true to say that these fibres could have been consistent with other clothing?'
> 'The pink fibres under the fingernails came from a garment of the same shade as Mrs Chesney's cardigan.'

The evidence did show that Chesney had been in close proximity with his alleged victims but it could not be stated exactly when this had occurred. Fingerprint evidence was also lacking and Superintendent Livings stated that no finger or palm prints had been found in the house which matched Chesney's. Surfaces had been suspiciously wiped clean, especially in the bathroom.[40]

Daws then described the bodies and their immediate surroundings, and that the defective French windows at the back of the house would have made entry easy to someone who had that knowledge. He detailed his findings on his trip to Germany. He claimed that there had been a 'life and death' struggle in the front room before Mrs Menzies died. He added that Sonia had told him that there had been no bruises on Chesney's arms when he left for England but there were on his return. Various members of Dutch airport staff stated that they recognised Chesney on his way to and from England on 10-11 February. Then Maling, Boyd and Pickersgill stated that they knew Chesney wanted to kill his wife and had offered the latter two money to do so.[41]

39 *Middlesex County Times*, 27 March 1954.
40 Ibid; TNA, MEPO 2/9542.
41 Ibid.

Money was the next topic. The Public Trustee stated that £8,400 had been settled on Mrs Chesney in 1929 for life. A letter from Chesney was read out to the effect that Chesney desired this money to go to Sonia.[42]

The inquest was then adjourned and resumed on the following day. Mrs Cooper was the first to give evidence to the effect that she heard footsteps on the night of the murders. Two witnesses from the previous day were then recalled to state that Mrs Chesney had 8 units of alcohol in her body on death and that Chesney's passport was in the name of Chown. The latter denied all knowledge of Chesney's using his name to secure a passport (understandable lies, of course). His solicitor resisted further attempts at questioning his client. This line of questioning ended, and various witnesses stated that they had seen Chesney on his journey from Holland to Ealing on 10 February and that he had used a passport in Chown's name. Kommissar Kunn gave his evidence in German and this was translated by Chadburn.[43]

Broadbridge summed up all the evidence in a speech lasting 45 minutes. He suggested to the jury that Mrs Chesney's death had been arranged so as to pass it off as an accident and suggested, 'Was the attacker surprised by "Lady" Menzies as he was leaving?...You may well think that if this did happen there was no question of Mrs Chesney's death being accidental. Did he then decide that for his own safety he would have to deal with "Lady" Menzies?' He said that there was scientific and medical evidence pointing towards Chesney, though he reminded them that no one had seen him enter the house nor attack either woman. They must return a verdict with the same seriousness as if he was still alive. The jury then departed for 35 minutes. On their return, 'There was a tense hush in the crowded Queen's Hall' and the foreman gave the jury's unanimous verdict – murder on both counts by Chesney.[44]

Afterwards, Broadbridge complimented Daws and his colleagues on their methodical and painstaking way in which they had collected the evidence. Mr Seaton stated that the co-operation of the German police had been invaluable. It was announced that the house would be returned to Ealing Council, the furniture and contents would be sold and hopefully a good home would be found for the two dogs (Tinker

---

42 Ibid.
43 Ibid; *Daily Telegraph*, 25 March 1954.
44 Ibid.

and Chow Chow).[45]

One reason why Chesney is perhaps not as known as other notorious murderers of this era (Heath, Haigh and Christie), is that there was no trial. Chesney cheated not only the hangman, but also the press and the public. Trials of multiple murderers, especially one with such a murderous past as Chesney and with a strong sex angle, were manna from Heaven for the tabloid press and were lapped up by the public, especially women. There is all the build up to the trial, with appearances at magistrates' courts, the trial itself and then the aftermath, including an execution. All these attract large numbers of people to view the accused (especially if good looking) as well as column inches. As a former naval officer in the war and as a larger than life character who was attractive to women, Chesney would have been a huge hit as the handsome womaniser Heath had been, and as was the dapper Haigh, too. There would probably also have been the life story of the killer written by himself, probably to finance his defence costs (as with the three just mentioned; as with them Chesney was virtually penniless) and appearing in a serial in *The Sunday Pictorial* or the *News of the World*. As it was, these two had to make do, respectively, with accounts written by Gerda and Sonia. From the historian's viewpoint it is a great shame that he did not stand trial for his memoir might have shed a light on his upbringing and early life; though much of his account might well have been somewhat fictional.

It has been suggested that the case against Chesney was not complete. Rupert Furneaux, writing about the case later that year noted, 'it is unlikely that, had he faced it out, he could have been convicted of murder; no single clue in the house pointed to him'.[46] A police officer stated on the day after his death, that if Chesney had walked into a police station, 'it would be quite embarrassing for us'.[47]

Had Chesney stood trial – it would have been at first at Ealing Magistrates' Court for the preliminary hearings and then at the Old Bailey - it is unlikely that the defence would have been one of Guilty but insane, as was the case with the era's trio of infamous multiple murderers (Haigh, Heath and Christie). There seems to have been no mental health issues in his family unless his uncle who died in an

---

45 *Middlesex County Times*, 27 March 1954; *Daily Telegraph*, 25 March 1954; TNA, MEPO 2/9542.
46 Furneaux, *Famous Criminal Cases I* (1954), pp.193-4.
47 *Daily Mail*, 17 February 1954.

asylum was brought into the equation, which would have been rather tenuous. It would have had to have been 'Not Guilty' as it had been in 1927. The defence would have had to have stressed that there was little or no evidence that Chesney was in the country at the time, and if he was, it could not be proved beyond reasonable doubt that he was responsible for the murders. The prosecution would have chosen which murder they were going to charge him with. It might seem obvious that the charge would have been that of killing his wife, as he had a clear financial motive, though motives do not have to be proved to find a defendant guilty (none was proved in the case of Christie who was found guilty of his wife's murder) and it is possible that the defence could have argued that it could not be definitely ruled out that the death of Mrs Chesney was an accident or suicide, though the bruises on the arms might have raised doubts as would the locked bathroom door. If they had proceeded with the murder of Mrs Menzies, a death that there was no doubt was one of murder, they might have been on stronger ground, chiefly because of the forensic evidence available, though Clarke had challenged this at the inquest. However, Chesney's entry into the country and his presence near Montpelier Road that night could have been verified by sufficient witnesses and the evidence of staff at the airport and elsewhere could have been utilised. It would seem unlikely that he would have been found not guilty and therefore would have faced the death penalty. After all, the jury at the inquest had found him guilty after a relatively short time.

One question worth posing is the hypothetical one concerning what would have happened if Chesney had not run into his mother-in-law on his exit. Firstly, the corpse of his wife would have been found far quicker. Yet as stated it could have been argued that this was an accidental death. However it was known that she and Chesney had been in dispute about money and there is no doubt that he would have been suspected. He could have been traced as having arrived in England on the day of the murder and having left on the following day. The evidence needed to convince the department of the public prosecutor to take the case to court as well as to convict would have been the lesser. That found on Mrs Menzies would not have existed, and that on his person (alive or dead) that had resulted from the struggle with her would also not have existed. There would have been some evidence; that of fibres of his wife's jumper being under his fingernails, but had he bathed before being taken by the police these would have disappeared. Mary Menzies could have testified against him, too, as she must have known of her daughter's fears about her estranged husband. Evidence of motive and opportunity could have been presented. Yet he would certainly have had a chance of escaping conviction, but even then, it was uncertain, and so the idea of a perfect crime was another of his fantasies. He had to lock the bathroom door to prevent an early discovery, but in doing so he branded the death as murder as well as that of his mother-in-law.

Murder cases involving sums of money often end up in other courts; as had happened in 1950 to resolve the disposal of the assets of Dr Archibald Henderson, murdered two years previously by John George Haigh, the 'acid bath murderer'. This case was no exception. On 16 February, Messrs Edward Mackie and Co. of 39 The Mall, Ealing, acting for the relatives of Mrs Chesney and Mrs Menzies, issued a statement that they were anxious to trace their wills. They had already heard that a London firm of solicitors had Chesney's. Ronald Politeyan, principal solicitor for Mackies', later found that a second will made by Chesney had been found (the one composed by Clarke). Both appeared to be valid, but they were undated; one was in the name of Merrett and the other in the name of Milner.[48]

It was not just that neither of the murdered women had left wills; the courts relatively quickly decided that their money should go to their next of blood kin. Mrs Chesney's money: £1774 5s 9d went to Mrs McNeish, as decided by the courts and Mrs Menzies' £376 12s 4d to the same in the following year. On 22 October 1954 Chesney's will for £20 was directed to be given to Sonia. For him, crime clearly had not paid.

The real problem was what to do with the sum that Chesney had settled on his wife in 1929; which was hers for life only and she could not touch the capital. The case was heard at the Chancery Division of the High Court of Justice on 27 October 1955 before Mr Justice Wynn Parry. The Court was called to determine whether the trustees of the settlement could transfer the funds to the representative of the settlor (Chesney), but the difficulty was of course that the settlor had murdered his wife. If they could not make this transfer, could the funds go to the wife's representatives or should they go to the Crown as bona vacantia. Finally, should Mrs Trull, now living in Lewes, be

---

48 *Middlesex County Times*, 27 February 1954.

entitled to any of it. Each of these five parties was represented by solicitors.[49]

The trustees' solicitors explained the details of the trust, that no children were born from the marriage, that Mrs Chesney died on 11 February and her husband five days later. Mrs Trull had never been legally adopted. There was discussion whether a murder enquiry need be made but it was agreed this was unnecessary because of the verdict at the coroner's court, unless anyone could show that Chesney was innocent of the double murder. Maurice Berkeley, acting for the settlor's estate said that that estate was entitled to benefit from the fund and that Equity courts had never ordered that a felon's estate be made over to the victim's estate or to the Crown. The solicitor representing Mrs Chesney claimed that that estate was entitled to compensation for the loss of her life interest.[50]

Anthony Charles Goodall, representing Mrs Trull, admitted that she had no legal claim, but she had a strong moral claim and supported the case for bona vacantia. He argued that a felon could not take any benefit from his crime and this principle should be applied as widely as possible. The Treasury Solicitor argued that the wife had a life interest only which was removed at her death, that the settlor had no claim because he had killed his wife and therefore the fund should go the government. The judge claimed he had some sympathy with the idea that the settlor's estate should not be excluded, but in the end he reserved his judgement.[51]

A week later the case was concluded. The judge summarised the case and pointed to precedents. He said that had Chesney not died he would not be in a position to benefit from his crime. His interest was indefeasible. On the assumption that he had killed his wife, the whole of the trust settlement went to the Crown as bona vacantia.[52]

In 1956, Mrs Alice McNeish died and was buried where she was born, in Coatbridge, a suburb of Glasgow, after a requiem at Ealing Abbey. Her unmarried daughter carried on with running St. Anthony's Home until its closure in the 1970s. She later ran another home and in both she was remembered as being efficient and caring. She died in Ealing in 1998. The Nixon-Pearsons had six children between 1953-1962

49 *The Times*, 28 October 1955.
50 Ibid.
51 Ibid.
52 Ibid, 3 November 1955.

and resided in Ealing for at least another two decades. The Trulls left Ealing by 1955 and moved to Lewes and then to Devon. The fates of Gerda Schaller and Sonia Winnikes are unknown (the former's sister worked in a British hospital and married an Englishman). Chesney's father returned to England from India and died in Surrey in 1966. It is unknown whether he ever tried to contact his son after his return to England; quite possibly not.

Eileen Thorpe married one Frank Mortimer in Ealing later in 1954. Daws became a detective chief superintendent in 1957 and then second in command of Scotland Yard's Research and Planning Branch. He retired in 1959 after 32 years' service. Yet in 1960 The Daily Sketch and Daily Graphic accused him of leading 'the Yard's private Gestapo' in spying on the uniformed and detective officers of the Metropolitan Police. Daws initiated a libel case against them and the case was heard at the Queen's Bench Division late that year. Daws was awarded damages and an apology. By now he lived at the Lodge Close, Cobham, Surrey. He did not have a long retirement, dying on 5 November 1961 at 87 Lodge Close, Stoke D'Abernon in Surrey, leaving £10,395 to his widow in the following year.[53]

Contrary to popular opinion, houses where terrible murders occur are rarely destroyed because of what happened there (the houses in north London where Denis Nilsen committed his murders in the 1970s and 1980s still stand); the demolition of 25 Cromwell Street in Gloucester following the Wests' murders in the 1990s is very much the exception which proved the rule. As with 10 Rillington Place in Notting Hill, 22 Montpelier Road was soon reoccupied after those resident there at the time of the murders moved out (Rillington Place was renamed and destroyed as part of more general slum clearance in the 1970s). On 4 March the aggrieved owner wrote to the council to request it be de-requisitioned and restored to him 'as a matter of urgency'. He noted that the property 'has now acquired an unsavoury and horrible reputation, which may have depreciated its value irretrievably'. A council spokesman suggested that it might be difficult to find someone to take it over. The council gave up possession on 10 May 1954.[54]

It was converted into flats by 1961 and was only demolished in about 1989 (along with numbers 21 and 23) and replaced by smaller

---

53 *The Times*, 22 November 1960.
54 ELHC, Civil Defence files 178/84.

houses in a very small road of 10 houses called Magnolia Close. The destruction of the original housing stock in north Ealing to be replaced by higher density housing was commonplace; having begun in the 1930s in any case; 16 Montpelier Road had been demolished in 1970 to be replaced by flats, for example. Ironically, in 1960 number 18 was converted for use as an old people's home; it still stands today being used for the same purpose.[55]

As to physical evidence, Scotland Yard's Crime Museum contains many grisly relics associated with serial killers and other murderers, but none more macabre than those for Chesney. The forearms severed from his corpse in Cologne are held in the museum. The coffee pot used against Mrs Menzies is also there. There is also a Colt automatic which is claimed to be the gun with which he committed suicide, but there is doubt as to its authenticity.

There have been several assessments of Chesney. McLeave, the first biographer, writing in the same year as Chesney's death, had this as a conclusion:

> *Chesney, enigmatic and unpredictable, could be both a charming husband and a ruthless and wily killer; he was something of a hero as his war record shows, and something of a weakling; he could be loyal to friends and yet betray and cheat others; he had an agile mind that could recognise the finer things, but his humour was often brassy and outrageously vulgar.*
>
> *The best that can be said of Chesney was that he was born 300 years too late. He belonged to the era of swagger and swashbuckling, even if his smuggling sometimes smacked of spivery.*
>
> *He loved the limelight and seems to have assumed his place in the gallery of the world's most notorious murderers.*[56]

Conrad Phillips wrote a book about the four most notorious British murderers in the decade after the Second World War and of these the fourth was Chesney. He had no sympathy for him and makes several references to him as being ape-like. He believed that only young hooligans had any liking for the man. As with McLeave, he likened him to a seventeenth century buccaneer, but discounted Chesney's war service as being merely that of a braggart and stated that he killed his mother; 'The pity is that this useless popinjay wasn't hanged then.

---

55 Ealing Electoral Registers and Ealing Building Inspection Books.
56 McLeave, *Chesney: The Fabulous Murderer* (1954), p.158-9.

Had he been two people might still be alive and living useful lives'.[57]

Finally there was Tom Tullett's biography, written two years after Chesney's death. As a journalist, Tullett talked to many people who claimed they knew Chesney over the years. It is hard to know how much truth there is in all the stories therein (there are certainly elements of fiction in some), but Tullett is certainly a good writer and spins an entertaining yarn. He noted that 'Smuggling, blackmail and murder came easily to Chesney whose powerful personality, surface charm and daring exploits made him a legend in his lifetime'.[58]

Numerous other books have referred to the case, but at most have only included a chapter about it.[59] The 69th issue of the Marshall Cavendish series of *Murder Casebooks* in 1990-1991 was devoted to Chesney; he also featured as a bit part in two other crime magazines. The former magazine retold the story, which was well illustrated but added little in the way of factual content to those studies of the 1950s. However, there was some context given on points such as the 'not proven' verdict and smuggling craft. There was also an attempt at analysis, chiefly that Chesney was a psychopath; seemingly charming, but deadly when thwarted in the pursuit of his selfish goals; a man to whom the closest ties of family or friends meant nothing when money was at stake.[60] Although there have been no films about Chesney, nor most criminals (10 Rillington Place and Dance with a Stranger (about Ruth Ellis) are very much the exceptions) there have been three televised dramas or semi-dramatisations about the case, more than for some better-known criminals (to date there has been only one about Heath and two about Haigh, for example). The first two focused entirely on the shooting of Mrs Merrett. The first of these was broadcast on BBC1 from 9.25-9.45pm on 23 July 1964 and was episode 4 of a season titled *Call the Gun Expert*. This was *The Teenage Murderer* and was written and narrated by MacDonald Hastings, Robert Churchill's biographer. Nicholas Bennett starred as Merrett. Twenty years later there was another TV drama, being the third in a series made by BBC Scotland, titled *Murder Not Proven?*. This episode used Betty Christie's description of Merrett 'A Big Romping Boy' as

57 Phillips, *Murderer's Moon*, pp.235-8.
58 Tullett, *Portrait*, endpage.
59 Stratmann, *Greater London Murders* (2010); Oates, *Foul Deeds and Suspicious Deaths in Ealing* (2006).
60 *Murder Casebook No. 69: The Barbaric Buccaneer* (1991), pp.2476-7.

its title. Broadcast on 31 May 1984 from 9.25-10.20pm, it starred Jasper Jacob as Merrett. Although described by *The Times* as being painstaking and of interest to students of jurisprudence, they also claimed it was 'a trifle dull' and lacking in tension since the title of the series gave the verdict away.[61]

On the night of 19 May 2014 there was an hour long drama documentary about his life and crimes, *All That Lies Behind Me* (to quote his final letter to Sonia) shown on the Gaelic channel Alba for the BBC. Unlike the previous two it covered the whole of his life, with his dealings with his wife and Gerda included as well. It starred Sean Baillie as the young man and Robert Yates as the older one, with others playing the parts of Mrs Sutherland, Mrs Merrett and Gerda (all non-speaking parts). It was presented by John Morrison. David Leslie, former crime journalist and author, provided some of the commentary, together with a psychologist and a retired lawyer. Although it tells the story fairly well in a general way, concentrating on the Scottish part, assumptions are often passed off as fact, there are a few errors of fact and there is nothing new therein.

---

61 *The Times*, 23 July 1964; 31 May 1984.

Conclusion

What else can be said about the life and career of John Donald Merrett alias Ronald Chesney? He had been a murderer, a smuggler, a fraudster a sailor and a womaniser in his time. Money was the root of his criminal career, rather than a love of power or pain, as with some other of the known British post war murderers. His lifestyle needed a high level of income to feed it and so crime seemed to provide an answer; from his teens to the end of his life.

Chesney seems to have had few virtues; a coarse form of sociability and a kind of heroism in the cannon's mouth at Tobruk and in making three escape attempts. His black market and smuggling activities may have won envious admirers in austerity Britain of the later 1940s. He was also attractive to women; Betty Christie, though she may have liked his money if not himself, Isobel, then Gerda, Sonia and Christa. The three latter may have been attracted, as suffering post war Germans, to the security he may have represented, as a British officer, though this would have been less so after about 1950, though the attraction of the older man may have played a part as all these women were in their 20s to his 40s. He treated those who loved him badly; with his deceit, theft and adultery, yet Gerda's love for him revived after their split and his wife had sobbed bitterly when he was sentenced to gaol in 1928.

Chesney can be fairly deemed to be a psychopath. He had a veneer of charm which was on display to his many acquaintances; he had few if any real friends. His ego was immense as was his physical build. Lies were nothing to him if they forwarded his ends. He was unable to sustain long-term relationships, due partly to his promiscuity. He had no realistic long-term goal and acted on impulse throughout his life. He was capable of inspiring love and of giving it, but only intermittently. It is unknown how much of his character was shaped by an inadequate childhood, but it was certainly a peripatetic one and one, for which most of the time at least, he lacked a father.

It is also probable that he suffered from bi-polar disorder, and which then was termed manic depression following the work of Emil Kraeplin (1856-1926) who diagnosed this mental illness as a form of psychosis. Apparently it often derives from a traumatic childhood, and certainly Chesney's childhood; travelling between different countries and not putting down roots anywhere, as well as having parents who separated, would fit the bill. Likewise his behaviour would also fit. In the manic state, the individual is abnormally happy, excitable, eager for excessive spending and sex, makes poorly thought out decisions with little regard to the consequences. The depressive has an extremely negative view of life, feels his cause is hopeless and is very likely to try and commit suicide. All this would fit Chesney's known personality and actions.

He was at odds with society. He has been called a buccaneer who had the misfortune to inhabit the wrong century; though piracy in former centuries was no more romantic to contemporaries than muggers are to our society. He was certainly unable to live the conventional life of having a steady family life involving regular work. His desire for an alternative life needed an alternative and thus illegal income stream. He was not intrinsically a violent man but felt no compunction about using violence if it served his needs. His end was a tragedy for himself; his life a tragedy for others.

Bibliography

Archives

The National Archives, Kew:
  ADM 187/9-55
  ADM 199/799
  ADM 208/1-9, 19-35
  DPP 2/2338
  IR 26/7420
  MEPO 2/9542
  WO339/10556

Ealing Local History Centre:
  Civil Defence personnel cards
  Civil Defence files, 178/84, Requisitioned property file -
  22 Montpelier Road.
  Building Inspection Books

London Metropolitan Archives
  Marlborough Street Court Register, PS/MS/A/01/215-219
  Wandsworth Prison Register. ACC3444/PR/01/230
  Coroners' Records, COR/MW/1949/140/01/244;
  COR/LW/1954/184/01/163

Ministry of Defence: RN Disclosures
  Papers of Ronald Chesney

Edinburgh University Archives
IN1/ADS/STA8

Glasgow University Archives
FM/2B/20/1-7

National Records of Scotland
AD15/27/1
JC5/27
JC9/20
JC26/1927/27

Edinburgh City Archives
ED6/13

Wills
Will of William Henry Milner, 1899
Will of John Donald Merrett, 1954

Electronic Sources
Ancestry.com (census returns, wills, electoral registers, civil registration certificates, shipping registers, Institute of Mechanical Engineers; Royal Aeronautical Club Aviators' Certificates)
Find My Past (marriages overseas; 1939 registers)

Primary sources

Newspapers
Aberdeen Evening Press, 1954
Aberdeen Journal, 1927
Blackburn Standard, 1864
Buckinghamshire Free Press, 1926
Cheshire Observer, 1899
Daily Mail, 1954
Daily Record, 1928
Daily Telegraph, 1954
Dundee Courier, 1926-1928, 1930
Edinburgh Evening Despatch, 1926-1927

Edinburgh Evening News, 1926-1927
Empire News, 1954
Evening Standard, 1954
Evening Telegraph, 1926-1927, 1930
Glasgow Herald, 1927
Hastings and St. Leonards Observer, 1953-1954
Illustrated [rest of title unknown], 1954
Lancashire Evening Post, 1905
London Gazette, 1935
Manchester Guardian, 1954
Middlesex County Times, 1949, 1954
Morning Post, 1899
Newcastle Evening Chronicle, 1928
Newcastle Weekly Chronicle, 1928
News Chronicle, 1954
News of the World, 1954
The Scotsman, 1927
St. Benedict's Parish magazine, 1954
Sun Herald, 1954
Sunday Despatch, 1954
Sunday Express, 1954
Sunday Mail, 1949
Sunday Pictorial, 1954
Sunday Post, 1926
Sussex Express and County Herald, 1951
The Times, 1927, 1954, 1955
Weekly Record, 1928
Western Daily Press, 1926, 1930
Woman's Sunday Mirror, 1957.
York Herald, 1884

Published Books and articles
Chesney, I.V., 'To Wide Horizons New', *Yachting Monthly*, vol. 66, no. 393, (January 1939)
Ealing Official Guide (1950)
Edinburgh University Calendar, 1925-1926
Hastings, M., *The Other Mr Churchill* (London: Harrap, 1963)
Hatherill, G, *A Detective's Story* (London: Deutsch, 1971)
Lloyd's Registers of Yachts, 1931-1939, 1947-1953

McLeave, H., *Chesney: The Fabulous Murderer* (London: Mark Goulden, 1954)
Phillips, C., *Murderer's Moon* (London: Arthur Barker, 1956)
Roughead, W. (ed.), *Trial of John Donald Merrett* (Edinburgh: William Hodge, 1929)
Simpson, K., *Forty Years of Murder* (London: W.H. Allen / Virgin Books, 1978)
Smith, S., *Mostly Murder* (London: Harrap, 1959)
Tullett, T., *Portrait of a Bad Man* (London: Evans Bros, 1956)
Webb, D., *Deadline For Crime* (London: Muller, 1955)

Secondary Sources

Adam, H.L., *Murder by Persons Unknown* (London: Collins, 1931)
Archibald, T.W., *A History of the Lothian and Border Police* (n.p., 1990)
Browne, D.G. and E.V. Tullett, *Bernard Spilsbury: His Life and Cases* (London: Harrap, 1951)
Evans, C., *The Father of Forensics: How Sir Bernard Spilsbury Invented Modern CSI* (Thriplow: Icon, 2007)
Fry, M., *Edinburgh: A History of the City* (London: Macmillan, 2009)
Furneaux, R., *Famous Criminal Cases 1* (London: Wingate, 1954)
House, J., *Murder Not Proven?* (Glasgow: Drew, 1984)
Konstam, A., *British Motor Gun Boat 1939-1945* (Oxford: Osprey, 2010)
Kynaston, D., *Austerity Britain, 1945-1951* (London: Bloomsbury, 2007)
Lenton, H.T. and J.J. Colledge, *Warships of World War II* (London: Ian Allan, 1964)
MacDonogh, G., *After the Reich* (London: John Murray, 2007)
Massie, A., *Edinburgh* (London: Sinclair-Stevenson, 1994)
Murder Casebook No. 69: The Barbaric Buccaneer (1991)
Oates, J., *Ealing: A Concise History* (Stroud: Amberley, 2014)
———, *Foul Deeds and Suspicious Deaths in Ealing* (Barnsley: Wharncliffe, 2006)
Pevsner, N., *The Buildings of Scotland: Edinburgh* (Harmondsworth: Penguin, 1984)
Phillipson, D., *Smuggling* (Newton Abbot: David and Charles, 1973)
Rose, A., *Lethal Witness* (Stroud: Sutton, 2007)
Roughead, W., *Classic Crimes* (London: Cassell, 1951)

Stratmann, L., *Greater London Murders* (Stroud: Sutton, 2010)
Thomas, D., *Villains' Paradise* (London: John Murray, 2005)
Upton, D., *Ealing at War, 1939–1945* (Stroud: The History Press, 2005)
Whittington-Egan, R., *William Roughead's Chronicles of Murder* (Moffat: Lochar, 1991)
Williams, N., *Contraband Cargoes* (London: Longmans, Green & Co., 1959)
Wilson, J.G., *Not Proven* (London: Secker & Warburg, 1960)

Electoral Registers for Ealing
Directories for Sussex, Berkshire, Edinburgh, Chichester, Ealing
Oxford Dictionary of National Biography

Index

Aitchison, Craigie, 74-87, 91-93, 96-97, 100-102, 107
Alness, Lord, 74, 79, 82, 89, 91, 97-100
Anderson, Agnes, 27-28, 48, 55, 89
Anderson, Robert, 25, 89
Appledram, 118-119

Barratt, Chief Superintendent Tom, 13, 15, 207
Beard, Thomas, 148
Bell, Dr Richard, 42-43, 77-78
Bexhill, 110, 112-113, 115
Birkdale, 18
Blackburn, Major Thomas, 21, 23, 25, 29, 31, 67-68
Blomfield, Sydney, 149
Blomfield, William, 148
Bonars, *see*
    Menzies, Mary and Chesney, Isobel
Bosham, 19, 23, 118
Boyd, Herbert, 174-176, 195-196, 208
Broadbridge, Dr Harold, 13, 148, 206, 209
Brussels, 140, 157, 159-161, 163
Buckingham Terrace, Edinburgh, 25-26, 30, 32-33, 35, 37, 39, 45-46, 50, 54-55, 67-68, 103
Burgess, Fred, 175
Buxtehude, 151, 154, 167, 183
Cairns, James, 32

Chadburn, DS, 203, 209
Chadwick, Mary Louisa, 17-18, 49
Chadwick, Rev William, 18
Chesney, Isobel, 6-16, 110-127, 130-131, 135, 137-138, 141-144, 146-152, 155, 157-159, 161-162, 166-169, 172-175, 177-179, 182-184, 186-188, 190, 192-195, 200, 203-204, 206-209, 211-213, 219
Chesney, Ronald John, appearance, 15, 71, 76, 90, 100, 152, 165, 167-168, 176, 181, 192, arrests, 70, 113, 154, 156, 159, 172, 176 birth, 17, 20, buys gun, 30-31, 39, character, 25, 29, 68, 71, 90, 98-99, 116-118, 123, 125, 128-131, 136-137, 141, 143, 152-154, 163-164, 167-168, 181-182, 188-189, childhood, 20, courtship and marriage, 111-112, 114, death, 199-201, death of mother, 56-57, 67, divorce attempts, 155, 157-158, 161-162, 169, 179-180, 182, 184-185, dramatisations, 216-217, employment, 116, 119-120, 185, evaluations of, 101-107, 204-206, 210-212, 215-216, 219-220, explanations of mother's death, 38-39, 42, 44, 48, 51, 53, 55-56, 105-106, 153, 159, fears arrest, 195-199, forgery, 33, 46, 51, 60, 64, 76, 87, 104, 185 frauds, 112-113, 153, 156, 164,

181, 185, gambling, 3, 29, 126, 131, 135, 155-156, 158, 185, mentioned, 3-4, 15-16, 35, 50, 58, 69, 72, 151, 170, 190, 210-214, murder of wife and mother in law, 193-194, 204-205, 207-209, preparations for murder, 171-172, 180-181, 186, 191-192, prison career, 70-72, 75, 100-101, 109-110, 114-115, 154-156, 159-161, 164, 174-176, 179 relationships with women, see also, Chesney, Isobel, Christie, Betty, Romm, Christa, Schaller, Gerda, Winnikes, Sonia, relationship with mother, 21, 25-29, visits mother in hospital, 42-43, 45, 48-49, 51-52, 57, relationship with wife, 116-117, 130-131, 141-143, 167, 173, 177, see also divorce attempts, religion, 153, 156, 174, 182, 185 schooling, 3, 21-23, sailing, 116, 120-127, seeks murderer, 174-176, 178-179, 187, smuggling, 126, 139-141, 151, 155, 172-174, 176, 179, 182-183, 186, social life, 25, 27-30, 32, 44-46, 67-69, 116-117, 143, spending habits, 29, 30-32, 51, 67, 117-118, 157, 166, suspected of murder, 60-61, suicide attempts, 183, 189, 192, 198-201, trial for murder, 73-100, 164, trials, 114, 154, 164, 173-174, university career, 3, 23, 24, 27-28, 32, 47, 68-69, 71, war career, 3, 127-137, 141, 153, 166

Chorlton, 17-18

Chown, Leslie, 180-181, 188, 191, 193-194, 209

Christie, Elizabeth, 29-31, 44-46, 67, 83, 104, 216, 219

Christie, John, 3, 210-211

Churchill, Robert, 64-66, 84, 93-94, 101, 104, 216

Clark, John, 6, 8, 150, 167-168, 191-192

Clarke, Stephen, 180, 196-199, 208, 211-212

Cologne, 140, 160, 165-166, 183, 186, 194-198, 202-203, 215

Cooper, Betty, 5, 209

Cummings, George, 6

Davidson, PC, 30, 89

Daws, Superintendent Edmund Walter, 10-12, 14-15, 193, 203, 207-209, 214

Doyle, Sir Arthur Conan, 24, 66, 74

Dueren, 165-166, 170, 176, 183-186, 190, 194, 196-198, 202

Dunedin Palais de Danse, 28-29, 45, 67, 69, 72, 79, 89

Ealing, 5, 16, 126-127, 137, 143-147, 151, 157, 167-168, 173, 181, 188-189, 192, 194, 198-199, 206, 209-210, 212-215

Ealing Priory, 144, 151 192, 206, 213

Ealing Town Hall, 143, 148, 206-207

Earl's Court, 170, 175, 178, 180-182, 185, 187

Eccles, Clara 6

Edinburgh, 23-26, 28, 30, 32-33, 42, 44, 46-47, 52-55, 58, 61, 66, 68-71, 73-74, 80, 82-83, 87-89, 93, 105-106, 109-110, 119

Edinburgh Royal Infirmary, 38, 42, 44-48, 50, 52-53, 55, 57, 98, 102

Edinburgh University, 23-24, 27-28, 47, 55, 57, 61, 67-68, 72, 92

Faithfull, PS William, 70

Fleming, Inspector David, 40-42, 44, 50, 54-57, 76-77, 90-91

Gibraltar, 121-123, 171

Gibson, PC, 42, 50-51, 76

Glaister, Professor, 63-64, 86, 98

Glasgow, 63, 83, 111-112, 118, 213

Glass, Alexander, 148-149

Gorky, Dr, 148-149

Grant, Elizabeth, 43, 45-46, 51, 52, 57, 60, 79-80

Greech, Joseph, 178

Groom, Margaret, 163-164

Gurrin, Gerald, 64, 87-88, 95

Haigh, John, 120, 195, 201, 210, 212, 216

Index

Hambach, William, 197-198, 202
Hamburg, 139, 151, 154, 183, 186
Hardie, Elizabeth, 25, 27, 54, 92
Harley, Frank, 8
Hastings, 117, 178, 180, 197, 206
Haynes, Inspector Frank, 149
Heaslewood, Peter, 8
Heath, Neville, 103, 201, 210, 216
Heathrow Airport, 191-192, 194
Henderson, Peter, 6
Henderson, PS, 40-42, 91, 96
High Wycombe, 69-70
Hill, Bertha, 21, 24, 27, 45-49, 57, 80-81, 95
Holcombe, Dr Roy, 43, 47, 49-53, 56, 61-63, 77-79, 81, 85, 95
Hughenden, 69-70

Innes, Jean, 47, 80
Izatt, PC, 37-39, 42, 66, 77

Jackson, Ted, 180, 187, 189, 194
Jenks, William, 20-22, 53, 82

Kinross, Lord, 60, 74-76, 99
Kirby, Superintendent George, 70
Kunn, Kriminal Komissar, 201, 209

Lawson, John, 69
Lerman, Jacob, 145, 147, 214
Lewes 173, 212, 214
Littlejohn, Professor, 47, 57, 61-65, 80, 84-86, 94, 96, 98, 107
London, 19-20, 22, 46, 49, 52, 60, 64, 66, 68, 109, 119, 143, 155, 164, 170, 174, 177, 188, 191, 194, 195, 203, 212

Macnaughton, Alan, 83-84
McNeish, Alice, 110, 119, 126, 192, 193, 212-213
McNeish, Phyllis, 9-11, 13, 15, 145, 187, 192, 206-207, 213
MacPherson, Charles, 47, 91
Maling, Irwin, 171-172, 204, 208
Malta, 123, 125, 126, 130
Malvern College, 22-23

Manchester, 17, 20, 59, 81
March, Patricia, 5-6
Massey, Dr Alan, 13
Menzies, Mary Ann, 6-9, 12, 14-15, 110-111, 113-114, 118-119, 123-127, 137, 144-150, 161-162, 167, 177-178, 186-187, 191-194, 203-204, 208-209, 211-212, 215
Menzies, Thomas Chalmers, 118-119
Merrett, Bertha, 17-61, 72, 75-84, 86-98, 102-106, 110, 153, 158-159, 166, 216-217
Merrett, John Alfred, 17, 19-20, 22, 27, 30, 39, 75, 80
Merrett, John Donald,
  see Chesney, Ronald John
Middlemiss, PC, 37-40, 42, 60, 77
Milner, John Donald,
  see Chesney, Ronald John
Milner, Elizabeth Ann, 17-18
Milner, James, 17-18, 81
Milner, William Henry, 17-18, 59, 67, 75, 115
Mitchell, MacGregor, 75, 87-88
Montpelier Road, Ealing, 5-9, 11, 14, 16, 145-146, 148, 151, 167, 172, 175, 180, 191-193, 199, 206, 211, 214-215

Neish, Sheriff Substitute, 70
Newcastle, 112-115
Newhaven, 170, 172
New Zealand, 17, 19, 21, 61, 135, 153, 155
Nickolls, Dr Lewis, 15, 204, 208
Nixon-Pearson, John, 9, 120, 123, 147, 151, 203

Ostend, 157, 159, 161, 163, 171, 186, 196, 203

Paris, 19, 55, 154-157, 159-160, 163, 175, 176
Parry, Justice, 212, 213
Paton, James, 51, 89
Pearce, Evelyn, 69

Penn, Eliza Annie, 17-20, 23, 29, 31, 49, 51-54, 60, 67-68, 71, 79-82, 90, 95, 97, 101, 115, 118
Penn, Walter, 19, 52-54, 67, 71, 79, 81-82, 95, 115, 118
Phillips, Conrad, 14, 126, 215
Pickersgill, William, 174-176, 208

Reading, 22, 69
Rillington Place, 13, 146, 214, 216
Robertson, Professor George, 92-93, 97
Rom, Christa, 185, 187-190, 219
Rosa, Dr Lewi,s 46, 56, 72, 76-77, 91, 96
Roughead, William, 46, 73-75, 82, 87, 99-102, 105, 109-110, 114-115

St Leonard's, 117, 178, 182, 196, 199, 207
Saxton, Donald, 21, 29
Scott, George, 28, 31-32, 45, 46, 67, 89, 104
Schaller, Barbara, 151, 155
Schaller, Gerda, 105-106, 111, 140, 151-162, 165-166, 182, 197, 202-203, 205-207, 210, 214, 217, 219
Sharp, Joan, 25, 27
Slater, Clarence, 149
Slattery, Ann, 192
Smith, Sir Sydney, 61, 65-66, 85, 93, 97, 101, 103, 107
Solomon, Martin, 133, 135, 160, 176, 183, 204

Smith, William Robinson, 88, 97
Spilsbury, Sir Bernard, 65-66, 84-85, 93-94, 97, 101-103, 107
Stott, Charles, 30-31
Sutherland, Henrietta, 26-27, 29-30, 35-40, 46, 49-50, 56-58, 66-67, 72, 76-77, 82, 90-91, 95-96, 98, 103-104, 106-107, 217

Teare, Dr Donald, 13-14, 148, 206, 208
Thom, Colonel, 44, 91
Thorpe, Eileen, 7-11, 13, 187-188, 192, 208, 214
Timberlake, Peter, 190
Tobruk, 132, 135, 160-161
Trull, Elizabeth, 9-11, 13, 120, 123, 147-149, 151, 153, 166, 189, 192, 207-208, 212-214
Trull, Frederick, 9-10, 13, 111, 151

Waitaki School, 21-22, 29
Wandsworth Prison, 174, 176
Watson, William, 74, 79-80, 82, 86, 88, 91-95, 99-100
Watt, PC, 42, 49-51, 56, 76-77
Weybridge, 119
Whitmore, Elizabeth, 6, 8
Williams, Alvan, 169, 190-191
Winnikes, Sonia, 165-176, 179-180, 182-190, 194-200, 205, 207, 210, 212, 214, 217, 219